SO HIGH A BLOOD

SO HIGH A BLOOD

The Life of Margaret, Countess of Lennox

Morgan Ring

B L O O M S B U R Y
LONDON • OXFORD • NEW YORK • NEW DELHI • SYDNEY

Bloomsbury Publishing
An imprint of Bloomsbury Publishing Plc

50 Bedford Square
London
WC1B 3DP
UK

1385 Broadway
New York
NY 10018
USA

www.bloomsbury.com

First published in Great Britain 2017

British Library Cataloguing-in-Publication Data
A catalogue record for this book is available from the British Library.

ISBN: HB: 978-1-4088-5966-7
TPB: 978-1-4088-5967-4
EPUB: 978-1-4088-5968-1

2 4 6 8 10 9 7 5 3 1

Ty ... ndia
Printed a ... on CR0 4YY

To find ... ury.com.
Here ... ming

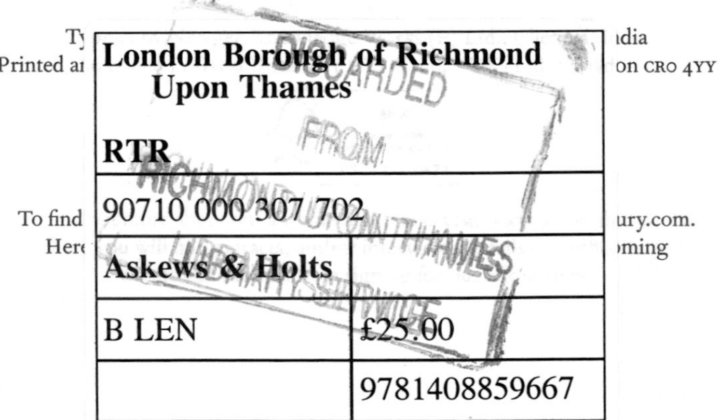

For my parents

CONTENTS

AUTHOR'S NOTE

DATES: Dates are given in Old Style, with the year taken to have begun on 1 January rather than 25 March.

SPELLING: Spelling and punctuation have been modernised throughout the text, though original spellings for the titles of printed works are retained in the Notes and Bibliography. I have followed convention by using the English spelling of Stewart for both the Scottish royal family and the earls of Lennox.

TRANSLATIONS: Translations from Latin, French and Italian are my own. Translations of the Scots mottoes on the Lennox Jewel are from Kirsten Aschengreen Piacenti and John Boardman's *Ancient and Modern Gems and Jewels in the Collection of Her Majesty the Queen* (London: 2008, pp. 183–5).

The Royal Stewarts and the Earls of Arran and Lennox

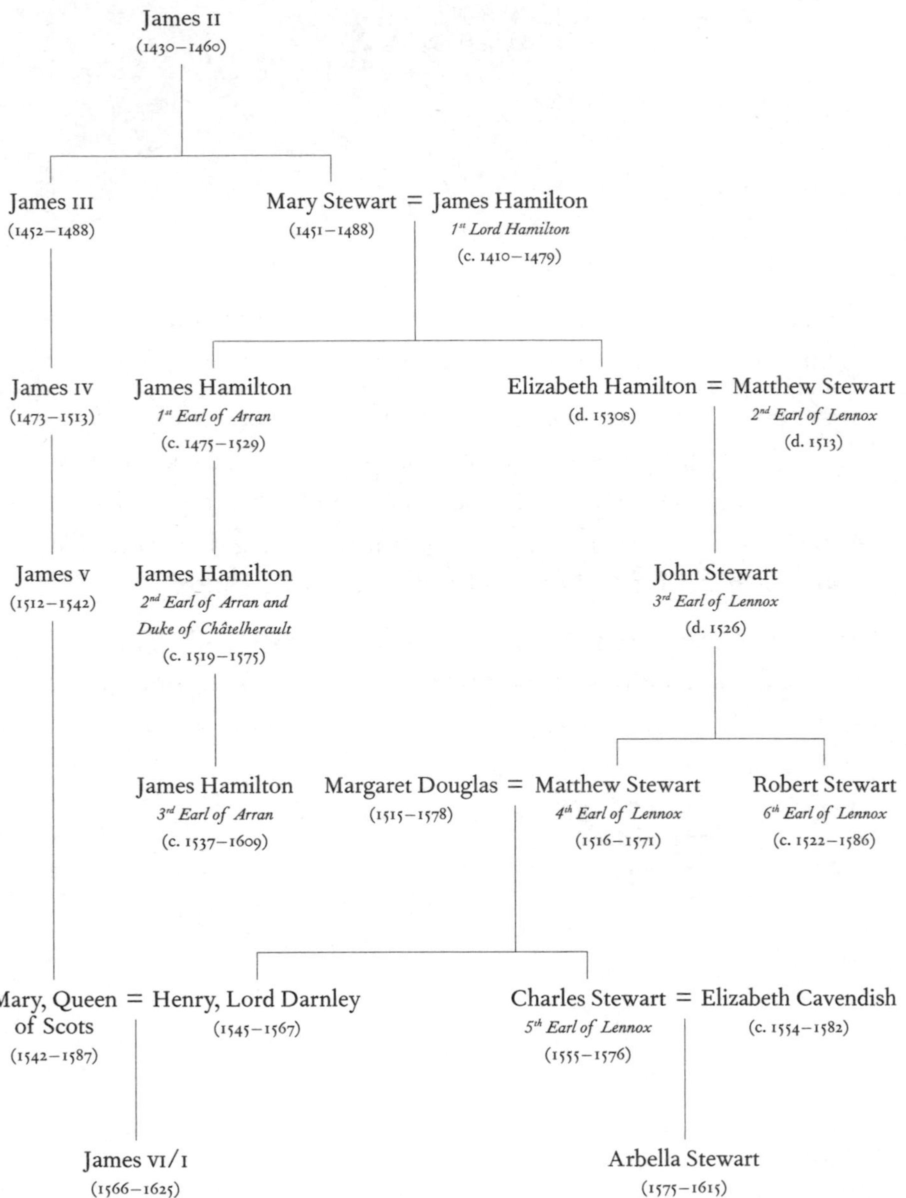

Earls of Angus

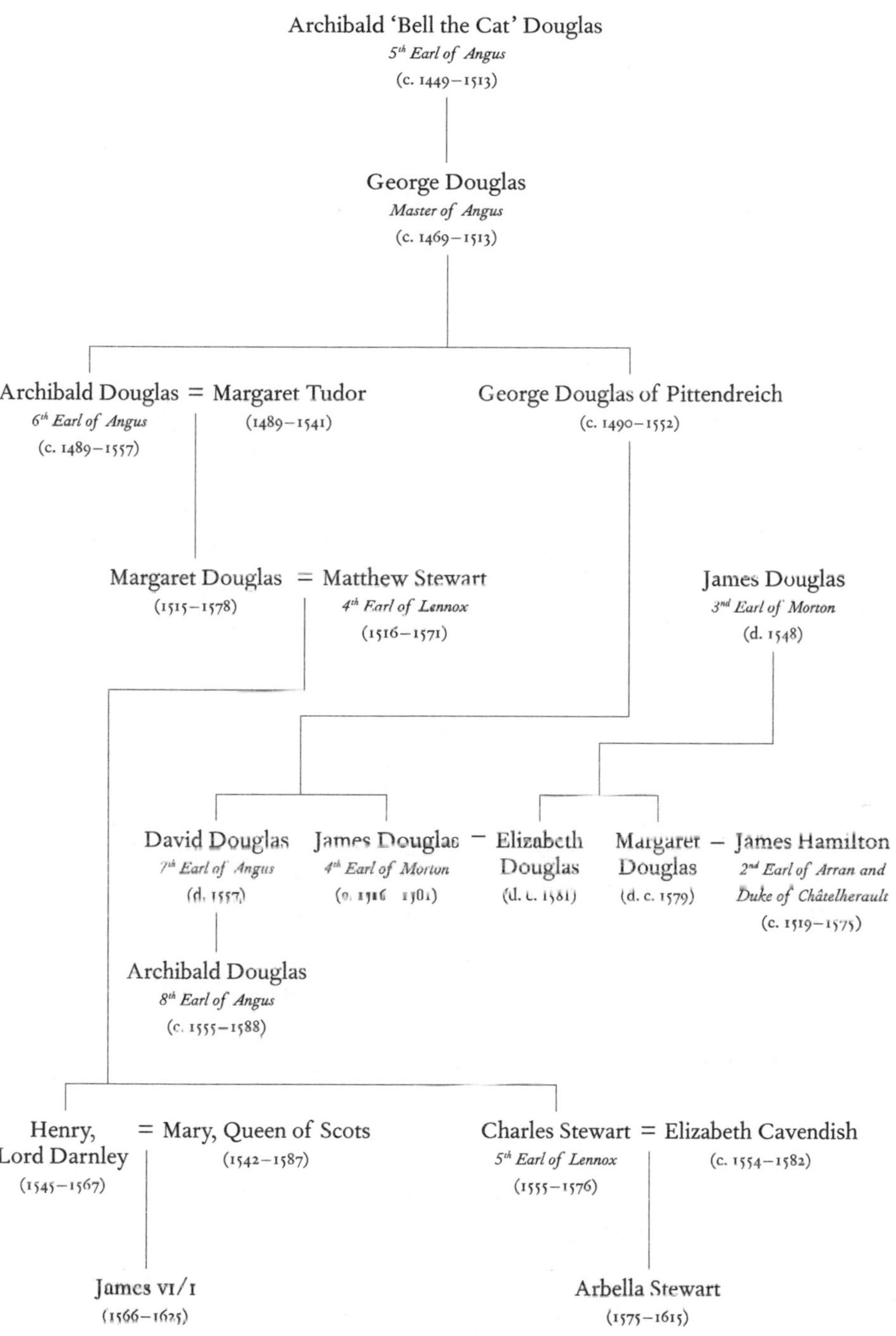

Archibald 'Bell the Cat' Douglas
5th Earl of Angus
(c. 1449–1513)
George Douglas
Master of Angus
(c. 1469–1513)
Archibald Douglas = Margaret Tudor
6th Earl of Angus
(c. 1489–1557)
(1489–1541)
George Douglas of Pittendreich
(c. 1490–1552)
Margaret Douglas = Matthew Stewart
(1515–1578)
4th Earl of Lennox
(1516–1571)
James Douglas
3rd Earl of Morton
(d. 1548)
David Douglas
7th Earl of Angus
(d. 1557)
James Douglas = Elizabeth Douglas
4th Earl of Morton
(c. 1516–1581)
(d. c. 1581)
Margaret Douglas = James Hamilton
(d. c. 1579)
2nd Earl of Arran and Duke of Châtelherault
(c. 1519–1575)
Archibald Douglas
8th Earl of Angus
(c. 1555–1588)
Henry, Lord Darnley = Mary, Queen of Scots
(1545–1567)
(1542–1587)
Charles Stewart = Elizabeth Cavendish
5th Earl of Lennox
(1555–1576)
(c. 1554–1582)
James VI/I
(1566–1625)
Arbella Stewart
(1575–1615)

The Children of Henry VII and Elizabeth of York

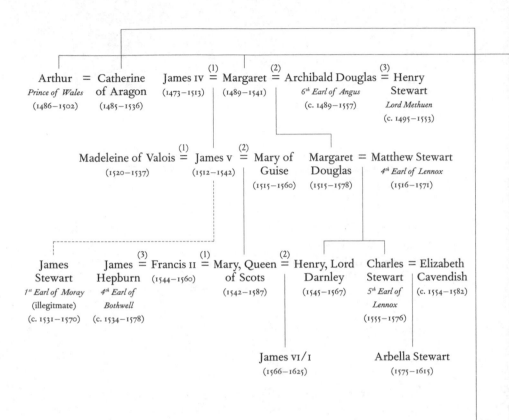

Arthur = Catherine of Aragon
Prince of Wales (1486–1502) — (1485–1536)

James IV (1) = Margaret (2) = Archibald Douglas (3) = Henry Stewart
(1473–1513) — (1489–1541) — *6th Earl of Angus* (c. 1489–1557) — *Lord Methuen* (c. 1495–1553)

Madeleine of Valois (1) = James V (2) = Mary of Guise
(1520–1537) — (1512–1542) — (1515–1560)

Margaret Douglas = Matthew Stewart
(1515–1578) — *4th Earl of Lennox* (1516–1571)

James Stewart
1st Earl of Moray
(illegitimate)
(c. 1531–1570)

James Hepburn (3) = Francis II (1) = Mary, Queen of Scots (2) = Henry, Lord Darnley
4th Earl of Bothwell (c. 1534–1578) — (1544–1560) — (1542–1587) — (1545–1567)

Charles Stewart = Elizabeth Cavendish
5th Earl of Lennox (1555–1576) — (c. 1554–1582)

James VI/I
(1566–1625)

Arbella Stewart
(1575–1615)

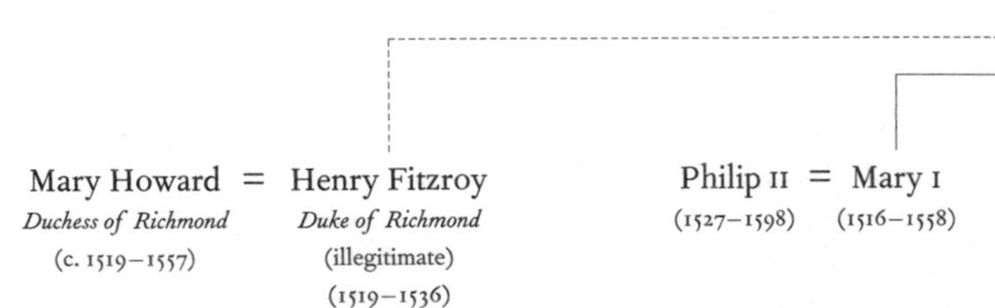

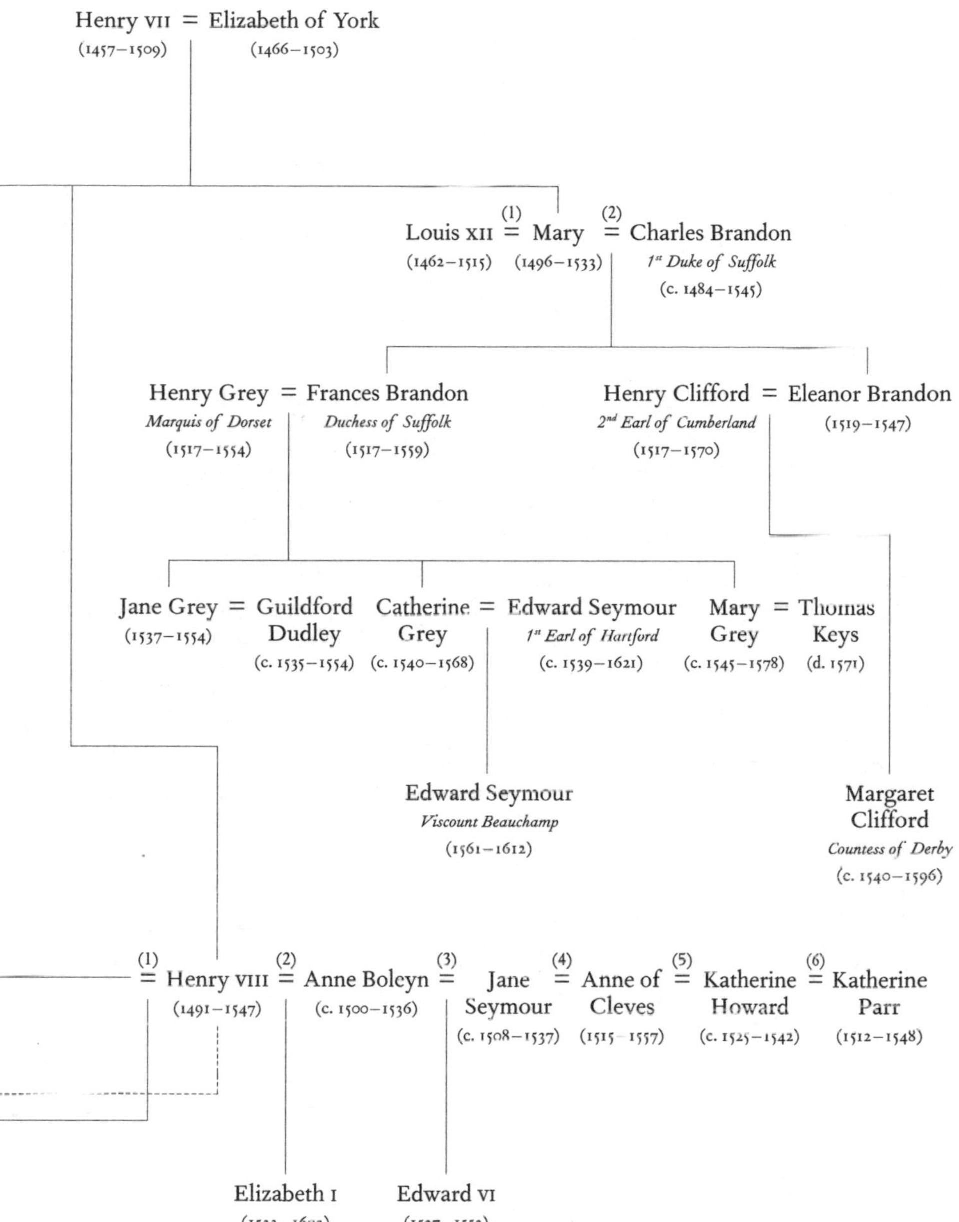

Henry VII = Elizabeth of York
(1457–1509) (1466–1503)
Louis XII (1) = Mary (2) = Charles Brandon
(1462–1515) (1496–1533)
1st Duke of Suffolk
(c. 1484–1545)
Henry Grey = Frances Brandon
Marquis of Dorset
(1517–1554)
Duchess of Suffolk
(1517–1559)
Henry Clifford = Eleanor Brandon
2nd Earl of Cumberland
(1517–1570)
(1519–1547)
Jane Grey = Guildford Dudley
(1537–1554) (c. 1535–1554)
Catherine Grey = Edward Seymour
(c. 1540–1568)
1st Earl of Hartford
(c. 1539–1621)
Mary Grey = Thomas Keys
(c. 1545–1578) (d. 1571)
Edward Seymour
Viscount Beauchamp
(1561–1612)
Margaret Clifford
Countess of Derby
(c. 1540–1596)
(1) = Henry VIII (2) = Anne Boleyn (3) = Jane Seymour (4) = Anne of Cleves (5) = Katherine Howard (6) = Katherine Parr
(1491–1547) (c. 1500–1536) (c. 1508–1537) (1515–1557) (c. 1525–1542) (1512–1548)
Elizabeth I
(1533–1603)
Edward VI
(1537–1553)

Preface
LOCKET

There is a locket in a cabinet in Edinburgh, small enough to fit into a child's palm but burdened with the weight of ancient jewels and dreams. The woman who commissioned it some 450 years ago planned each detail of its intricate symbolism: the heart-shaped frame; the unsettling images of dying knights, captive queens and hidden skulls; the cryptic Scots mottoes twisting around its edges.

Once, ambassadors to the court of England had praised the woman's beauty, and one unfortunate young courtier had died in the Tower of London for daring to love her. By the time she created the locket, she was haggard, worn by prison, loss and fear, her merry half-smile flattened into thin-lipped resolution. For the white enamel border surrounding the locket's face she chose the legend *Qvha hopis stil constantly vith patience sal obteain victorie in yair pretence*: 'Who hopes still constantly with patience shall obtain victory in their claim' – a prediction, a promise and a prayer.

The woman was Margaret Douglas, Countess of Lennox. Half-English and half-Scottish, she had arrived at the court of her uncle, Henry VIII, amidst the Christmas revels of 1530. In the four decades that followed, she transformed herself into a powerful, political noblewoman wielding influence in both England and Scotland. As the Protestant Reformations unfolded across the British Isles and the Tudor line of succession remained in constant doubt, she envisioned a united England and Scotland, ruled by one royal family, sharing a common Catholic faith. When her niece Mary, Queen of Scots, was widowed in France, Margaret helped set in motion shattering events that would see her descendants succeed to the crowns of England, Ireland and Scotland.

Most of the sixteenth-century women who made their way into the records of the era were born into wealthy, powerful families. They were expected to play a part, with a different leading man for each act of their lives: daughter, wife, mother. There were different obligations attendant on each of these positions, and women were judged by how successfully they met them. There was conventional praise for women who came up to expectations and conventional censure for those who did not: the good were all virtuous, beautiful and wise; the bad were vicious, domineering and blind to their own foolishness.

Margaret's friends often spoke of her as though she had never had a political idea in her life and simply wanted to see her children married as well as any devout Catholic mother could wish. She understood her stock part perfectly and took care to portray herself as a model noblewoman: irreproachably loving wife and mother, competent to manage the people and finances of large family estates, but unsuited to high politics. Her enemies, on the other hand, talked about her as though she were a sort of fairy-tale villainess. In their descriptions, she was a woman who consulted witches and fortune-tellers, dominated her weak-willed husband while entertaining the affections of other men, and plotted to foist her feckless, spoiled son Henry, Lord Darnley, on the ill-starred Queen of Scots.

Her contemporaries disagreed so deeply about Margaret's character that it is no shock to discover she has remained overlooked and enigmatic – one more lovely Tudor rose on the royal family tree, or horrible lord Darnley's horrible mother. The truth was that the character shorthands and commonplaces of the sixteenth century could not capture her. Margaret Douglas, a woman who made unfixable mistakes but also realised tremendous ambitions, was simply too human and too complex. To recover the Countess of Lennox, we must return both to the accounts of her actions and to her own words and writings. Through them, a story emerges. That story, of constant hope and dynastic dreams, of great triumph and terrible grief, was played out largely in secret, enacted in isolated manors and palace corners by spies, intelligence-gatherers, and by a woman unshakeably convinced that her descendants would one day rule throughout the British Isles.

Part One

THY PROMISE WAS TO LOVE ME BEST

I

'O Come Ye in Peace Here, or Come Ye in War?'

With the dead still unburied and the wounded scarcely borne away from the field at Bosworth, Henry Tudor gave thanks to God for his triumph over Richard III. The last king of the House of York had reigned for just two years after seizing the crown from his young nephew, Edward V. Richard had died with his sword in his hand, struck down as the men around him had tried to flee. Now, the victorious soldiers cheered: Thomas Stanley took up the slain king's crown and set it on Henry's head.[1]

That day at Bosworth in late August 1485 marked the violent end to a tumultuous seventy years. In the aftermath of Henry V's victory at Agincourt in 1415, it appeared that the House of Lancaster would rule a lasting cross-Channel empire as undisputed monarchs of both England and France. But that imperial vision faded during the reign of the great king's heir, the devout, sickly Henry VI. England surrendered all its French territories save Calais – perhaps for ever. The Lancastrians lost their crown to their Yorkist rivals, who were soon mired in usurpation, murder and rebellion. By 1485, a generation of English and Welsh people had lived and died without knowing a stable monarchy.

By strict dynastic reckoning, the crown did not belong to Henry Tudor. His father Edmund Tudor, first Earl of Richmond, had had no claim to it. His mother, Margaret Beaufort, was a great-great-granddaughter of Edward III, but her grandfather John Beaufort had been born a bastard. It had taken a papal bull and an act of parliament to legitimise him, and even then he was barred from the royal succession.[2] But although there were others with stronger rights – and Henry Tudor would always face pretenders to his throne – he had obvious advantages: allies; an army; and, it seemed that day at Bosworth, the blessing of God.

With an eye for the practical as well as the symbolic, twenty-seven-year-old Henry asserted his rule. He held his coronation in October 1485, becoming Henry VII, anointed King of England and Lord of Ireland, crowned with the same regalia and by the same rites as any of his predecessors.[3] As he had sworn to do should he ever become king, he married Elizabeth of York, sister of the dead child-king Edward V, and gave his new dynasty a new emblem: the Tudor rose, uniting his Lancastrian red to Elizabeth's Yorkist white. Nine months later, they had an heir and called him Arthur. England's first printer, William Caxton, had just published a translation of Sir Thomas Malory's medieval epic *Le Morte d'Arthur*, and Henry and Elizabeth gave their son the name of the mythical king whose dominion had extended throughout Britain: 'He shall be long king of all England,' predicted Merlin the magician, 'and have under his obeisance Wales, Ireland, and Scotland.'[4]

Over the ten years that followed, Henry and Elizabeth had three more children who lived to adulthood: Margaret, Henry and Mary. For the king, these young princes and princesses meant that his family's dynasty would survive him and that he could make marriage alliances with European powers, vital considerations for a new royal house trying to signal its permanence and prestige.

Henry's first move was to shore up England's friendship with Spain, enormously wealthy and newly centralised under the rule of Ferdinand of Aragon and Isabella of Castile. In the spring of 1488, England and Spain commissioned envoys to arrange a match between Prince Arthur and Katherine of Aragon, youngest daughter of the Catholic monarchs.[5] They agreed that the children would marry once they came of age, but were nearly confounded by the challenge of agreeing the bride's marriage portion. At one point the exasperated Spanish ambassadors revealed how little faith they had that this new dynasty would survive any longer than the last, and told their English counterparts 'bearing in mind what happens every day to the Kings of England, it is surprising that Ferdinand and Isabella should dare to give their daughter at all'![6]

While the diplomats wrangled, Henry's queen, Elizabeth, gave birth to a daughter at nine o'clock in the evening of 28 November 1489. Two days later, the royal family and aristocracy gathered to see the girl brought to the porch of St Margaret's church, next to Westminster Abbey. The Bishop of Ely baptised her with chrism, salt and Holy Water. Then, four knights held a canopy above her as she was carried through the candle-lit church to the high altar, where the Archbishop of York confirmed her. Her newly made godparents gave her gifts: gilt flagons, a jewel-encrusted vessel containing Holy Water, a silver chest filled with gold. In honour of her grandmother Margaret Beaufort, who also served as godmother, she was named Margaret Tudor.[7]

In the religion of late medieval England, there was a saint for every place, profession and occasion, a patron who could intercede with God on behalf of mortal Christians. The christening connected the newborn princess with two particular saints among this vast communion. It took place on the morning of the feast of St Andrew, the fisherman-turned-apostle who had been martyred on a saltire and adopted as the patron of Scotland, and the child was given a name that she shared with the eleventh-century Scottish queen who had become one of that country's most beloved saints. This proved a lucky pair of coincidences, for in 1496, Henry began to pursue a marriage for his young daughter with James IV, King of Scots.[8]

It was an idea with possibilities. If the scheme worked, it would secure England's northern border and draw Scotland into the Anglo-Spanish alliance. But it was also a touch far-fetched. Scotland and France had an 'Auld Alliance', and English kings lived with the fear of French invasion through Scotland. England, for its part, was the only country in a position to invade Scotland, and its kings traditionally upheld a spurious claim to be the feudal lords to Scotland's monarchs. The border region was notoriously unstable, and although there had been long stretches of entente – Henry himself had received Scottish support for his claim to the throne – the two countries were 'ancient enemies'.[9]

Scotland faced its own political trials. The Stewart dynasty had held power for more than a century, but its kings had tended to accede young and die young. Throughout the fifteenth century every single Stewart ruler had come to the throne as a child. In these circumstances, Scotland's nobles usually became responsible for governing the country, with the late king's widow keeping custody of their child-king son, and either the next-in-line or specially appointed senior nobles acting as Regents.[10] This string of minorities, added to the fact that the crown lacked the money to enforce its will without the support of the nobility, meant Scottish aristocrats were powerful figures.

Scottish kings, however, were just as eager as their fellow European rulers to expand their own political power. It was the time of Renaissance monarchy, when kings not only cultivated new artists and writers but tried to make themselves masters over their clergy, nobility and ordinary subjects – in short, to be emperors in their own kingdom.[11] James IV, according to the Spanish ambassador Don Pedro d'Ayala, had all the makings of such a king. He was courageous, pious, loved by his subjects.

It helped that he was a good-looking, virile man, bearded and physically strong. Hunting was among his chief pleasures. D'Ayala was impressed by James's talent for languages and his abstemiousness in eating and drinking – 'such a thing seems to be superhuman in these countries'. Although young, the king was a wise man who both heard counsel diligently and knew his own mind. James also had his imperfections: in d'Ayala's estimation, he was a rash commander, brave but with a tendency to leap into battle himself before he had made his orders clear. Moreover, he had a tremendous ego, 'as much as though he were lord of the world' – and he wanted to make a major international alliance through his marriage.[12]

Although both Henry and James stood to gain from the match, the Anglo-Scottish marriage talks dragged on for five years, brought to frequent halts by outbreaks of war. Finally, however, Henry secured the marriages he wanted for his eldest children. Prince Arthur married Katherine of Aragon in November 1501. Two months later, England and Scotland concluded the Treaty of Perpetual Peace at Richmond Palace. Margaret Tudor would move to Scotland the following year, taking a dowry of 30,000 gold English nobles. In return, she would have lands worth £2,000 annually, with a further allowance of 500 marks per year.[13]

On 25 January 1502, Princess Margaret heard High Mass in the chapel of Richmond. It had been completed just the year before and it glittered. The choir was decked in cloth of gold, the altars were set with jewels and contained relics of the saints, the walls were hung with arrases and images of the English kings.[14] There in the Queen's Great Chamber, before her parents, her younger brother and sister, the lords spiritual and temporal of England and diplomats from across Europe, Margaret listened to the Earl of Bothwell pledge the faith of the absent Scottish king. Then, twelve years of age and therefore considered old enough to marry, she swore to have 'the said James king of Scotland unto and for my husband and spouse, and all other for him forsake, during his and mine lives natural. And thereto I plight and give to him . . . my faith and troth'. As she finished her vows, trumpeters and minstrels began to play, filling the room with 'the best and joyfullest' music.

Margaret had been brought up for this moment, but she was young and overwhelmed. Her father left the room, taking the Scottish representatives with him. Amidst the clamour of the musicians and the courtiers, her mother took Margaret's hand. Queen Elizabeth led her young daughter away to dinner, and sat beside her throughout the meal. Jousts and banquets went on for another day of celebrations, and Henry, showing a liberality at odds with his later reputation, gave lavish gifts to the Scots, from golden cups to velvet gowns. Margaret, Princess of England, was now known as Margaret, Queen of Scots.[15]

But Henry's double diplomatic triumph depended on the lives of Arthur and Margaret, and in early modern families of all degrees and conditions, parents often outlived their children. Fifteen-year-old Arthur suddenly died on 2 April 1502. Arthur and Katherine had been living at Ludlow Castle in the Welsh marches, and it took two days for news to reach the court at Greenwich. Early on the morning of the third day, the king's confessor woke Henry, turning to the Book of Job as he struggled to put the horrifying message into words: 'Shall we receive good at the hand of God, and shall we not receive evil?' Elizabeth tried to comfort the king, urging him to give thought to his own health and the well-being of his kingdom, before she broke down herself. Henry had already resolved 'that he and his Queen would take the painful sorrows together', and now repeated 'her own wise counsel' to her: that they had three surviving children and were still young enough to have more.[16] But the second tragedy came soon afterwards. The thirty-six-year-old Elizabeth did become pregnant again that year, only to die in childbirth in February 1503.[17]

Grief-stricken, Henry now confronted the full implications of his diplomacy. He still had a son and heir, the young Henry, Duke of York, who was soon engaged to the widowed Katherine of Aragon. But the duke was still a boy, and it was clearer than ever that no child was guaranteed to survive to adulthood. Margaret's marriage assumed new importance and new danger. Matching his eldest daughter with the King of Scots might someday mean that the rulers of Scotland would have a claim to the English throne. Henry's shrewd gambit now threatened graver ends: if Margaret's surviving brother died and she inherited the crown, her husband could become King of England.

Even so, Margaret set out for Scotland four months after her mother's death. Her month-long procession began on 27 June 1503, when she left Richmond in the company of her father. He went with her as far as his mother's palace of Collyweston in Northamptonshire. As a parting gift, he gave her a Book of Hours with Flemish illuminations. He left a note asking her to remember him in her prayers, inscribing it on the feast of George, England's patron saint.[18] From Collyweston she travelled north, at some times riding on a palfrey and at others carried in a litter supported by two strong horses. The Earl and Countess of Surrey headed her retinue, which also included peers, clergy, ladies, gentlemen, musicians and minstrels. At every town along her route, there were celebrations. Local dignitaries lavished money on elaborate feasts and displays – the Lord Abbot of St Mary's, York, hosted the retinue for a mere two days and knocked down part of the abbey wall to build a new gateway for the occasion. Churches brought out their most cherished relics and filled the streets with the sounds of chanted anthems and ringing bells. On 1 August she crossed into Scotland. Two days later, at Dalkeith Castle on the River Esk, Margaret at last met James.

The king, dressed in crimson velvet trimmed with cloth of gold, was sixteen years older than his bride to be. For several days he played the role of chaste and chivalrous knight, listening to her play the lute, presenting her with gifts of horses, riding out with her to hunt harts. Then it was on to Edinburgh; the capital had prepared a show.

Fountains flowed with wine and church bells 'rang for mirth' at the entrance of the new queen. People filled the streets and leaned out of crowded windows to catch a glimpse of her. On specially constructed scaffolds, actors played out tableaux of Christian and classical scenes: maidens dressed as the four virtues of Justice, Fortitude, Temperance and Prudence trampled tyrants and sinners under their feet; the archangel Gabriel greeted the Virgin Mary; the Virgin married Joseph. More ominously, one scene showed Paris giving the apple of discord to Venus, setting in motion the events that led to the founding of Rome – but only after ten years of war and the ruin of his family's kingdom.[19]

On 8 August 1503, Margaret was led to the abbey church of Holyrood, a Gothic monastery that James had transformed into a palace. Sitting at the base of Arthur's Seat, Holyrood offered Margaret new apartments, extensive gardens and respite from the noise of the city.[20] There, she and James were married and Margaret was crowned. Escorted by English and Scottish noblewomen, dressed in crimson velvet and wearing a collar of pearls, her hair loose, she was anointed and presented with a sceptre by the king himself. Bonfires roared throughout Edinburgh. Margaret, James and their guests feasted on wild boar's head before spending the afternoon dancing and the evening in yet another banquet.[21] The poet William Dunbar saluted her with a rhythmic Scots ballad that celebrated her Tudor blood and hailed her as queen: 'Welcome the rose both red and white/ Welcome the flower of our delight/ Our spirit rejoicing from the sunbeam/ Welcome of Scotland to be queen!'[22] When the festivities had concluded and the English delegation had returned home, Margaret Tudor was left to fulfil her new role as Queen of Scots and wife of the king.

It was not always an easy marriage. Margaret was thirteen, whereas James was thirty. She was technically old enough to marry, but young brides often did not consummate their marriages until they were sixteen, and James already had mistresses and a nursery full of children by them. In spite of her English retinue, the new queen was lonely, and worse, homesick. Shortly after her arrival, she dictated a letter to her father, her words full of anxiety, inexperience and unguarded emotion. She began with formal commendations, then moved on to her sense that she had been cut out of the political loop: her chamberlain was not part of the daily meetings James had with his counsellors, and she could only pray 'God send me comfort', hoping that she and her household 'that been left herewith' would be well treated. At last, she seized the pen from her secretary and wrote in her own blocky, childish script: 'I would I were with your grace now and many times more.'[23]

As she became older, however, Margaret Tudor grew into her role. She became attached to the dashing James, whom she would later call 'my dearest spouse and husband'.[24] Once Margaret was sixteen, they began having children. Their first child was sickly: James went on a pilgrimage to the shrine of St Ninian, praying that their son would live, but the boy died young. So did their second and third children, but their fourth, a boy named James who was born on 10 April 1512, would outlive his father. Margaret played the part of queen consort adeptly, becoming a patron, ready to intercede for those who needed her husband's mercy. But this relatively successful royal marriage was not enough to preserve the peace between England and Scotland.[25]

Henry VII died on 21 April 1509 and was succeeded by his surviving son, Margaret's younger brother, Henry VIII. In the first weeks of his reign, the new king married his former sister-in-law Katherine of Aragon and then had her crowned alongside him at the June coronation.[26] Henry was in love with his brother's strong-willed widow, and as he declared to Katherine's father Ferdinand, 'if he were still free he would choose her in preference to all others'.[27] The marriage also had the effect of reaffirming England's alliance with Spain. Upon Henry's accession, the Venetian ambassador declared him 'magnificent, liberal, and a great enemy of the French'.[28] Henry VIII saw himself in the tradition of his conquering Lancastrian forebear, Henry V – also the heir of a dynastic founder who had lacked the taste for foreign adventures – and he wanted to reclaim the lost French lands once held by England's medieval kings. His counsellors were unenthusiastic, but by 1511 Henry had overruled them and joined an anti-French alliance led by the papacy and known as the Holy League.

At first, England and Scotland remained on cordial, even familial terms. Henry renewed the Treaty of Perpetual Peace in August 1509.[29] Ferdinand had reminded Katherine that '[a]s the King and the King of Scots are brothers it would not become them to quarrel'.[30] But when it became obvious that Henry was going to go to war with France, James found himself caught between two alliances – a new one with the ancient enemy, England, and an old one with the traditional ally, France. The new seemed profoundly unreliable: not only was Henry refusing to pay his father's bequests to Margaret Tudor, a decision she resented, but he also chose January 1512 to reassert the English kings' old claim to be overlords of Scotland. That summer, James retaliated by cementing the French alliance with a new treaty.[31]

James and Henry had put Margaret Tudor in an invidious position. She loved her husband, whom she had lived with for nearly ten years, in which time she had not seen her brother, who was doing little to maintain her friendship. Still, she did not want to see England and Scotland go to war. As Thomas Dacre, Henry's Lord Warden of the Marches, reported, she was 'sorry any cause of grudge be between' Henry and James.[32]

In June 1513, Henry set out to wage war against France, and captured the northern towns of Thérouanne and Tournai, leaving Katherine of Aragon in charge of the government of England. The king was still absent on the Continent when the Scots invaded Northumberland in August, setting up camp on Flodden Hill at the beginning of September and earning James an excommunication in the process. English forces under Thomas Howard, Earl of Surrey, marched north to meet them, and brought them to battle on the afternoon of 9 September.

It was a brutal, confused encounter. The survivors would never forget it. James's army marched down from the hill, clashing with the advancing English. The long pikes favoured by the Scottish troops were worse than useless in the close hand-to-hand fighting that followed, and the English dispatched Scot after Scot, noble and foot soldier alike. James, justifying d'Ayala's analysis of him as a reckless commander but a brave man, fell in the midst of the carnage, a spear-length away from Surrey. As light faded from the battlefield, the Scots fell back, pursued by the English, who devastated the retreating troops.[33] For the English, there were spoils – horses, prisoners, ordnance.[34] For the Scots, there was little beyond terrible, traumatic grief – they had lost their army, their nobility and their king.

Before long, the almost unbelievable news reached the English court. Katherine of Aragon saw it as a God-given triumph over a detested enemy, writing to Henry that it was 'the greatest honour that could be and more than ye should win all the crown of France'. She reduced James from a king to a trophy, sending his bloodied shirt to Henry only after her advisors talked her out of sending the corpse: 'I thought to send [James] himself unto you but our Englishmen here would not suffer it.'[35] Henry's instincts were just as polemical as his wife's. He wrote to the pope that he would not make peace so long as any Scottish nobles remained alive, free and allied to the French.[36] The poet John Skelton seized the chance to publish a bitter ballad mocking James's downfall: 'Before the French king, Danes, and other/Ye ought to honour your lord and brother.'[37]

Despite this jingoism, both Katherine and Henry tried to conciliate the widowed queen of Scots, as they could not be sure of her loyalties. At Katherine's wedding to Prince Arthur twelve years before, Margaret and Henry, both still children, had danced together so energetically that he had 'suddenly cast off his gown and danced in his jacket', to the delight of their parents.[38] Now, Henry had word at Tournai that his sister was threatening vengeance on her native country.[39] He asked the pope for permission to bury James at St Paul's Cathedral in London, even though the Scottish king had died excommunicate – this never happened, and James's body was eventually lost. Katherine, for all her conviction that Flodden was a triumph 'so marvellous that it seemeth to be of God's doing alone', wrote sympathetic letters to her sister-in-law.[40] Henry and Katherine believed that James's death gave Margaret Tudor new political importance. It was Henry's hope that she would take his advice in governing Scotland and see that her young son, suddenly James V, King of Scots, grew up favourably disposed to England.[41]

In fact, Henry's sister had become even more important than he and Katherine realised. As queen dowager, Margaret Tudor could expect to keep custody of her son and serve as his tutor or guardian. James IV, however, had gone further. His will does not survive, but he seems to have decreed that Margaret would not only be their son's guardian, but his Regent – unless she remarried. Giving her the office was an innovation, and a mark of James's affection and respect for his wife.

He had not left her with an easy task. On 19 September, Margaret met the surviving lords spiritual and temporal. Together, they agreed to have the young king crowned in the chapel at Stirling and established a daily council to assist Margaret in the governance of the realm.[42] She was now Regent for her son, dealing with the enormous challenge of governing in the aftermath of Flodden. The men who had died on the battlefield had been Scotland's experienced political elite. This would have been a challenge for any ruler, much less one whose sex and nationality seemed, to some, to render her untrustworthy. Being pregnant – and still just twenty-three – did not help.

She gave birth to James's posthumous son Alexander, Duke of Ross, on 30 April 1514. Four months later, mistrusted by her counsellors and taken for granted by her brother, Margaret took a step that nobody had foreseen – she remarried.

Her new husband was Archibald Douglas, sixth Earl of Angus. He was the grandson of the previous earl, who had died soon after losing his two eldest sons at Flodden. The new earl abruptly became one of the most important magnates in southern Scotland.[43] Although the Douglases were not in line for the throne – their emblem was the red heart of Robert the Bruce, given to a forebear in token of his loyalty to the crown – they were a force to be reckoned with, having extensive lands near the border and a powerful network of supporters.

A good-looking widower in his mid-twenties, Angus was brave, affectionate and utterly loyal to his kin – his favourite oath was 'by Saint Bride of Douglas', an invocation of the parish church in his family's namesake village.[44] But he combined political inexperience with naked familial ambition – not a propitious mix of qualities for the husband of a female Regent.

Margaret's reasons for marrying Angus have never been wholly clear. She was often impetuous when under pressure: the chroniclers Polydore Vergil and Raphael Holinshed, writing several decades after the event, thought she feared Henry would make her leave her sons and marry a foreign king.[45] The secret marriage was certainly not a choice her counsellors advised. With characteristic Tudor faith in her right to act as she saw best, she later wrote 'I took my lord of Angus against all Scotland's will . . . I took him at my own pleasure'.[46]

On 18 September, Scotland's nobility gathered at Dunfermline to denounce Margaret and demand that she be replaced as tutor to the king. She had 'contracted marriage and passed *ad secundas nuptias*' – second marriage – and therefore she should have nothing more to do with 'matters pertaining to the crown'.[47] They wanted a new governor, and so they sent an invitation to John Stewart, Duke of Albany.

Albany was a half-French cousin of the late king who had been born and raised on the Continent. Strong-jawed and soldierly, Albany was heir presumptive to Margaret's children. England protested that Albany, as next in line to the throne save James's brother, was a threat to the boys and should be kept in France. Nonetheless, he set out in the spring of 1515 and reached Scotland in mid-May.[48] The July parliament confirmed him as governor.[49]

Margaret Tudor was six months pregnant by her new husband, with little money and few allies, but she was not about to surrender her children to Albany. With Angus and her sons, she headed for Stirling Castle: high on a crag where the Highlands meet the Lowlands, it was a modern fortress, built to withstand the most determined attackers. She did not give in when Albany's messengers approached with the orders to give up the boys. Instead, she ordered that the portcullis be lowered, insisted that Stirling was hers, and that her late husband had made her protector of their children. Although she asked for time to make up her mind, she already had a desperate plan. If Albany besieged Stirling, she would place young James on the walls and make it plain that the duke was waging war against Scotland's crowned king.

The queen's instinct for imagery was not enough to prevent Albany's arrival on 4 August. As Margaret would later recall, she found herself with only her women, loyal servants and a handful of soldiers. Margaret Tudor was a princess of England, dowager Queen of Scots, and convinced she was Regent for her son, but nothing in her upbringing could have prepared her for the sight of Albany's force and artillery arrayed against her, or for the sight of her defenders fleeing.

Out of options and allies, she surrendered, asking Albany that he show favour to her sons and her husband. He replied that he would help her and the boys, but not traitors. 'And there by reason of his great might and power as an usurper with violence . . . [he] did take from me the king and duke my said tender children.'[50]

The queen had lost her sons. In the weeks that followed, the question became how she could get them back and get to safety, and it was agreed that she should flee to England even though she was soon due to give birth. At the end of September, she left Scotland. She made it as far as Harbottle Castle in Northumberland, where she went into labour two weeks early – 'to my great peril and extreme danger'. Margaret would later say that the birth and its aftermath were so difficult and dangerous that many believed she had died. But she survived, as did her daughter, born on 8 October 1515: Lady Margaret Douglas.[51]

Thomas Dacre, Warden of the Marches, and his colleague Thomas Magnus, archdeacon of the East Riding of Yorkshire, wrote to Henry VIII ten days later. His sister, they informed him, had come into England and been 'delivered and brought in bed of a fair young lady'. They were far from court and working in a 'barren and wild country', so there was no chance to arrange a spectacle to stand comparison with Margaret Tudor's royally appointed Westminster baptism, but they assured Henry that his new niece had been christened the very next day.[52] Although Dacre and Magnus did not go into details, Margaret had been assigned godparents at this hasty christening, Thomas, Cardinal Wolsey, among them. He was not only Archbishop of York, the diocese in which she had been born, but also England's only prince of the Church and Henry VIII's chief minister.

For her part, Margaret Tudor had already written to Albany, telling him that she had 'been enforced for fear and danger of my life . . . to depart forth of the realm of Scotland into this the realm of England', where:

> by the grace of almighty God I am now delivered and have . . . a young lady, desiring you in God's name and for your honour as right and good justice reigneth that ye suffer me as tutrix of the young king and prince my tender child . . .[53]

It was telling that the newborn daughter did not merit a sentence to herself.

2

Childhood

Margaret Douglas was a child of the border: half-Scottish, half-English, born in flight from one country to the other, of royal blood but of uncertain status. Although she was Henry VII's first granddaughter, she was not the centre of attention at Harbottle Castle in the first weeks of her life. It would be some time before anybody was quite sure what to do with her.

Margaret Tudor left Harbottle for Dacre's fortress at Morpeth five weeks later in November 1515, probably taking her daughter with her. The Warden of the Marches had Morpeth fitted out for his royal guest, and at least one observer noted that he 'never saw a baron's house better trimmed in all his life'. There were new tapestries, gold cups and silver dishes, the best food that could be had. It was nearly Christmas, and King Henry was seasonally generous with his gifts, sending his sister two gowns, one of cloth of gold and another of tynsen, a kind of shimmering cloth woven with metallic thread. Angus crossed the border, was reunited with his wife and met his newborn daughter, while the dowager Queen of Scots, temporarily absolved of all political responsibilities, tried her best to return to normality: she spent a good deal of time ordering clothes to replace the ones abandoned in her flight and writing reproachful letters to the English and Scottish courts.

But there was an undercurrent of anxiety to Margaret Douglas's first Christmas. In the course of escaping and giving birth, Margaret Tudor had pinched her sciatic nerve. Her right leg was in constant pain from hip to ankle, and the trip from Harbottle had exacerbated the damage. Morpeth rang with her shrieks whenever her servants tried to help her out of her sickbed. Despite Dacre's lavish provisions, she took only a bit of roast meat with jelly and turned down everything else on offer, from boiled meat to almond milk to pottage.[1] Above all else, she missed her sons, and spoke especially often of baby Alexander. Nobody could find the heart to tell her that the boy had died on 18 December.[2]

With the spring, however, Margaret Tudor's health returned, and with it, her focus. The dowager Queen of Scots had three goals: get back control of her surviving son, secure her revenues, and decide what to do about Angus. Her new husband, not trusting that England would help him recover his lands, returned to Scotland and made peace with his enemies: a show, said Dacre, 'of falsehood and doubleness'. Although the betrayal stung, Margaret Tudor took comfort in the fact that she was about to set forth for her brother's court.[3] Come May 1516, she was back in London at last, riding on a white palfrey sent to her by Katherine of Aragon. The city was rife with plague and unseasonably hot, but she was no longer a fugitive.

Seeing his sister for the first time in more than a decade, it was hard for Henry to accept that she had married again and now had a legitimate daughter. Angus's about-face furthered the unreality of the business: 'Done like a Scot,' fumed the king.[4] Sebastian Giustinian, the Venetian ambassador in London, reported that Henry's counsellors were trying to extricate Queen Margaret from this new marriage so that she could marry again. If all Scotland had been under papal excommunication at the time, they reasoned, then Angus had not been able to legally wed, and Margaret Tudor could go off to Austria to marry the aged Emperor Maximilian I.

Even Margaret Douglas's godfather was reluctant to accept that Margaret Tudor was really married to Angus and could not be the emperor's bride. Bartholomew Ticcioni reported that Thomas Wolsey had told him he would 'gladly send back his [cardinal's] hat or lose a finger of his right hand so that she should be free' to make such an advantageous marriage.[5]

Few gave much thought to what this would mean for the infant girl. If her parents had, in good faith, thought themselves married, then Margaret Douglas might be called legitimate – and nobody wanted to say that the Queen of Scots had had a child out of wedlock. But if her parents had never been married, the child was a bastard – and her mother could marry again.

Fortunately for young Margaret, her mother was not ready to marry abroad for Henry VIII's convenience. Margaret Tudor's dower lands were in Scotland, where she was the king's mother. She did not want to be sent anywhere else, least of all to Austria, and Henry and Wolsey conceded that she might be a useful balance to Albany's French influence. In April 1517, Margaret Tudor received permission to return to Scotland and collect the revenues from her lands.[6]

Her old hosts Dacre and Magnus rode with her to the border. She was on the point of crossing back into Scotland when she suddenly faltered. As a teenager, she had thought England and Scotland equal, but now, she said, she saw 'the honour of England, and the poverty and wretchedness of Scotland'.[7] The two men had to talk her over the border. Margaret knew perfectly well that being the king's mother did not confer automatic power and happiness. She tried to build up her own faction in order to contest Albany, but had little success, and her marriage to Angus, never better than unstable, soon reached the point of collapse.

Angus had already shown himself to be untrustworthy politically, but now he compounded double-dealing with adultery, seizing one of Margaret's houses and living openly with Janet of Traquair, his long-term mistress. By October 1518, Margaret and Angus were no longer speaking to one another. After six months, worn down, she wrote to her brother, saying she wanted 'to part with him [Angus] for I wot [know] well he loves me not as he showeth to me daily' and that she 'shall never marry but where ye may like me nor never to part from your grace'.[8]

While her brother had once been prepared to pretend that Margaret's remarriage had never happened, the notion of divorce touched an orthodox nerve in Henry. He had not chosen Angus to be his sister's second husband, but her husband he was, and he might yet prove a useful ally. In the summer of 1519 the king sent a Franciscan friar named Henry Chadworth to mediate between the feuding spouses, and it seemed to work. Soon afterwards, Margaret Tudor reported that they had been reconciled and Angus thanked Henry for his role in persuading his wife to remain with him, 'according and conforming to all reason and laws both of God and halykirk [the holy church]'.[9]

But this newfound partnership did not last and Margaret Tudor, to the confusion and dismay of her brother and his counsellors, threatened to turn to France and to the Duke of Albany. He had terrified and humiliated her at Stirling, but now she wanted her dower lands, a divorce and a say in government, and only Albany was in a position to help her. By the end of 1521 the duke was back in Scotland. Angus vacillated, at first opposing Albany, then briefly allying with him, before finally turning against him and fleeing to France. Skirmishes and power struggles along the border threatened already shaky relations with England, kept steady by a series of short-term truces rather than a formal peace.

It is unlikely that Margaret Douglas had a clear idea of what was happening to her parents. There are almost no traces of her childhood. A much later account says that she went to Scotland with her mother, so it seems probable that she left England in 1517, but she does not seem to have been living regularly with either of her parents.[10] The reports of Angus's arrival in France do not mention a little girl, and when Margaret Tudor was pondering another flight back into England in 1523, she asked for aid for herself and for her servants – not for her daughter.[11] In her early teenage years her chaperone was a well-off Edinburgh widow named Isobel Hoppar, wife of her great-uncle Archibald Douglas, a man known by the martial epithet Greysteel. It seems credible, though it is not certain, that Margaret was in the care of women outside her mother's household, most likely her Douglas kindred.[12]

Many years later, Angus would say that his daughter was 'this thing in the world that I love best', but they were only rarely together during her childhood.[13] Margaret Tudor also saw little of her. The girl was worth considerably less to her mother than her half-brother James, both politically and personally: she was still a child and not guaranteed to survive to marriageable age; she was not in line to the Scottish throne; and she was the daughter of a much-regretted, impetuous second marriage.

Nonetheless, events would show that Margaret Douglas had much in common with both her parents. Like her mother, she had a certain disregard for consequences – which proved dangerous, as she also inherited her father's taste for political intrigue. Although they were only briefly together as a family, all three were courageous, decisive and usefully prone to being underestimated.

The Douglas estates extended across the Lowlands, but the greatest of their houses was Tantallon, the medieval stronghold where Margaret's grandfather and great-grandfather had been born. It was a formidable red castle perched on a cliff overlooking the Forth. In every room, blazes roared in great stone fireplaces, beating back the driving winds and rain. Down below, the

Bass Rock dominated the riverscape. It was a small island, home to thousands of gannets, white-feathered seabirds with black-tipped wings that dived in and out of the Forth to catch fish.

From her later writings it can be inferred that Margaret received an education that was solid, if unexceptional, for a girl of her rank. There were languages to learn: she read and wrote in English and French, and likely spoke some Scots as well. While some young women of the gentry and aristocracy were more scholarly, with Latin and even Greek at their command, Margaret would come to be particularly associated with books. Since it was assumed she would someday be mistress of a great household, she would have been introduced to estate management, perhaps with formal lessons and certainly by observation – as an adult, she was never good with money, but she knew how to earn the loyalty of her servants.[14] She also had to acquire the accomplishments expected in a noblewoman: a trained singing voice, lively dancing, a head for gambling and delicate needlework. In her teens and twenties she proved an adept courtier, suggesting she took to these lessons, and she remained a talented needleworker into old age.

Finally, she needed schooling in the Catholic faith. The liturgical seasons, feasts and saints' days gave shape to her year. Regular attendance at Mass offered ritual and order, the often-repeated Latin sentences slowly becoming fixed in her mind. Before she could read, she saw images from the Bible in Books of Hours and on the walls of churches, stories from the New Testament fulfilling the pledges and prophecies of the Old. Once she had mastered reading, there were devotional books to occupy her hours and deepen her faith: prayers, psalms and saints' stories to be learned, repeated and meditated upon.

Margaret was learning the basic tenets of the Christianity then practised in western Europe just as those very tenets were coming under new attack. Weeks after her second birthday, a

German monk named Martin Luther posted ninety-five theses to a church door in the university town of Wittenberg, arguing limits to the authority of the pope. Meeting with resistance from religious and political authorities alike, Luther responded by developing a new theology: salvation came not through faith and good works on earth, but through faith and grace alone. He was branded a heretic at the Diet of Worms in 1521, but he found powerful protectors who helped him to survive and spread his ideas – ideas that found a ready audience in England and Scotland. Central among these was the belief that ordinary Christians should read the Bible in their own language. In secret moments of religious conversion, men and women found that reading or hearing illegal English scripture brought them closer to God than they had ever known before.[15]

In England, Henry and his regime threw themselves into the struggle against this new heresy. In St Paul's Churchyard, site of the great pulpit of Paul's Cross and the home of London's bookselling trade, Lutheran works went up in righteous flames.[16] Henry did his part for traditional religion: he wrote a *Defence of the Seven Sacraments*, dedicated it to Pope Leo X, and earned himself the title 'Defender of the Faith'.[17] In Scotland, the July parliament of 1525 condemned Luther's 'damnable opinions of heresy', proclaiming that Scotland and its leaders had been orthodox since their first conversion to Christianity, 'clean of all such filth and vice', and banned the import of Luther's books.[18]

But there were more immediate concerns than heresy. In the two years that followed Albany's return to Scotland and Angus's departure for France, relations between England and Scotland deteriorated; Margaret Tudor, unable to restore peace, had nearly fled back to her native country. The situation changed in the summer of 1524. Albany left for France and Angus returned to England – an altered man, according to Cardinal Wolsey: 'it appeareth right well that since his being in the realm of France he is greatly amended, having now substantial, good and fresh understanding in matters of wisdom and policy'.[19] Margaret Tudor was useful to England, but Angus was potentially valuable as well, and he returned to Scotland in the autumn. As the cardinal wryly wrote to the Duke of Norfolk, 'it is no folly for a good archer to have two strings to his bow, especially whereas one is made by thread wrought by women's fingers'.[20]

The dowager Queen of Scots had no intention of sharing status with either Albany or Angus. The young King James, with her encouragement, assumed power himself in the summer, and Margaret Tudor started petitioning Henry and Wolsey to match her son with Henry's daughter, Princess Mary –'such a marriage', Wolsey wrote, 'as never king of Scots had the like'.[21] Mary, some five months younger than her cousin Margaret, was Henry's only legitimate child, and her marriage was a matter of serious consequence. By 1524, it was apparent that Katherine of Aragon was unlikely to have more children. Whoever married Princess Mary might become king of England through her.[22] Margaret Tudor was aiming very high for her son.

Margaret Douglas was now nearing her tenth birthday and was old enough to become caught up in her mother's political struggles, though the dowager Queen of Scots was less overtly ambitious for her daughter than for her son James. There seems to have been a plan to marry young Margaret off to James Stewart, Earl of Moray, one of James IV's illegitimate sons. On 22 February 1525, Magnus reported that Moray expected to get the wardship of the young earl of Huntly and 'to have in marriage my Lady Margaret, the Queen's and the earl of Angus's daughter and heir'.[23]

Nothing came of this, and the critical question remained the custody of James V. According to English accounts, the king was growing into an impressive young man: 'He sings, dances, and shows familiarity among the lords; than which nothing can be better in a young prince . . .'[24] He was, however, only thirteen by the summer of 1525. In the July parliament it was agreed that different groups of four nobles – Margaret Tudor not among them – each would share custody of James on a rotating basis, diluting the power that normally went with responsibility for a young king.

Angus was one of the first group. Come the end of his term in November, he demonstrated the problem with this scheme: it imagined that no noble, no matter how ambitious, would violate the terms. Angus, however, kept James rather than passing him on to the next group, and it soon became clear that he was not going to give him up.

Angus turned to his own family to fill the offices of state and keep control of the kingdom. Before long, he had lost supporters who had expected greater rewards, most dramatically John Stewart, third Earl of Lennox. Lennox tried to seize the king from Angus but died in the attempt, leaving his nine-year-old son to inherit the earldom. James was more or less a prisoner – a status that the young king resented enormously. For Margaret Douglas, however, her father's coup probably meant more and more frequent visits to court, and more relatives to meet.[25]

Little evidence survives to show what Margaret and her royal half-brother thought of each other, though they looked alike, with the same hooded eyes and long nose. Both were bright, if patchily educated, and both found it difficult to forgive those who crossed them. Equally, we do not know what she made of her cousin James Douglas, although they were near contemporaries and the family ascendancy almost certainly brought him to court as well. He was the son of Angus's younger brother, Sir George Douglas, and would eventually become Earl of Morton and Regent of Scotland. This young, blond boy did not have Margaret's part-English, part-Scottish heritage – he was a

Douglas through and through, and they would grow up to be implacable political foes.

In 1528, Margaret Tudor at last received confirmation that Rome would grant her a divorce from Angus. She was free to marry her new paramour Henry Stewart, Lord Methven.[26] An English clergyman acting at Henry's request sent Margaret a stern letter stating that she and Angus were 'inseparably knit together by the fast bond of just matrimony', and that the order of divorce was a 'shameless sentence . . . without order of justice'. He marvelled that she could so much as consider exposing her daughter to accusations of bastardy:

> the natural love, the tender pity, and motherly kindness toward the fruit of your own body, your most dear child and natural daughter, cannot but provoke your grace unto reconciliation, whose excellent beauty, and pleasant behaviour, nothing less godly than goodly, furnished with virtues and womanly demeanour after such a sort that it would relent and mollify a heart of steel, much more a motherly mind . . . what danger of damnation should it be to your soul with perpetual infamy of your renown slanderously to distain with dishonour so goodly a creature, so virtuous a lady, and namely your natural child procreate in lawful matrimony as to be reputed baseborn . . .[27]

But the queen, even in the face of this rather overwrought appeal, was unmoved.

Coming on Henry's orders, the letter was hypocrisy of the very highest order. Unwilling to leave his throne to his daughter, Mary, the king wanted to father a legitimate, male heir. He embarked on the long journey that would allow him to divorce Katherine of Aragon and take a second wife, Anne Boleyn.

Nearly twenty years before, Henry had needed a papal dispensation from Julius II so that he could marry Katherine, who was his brother's widow. Now convinced that this marriage violated Biblical law and would therefore never produce sons, he wanted the current pope, Clement VII, to declare that his predecessor had erred and overstepped his authority when he gave Henry and Katherine permission to wed. Clement, however, was not so accommodating as Julius. Even if he had been inclined to admit such an error on the part of the papacy, he did not want to antagonise Katherine. She was the aunt of Charles V, arguably the most powerful ruler in Europe. He was the Holy Roman Emperor and King of Spain, with a reputation as a wise man and a record as a successful general – among other victories, he had sacked Rome the year before. This insoluble problem – the king's 'Great Matter' – was Wolsey's to solve.

At last, in the spring of 1528, young James escaped from Angus, asserting his own authority as king. Infuriated by the insult of his captivity, he wanted revenge not only on the earl, but on all those who had benefited from his regime. For Margaret Douglas, it was the first of many occasions on which she had to choose an identity: as James V's half-sister, was she an honorary Stewart? as the King of England's niece, a Tudor? or, as she was named, a Douglas?

If it was the last, she was in danger, along with the rest of her family. In August 1528, while Angus's uncle Archibald and his brothers George and William were eating dinner at Archibald's house in Edinburgh, Lord Maxwell, a close attendant upon the king and an enemy to the Douglases, burst in with several retainers and forced them to flee the city on horseback. On 3 September a parliament met and summoned Angus and the Douglases to appear on charges of treason. They refused to attend – Angus's secretary, sent in his stead, said that they were not lawyers themselves and could not get anybody to act for them – and were convicted of treason on 5 September.[28]

However Margaret Douglas saw herself, each of her parents was determined to decide her fate for her. There is a surviving report, made several decades after the fact, that suggested she became a political pawn at this moment of Douglas crisis. Alexander Pringle, a Scot who later moved to England, recalled that King James wanted to marry her to the Earl of Huntly, a young ward of the crown; Margaret Tudor wanted her to wed James Stewart, her own third husband's younger brother; and Margaret herself, by now a teenager, took a liking to the third Earl of Bothwell. Angus, unwilling to endorse any of these plans, resolved to get her out of the country.[29] Pringle's account is full of errors and it is hard to see what good Margaret Tudor thought she would do by marrying her daughter to her own brother-in-law, but some aspects are more credible. For one, the Earl of Bothwell was sixteen and handsome – exactly the sort of older boy a thirteen-year-old girl might like. For another, Angus, moved by some combination of paternal affection and political sense, wanted to keep control of his soon-to-be-marriageable daughter.

On the day they were declared traitors, Angus and his brother William spoke with Roger Lassells, steward to the Earl of Northumberland, the most powerful peer in northern England. Angus was not ready to surrender, but he wanted to be equipped for the worst, and asked that the earl provide rooms at Norham Castle for his relatives if they had to flee: for his daughter Margaret, for George, Earl of Huntly, and for Margaret's great-aunt Isobel, who was to look after them.

On 2 October, King James attacked another Douglas stronghold, Coldingham Abbey. Angus managed to escape before James arrived, rallied his forces, and, though badly outnumbered, 'pursued the king so fast that he drove him to Dunbar'. He then returned to Coldingham and expelled the king's men.[30]

But Angus could only keep James at bay for so long and he knew it. It is unclear whether or not Margaret was witness to any of these attacks on her father's family – although if Isobel was her governess, she may well have been in Archibald Douglas's Edinburgh house on the night of the invasion. If she had been staying with her father, she would have fled Coldingham with him. Either way, the Douglases were fighting for their survival and could not protect Margaret any longer. They had to get her out of Scotland. Within a week of the assault on Coldingham, Angus sent her south to Norham, just across the border in Northumberland.[31]

Only now did Margaret Tudor take up her pen to protest. On 25 November she wrote Magnus a letter outlining the 'great dolour' she had had at Angus's hands, particularly in the last three years, 'having no consideration of our person, honour, nor will but putting all in jeopardy'. Now, he 'would not suffer our own daughter' to remain in Scotland 'with us for our comfort' and her own: had she stayed with her mother, she 'would not have been disinherited'.[32] By refusing to let Margaret stay in Scotland, Angus had unilaterally decided that she was more Douglas than Tudor, with a stake in his family's struggle with James – and for the next two years, she would not live like a member of England's royal family.

While Angus lost his remaining fortresses and was forced to flee to England, his daughter stayed at Norham during the autumn, through Christmas and into the New Year, until the Earl of Northumberland declared that he could no longer keep her. At the end of April 1529, Angus brought Margaret, together with a gentlewoman and a manservant, to Berwick Castle, held by Wolsey. Meeting Thomas Strangways, the cardinal's controller, he explained that Northumberland was unable to shelter

Margaret and that he hoped Wolsey, her godfather, might have some place for her – for which he could pay. Wolsey was leagues away at court and preoccupied with his failure to arrange an annulment of the king's marriage, but Strangways, acting on the cardinal's behalf, agreed to take her in.

Margaret told Strangways that she was happy at Berwick, reassuring him that she had been 'never merrier nor better pleased and content than she is now'. She clearly knew the polite thing to say, but was it the honest remark of a girl who had been on the run and was glad to have found a haven, or the formality of a bored teenager, repeated often in the hope that it might become the truth? The controller did his best to keep her safe while also giving her as much freedom and amusement as he could, which, he observed to Wolsey, was 'rather more than she hath had'.[33] For Margaret, it was the first experience of a feeling she would come to know well: finding herself cut off from her family and having to rely on the loyalty of servants and on her own company.

While Margaret lived on at Berwick, first at no cost and then at Strangways's expense, Wolsey's career went into free fall. He surrendered the bishopric of Winchester and the abbey of St Alban's in February 1530, losing a major portion of his revenues. In spring he left the court and headed north, where, he wrote to Henry, he found his houses in decay, his pension insufficient and his creditors aggressive.[34] Thomas Cromwell, who had long been Wolsey's aide and was soon to replace him as the king's chief minister, did his best to advise and console his old master, observing how lucky the cardinal was to have the time to serve God and suggesting that he give up his expensive building works.[35] He was not to have the chance.

In one more minor betrayal, Strangways turned against Wolsey, alleging that the cardinal had not only compelled him to give up valuable property and offices so that he could resell them at a profit, but also failed to pay back the expenses he had incurred in his service – which included 200 marks 'for the bringing up of the lady Margaret Douglas'.[36] Henry ordered Wolsey to return to court in November, and the cardinal, already ill and certain that he would face humiliation, imprisonment and execution, died before reaching the king.[37]

Although it is not clear who gave the summons, Margaret was now invited to court. Strangways, deep in debt and only too happy to stop covering the living expenses of a queen's daughter and her servants, lost no time in bringing her to London.[38] By 23 December 1530 she was at court, where her uncle Henry VIII gave her ten marks 'to disport her with all this Christmas'.[39]

Margaret's godfather was dead, her mother was in another country, and her half-brother still refused to let her father return to Scotland, but for the moment, none of that mattered. After two years spent in draughty border castles, she was now nearly of age and being treated like a princess, with a new family and a new home: the Tudor court.[40]

3

The King's Niece

The grandeur of the Tudor court at Christmas 1530 outstripped anything fifteen-year-old Margaret had known before. She found herself at Greenwich, the riverside palace where Henry VIII had been born, and which he had refurbished with new stables for hunting and jousting, vast halls for feasts and entertainments, towers for spectators at the tiltyard.[1] Merriment and excess engulfed her. There were celebrations throughout the twelve days of Christmas, all culminating in the splendour of the Epiphany, when the great hall became a riot of masquing, dancing, banqueting courtiers.[2]

Yet just as at her first English Christmas, when her mother's illness had overshadowed the seasonal mirth, there was trouble behind the display. In the five years to come, anxiety and unease were constant attendants on the glamour and the pageantry: the court was one of the great arenas of Tudor politics. It was the place where nobles had to come and serve if they wanted a part in affairs of state and a reputation built on their own triumphs rather than on their ancient titles. Equally, it was the place where keen-witted lawyers, clergymen and minor aristocratic relatives – male and female – could use a post on the staff of some generous patron to make their way into royal service, winning office and influence far beyond that of their fathers. Adaptable and adventurous, Margaret quickly established a place for herself, winning friends and coming to be seen as what she was – not just the child of a beleaguered Scottish earl, but the king's niece and the daughter of a queen. It soon became clear, however, that politics could divide the closest of friends and that being part of England's royal family often meant secrecy, danger and heartbreak.

Henry was already maintaining Anne Boleyn, paying many of her expenses and keeping her near him at court. Wolsey was dead, and though Katherine of Aragon was still the acknowledged Queen of England, the efforts to win Henry his divorce were growing ever more audacious. The king had an illegitimate son, the eleven-year-old Henry Fitzroy, Duke of Richmond, and a legitimate daughter, the Princess Mary. Neither one was Henry's ideal heir: no bastard had sat on the English throne since the death of William the Conqueror, and no woman had ever been acknowledged as queen regnant. From Mary's childhood, Henry had made the most of her status as heir presumptive when trying to secure her a husband in the diplomatic marriage market, but he wanted a legitimate son, and promptly. There had to be time for his heir to grow up, to learn how to be a king, to inherit the throne only when he was old enough to govern for himself: 'Woe to thee, O land, when thy king is a child' – as the nearby Scots knew better than anybody.[3]

By the patriarchal logic of early modern England, Henry's fixation made sense. The basic duties of a monarch were traditionally male – defending the realm and administering justice. So was the task of perpetuating a dynasty. A married woman was subordinate to her husband, so if an English queen married an Englishman, she put herself in the impossible situation of being a ruler who was subject to her own subject; if she married a foreigner, she risked drawing England into any conflict her husband's country might enter. An unmarried woman might preserve her own authority, but only at the risk of throwing the realm into a succession crisis or even civil war at her death. Much simpler and safer, Henry believed, to have a son.

But Henry treated Margaret with a generosity that contrasted with his cruelty to his wife and daughter. Her parents were not going to give him money for her upkeep – in fact, Angus ended up in the king's pay himself, a useful servant on the borders to Henry and a perpetual irritant to the King of Scots – so Henry provided for her and her servants at his own expense.[4] She was welcomed into her Tudor family.

One day in October 1531, ten months after her arrival, Henry paid to have Margaret outfitted in royal style for the coming winter. The keeper of the Great Wardrobe delivered finery upon finery. There were yards of good Dutch linen for her smocks; twelve pairs of gloves; fourteen pairs of shoes, eight made of leather, six of velvet. Then there were the gowns, one trimmed with powdered ermine; the velvet and satin kirtles and sleeves; the two headdresses in the French fashion made popular by Anne Boleyn – rounded hoods, rather than the pointed gable style favoured by Katherine of Aragon. The clothes were meant to last, so Margaret's attendants took charge of all the ribbons, pins and needles needed to keep the wardrobe in good repair. She went about her days impeccably dressed, her black velvet hood fluttering behind her.

Soon after she came to court, Margaret made one of the most significant relationships of her life: she joined the household of her cousin, Princess Mary. It was an organisation of over one hundred and sixty men and women, from cooks to account-keepers to minstrels: Margaret brought her own two gentlemen attendants and her groom. John Hussey, a man in his mid-sixties who had served Henry VII and Henry VIII as courtier and diplomat, was the chamberlain.[5] Like Margaret, Mary was a goddaughter of the late Cardinal Wolsey.[6] Her governess was Margaret Pole, Countess of Salisbury, member of the House of

York. Although Lady Salisbury was daughter to 'false, fleeting, perjur'd Clarence', the treacherous brother of Richard III said to have been executed by being drowned in a butt of malmsey wine, she bore little resemblance to her disgraced father. The countess was famously pious and devoted to Mary. Her son Reginald Pole, a nimble-minded young man of fervent piety and feeling, was one of Queen Katherine's preferred suitors for Mary's hand.[7]

Margaret was only five months older than her cousin, making her one of the two noblewomen in the household close to Mary's own age, and they eventually became firm friends. The princess had a way of commanding loyalty. She looked like the king, with red hair and pale, penetrating eyes. Mary was exceptionally well educated and spoke graceful English, French, Italian, Spanish and Latin. A great European marriage had been awaiting her since her birth, though none of the talked-of alliances had come to pass. But, married or not, she was confident that she was her father's heir.

Through Mary, Margaret came to know the English nobility. The household entertained often, welcoming guests to eat and stay. Sometimes these were quiet, personal affairs. The Countess of Salisbury's younger sons, Lord Montague and Sir Geoffrey Pole, came to visit. The dowager Marchioness of Dorset visited more than once, on one occasion bringing her son Henry Grey, newly connected to the royal family by his marriage to Frances Brandon, eldest daughter of the king's younger sister Mary and the Duke of Suffolk. Occasionally, Mary would host banquets for local gentlewomen.[8] When not entertaining, Margaret and Mary had lessons with Mary's schoolmaster and devotions with her chaplains, and passed their free time in music, needlework and riding together. Margaret's long and lonely months at Berwick were firmly in the past.

Although they were removed from court, there was no idyllic remove from politics. Margaret's arrival coincided with a new approach to the marriage problem. Shortly before Wolsey died, Henry had been presented with the *Collectanea satis copiosa*, a collection of documents arguing that kings of England were head of the Church in their own realm and need not defer to the pope's authority. Here was the new strategy Henry needed. The clergy submitted canon law to royal authority the following year. Anne Boleyn's position was growing ever stronger.[9]

Convinced that Katherine had never been his lawful wife, Henry's conscience left him free to marry again. In January 1533 he and Anne wed in secret, and she took the queen's role in the Easter solemnities that April. Eustace Chapuys, the Spanish ambassador, was a scholar, cleric and diplomat who had been sent to England to deal with the divorce crisis. He reported that Anne 'went to mass in Royal state, loaded with jewels, clothed in a robe of cloth of gold'. Her cousin Mary Howard, engaged to the king's illegitimate son the Duke of Richmond, carried her train, and preachers offered prayers for her. In the same month, parliament passed the Act in Restraint of Appeals, banning legal appeals to the jurisdiction of Rome and declaring 'this realm of England is an Empire, and so hath been accepted in the world, governed by one supreme head and king'.[10] On 23 May, Henry got his sentence of divorce from the new Archbishop of Canterbury, Thomas Cranmer, and a week afterwards Anne was crowned queen.[11]

The new queen was pregnant at her coronation, and three months later she gave birth to a daughter: Elizabeth. She was not the hoped-for male heir, but Henry was not going to abandon the path that he had chosen. Elizabeth would be legitimate and a princess, with precedence over her half-sister Mary, so Henry began his efforts to force his elder daughter to surrender her status and her title. But when the order came through her own chamberlain that Mary was no longer to be called princess, she ignored it and her household followed her.[12]

One day in early October the earls of Oxford, Essex and Sussex rode up to the gates of Beaulieu Palace in Hampshire. They were all senior aristocrats on a mission from the king, and both Oxford and Sussex were strongly associated with Anne Boleyn's cause. Margaret was probably inside with Mary when they entered the house and asked to speak with the princess in private. Mary would only speak in front of all her attendants: justifiably, she thought she needed witnesses, and the household assembled. Margaret stood and watched as the three middle-aged noblemen tried to persuade the eighteen-year-old Mary to give up her title, only to have their threats met with implacable refusals – delivered, Chapuys later reported, 'with such great sobriety and wisdom that they could make no reply; and there was no person in the company that did not shed tears'.[13]

To Henry's mind, Mary's staff had 'put notions into her head' and kept her from obeying him.[14] By December 1533 he had grown so infuriated that he determined to break up her household and send her to live with her half-sister Elizabeth. Her governess offered to go with her at her own expense, but was told this was not allowed. Mary set off with only two servants, her fall from favour manifest.[15] Henry, however, had something else in mind for his niece: he summoned Margaret back to court and placed her in Queen Anne's household.

Margaret had been through more abrupt changes of fortune than this, and she adapted quickly. The king and queen were responsible for Mary's humiliation, but Margaret seems to have forgiven them both. She was delighted to be in Anne's circle and Henry, in turn, was delighted with her. At the New Year's celebrations in 1534 she gave him a gift and he called her to him so that he could give her a piece of plate in person.[16] Before long Margaret was a fixture of the court, 'beautiful and highly esteemed'.[17]

Henry was not acting from simple altruism or familial duty: with one daughter in the cradle and the other in disgrace, a marriageable Tudor teenager was decidedly welcome. Shortly after Margaret's reappearance at court, Henry spoke with the French ambassador, and told him that he no longer wanted to wed his daughter Mary to Alessandro de' Medici, the newly created Duke of Florence. She was still refusing to acknowledge his second wife and second daughter and Henry wanted to punish her. He might have added, although he did not, that he was reluctant to match Mary with a foreigner who might someday stage an invasion of England to claim the throne on her behalf. But, he pointed out, he did have a niece, 'whom he keeps with the Queen his wife, and treats like a queen's daughter, and if any proposition were made for her, he would make her marriage worth as much as his daughter Mary's'. No formal negotiations were opened – which was lucky, as Alessandro was an unpopular womaniser who was assassinated three years later – but Henry saw how useful Margaret could be.[18]

What did Margaret make of Henry's break with Rome, or of his reinvention as head of the Church of England, a role confirmed by the Act of Supremacy in 1534? The likeliest explanation is that she cared less about it than did many of her contemporaries. She was conventionally pious and attended by a chaplain, but it is unclear whether that chaplain was a conservative or a reformer. There is no evidence she resisted the royal supremacy – if anything, the opposite. In 1534, Henry saw her as obedient, unlike Mary, and six years later a book dedicated to Margaret called her 'niece to the most noble Christian prince King Henry the VIII . . . supreme head of the church of England'.[19] Margaret moved seamlessly from the Catholic atmosphere of her cousin's household to the Protestant one of Anne's, without appearing to sacrifice her friendship with the princess – now bastardised and officially known as 'the Lady

Mary'. The quarrels shaking court and country did not seem to touch her.

In Anne's household, Margaret found all the traditional occupations for noblewomen – needlework, music, dancing – alongside the equally traditional rituals of chivalry and courtly love. At the same time, the queen was a dedicated patron of emerging artists and Protestant theologians, and her chambers were filled with intellectual spirit.[20] Margaret reinvented herself once again, not just as the king's niece, but as one of the brightest of the bright young things at court. She fell in with a brilliant set of literary-minded courtiers, a circle dominated by Sir Thomas Wyatt. With his high forehead, full beard and unsettling eyes he was just over a decade older than Margaret and already had a reputation as a poet and diplomat. This group of noblemen and noblewomen wrote and exchanged poems, recording them in the quarto, or pocketbook-sized pages of a leather-bound paper book that has come to be known as the Devonshire Manuscript. They collaborated, sharing the manuscript amongst them, so that each poem was liable to spark an idea for a fresh new one in response. Writing in English, the authors tried on new voices and personas, writing about men, women, chivalry and love.[21]

Margaret thrived on the creative energy and made good friends. Chief among these were Mary Fitzroy, *née* Howard, who was newly married to Henry's illegitimate son, the Duke of Richmond, and Mary Shelton, a young cousin of Anne Boleyn so fond of verse that the queen once had to reproach her for writing 'idle poesies' in the margins of her prayer book.[22] Before long, Margaret became one of the busiest figures in the circle, responsible for many of the transcriptions in the manuscript. In the sphere of printed books, most writers were men, but in the world of handwritten manuscripts, women had a central role.[23] Margaret composed a handful of poems herself, and she was amanuensis to Wyatt, copying out his verses in her bold, clear script.

She filled the pages with her friends' stories of lovers – the steadfast and the faithless, the exultant and the unrequited: one lovelorn lyric in her hand starts with the refrain 'Thy promise was to love me best/And that thy heart with mine should rest/ And not to break this thy behest/Thy promise was, thy promise was.' Some of the poems are ballads, and she annotated one with the words 'learn but to sing it'. She went through the manuscript finding other poems to serve her purpose, and several of the manuscript's pages still carry her notes to herself: 'and this . . . and this . . . forget this'.[24] Mary Shelton, finding this last comment added to a poem beginning 'Suffering in sorrow in hope to attain/ Desiring in fear and dare not complain', rejoined with 'it is worthy' – though she did not say of what.[25] It was in this frank, back-and-forth world of new ideas, poetry and friendship that Margaret now lived. But there was grief behind the glitter in the queen's household: Anne miscarried a child in August 1534.

One of Margaret's new associates was Lord Thomas Howard, a fellow writer in the Devonshire Manuscript circle and uncle to Anne Boleyn, although he was ten years younger than his royal niece. He and his elder brother Lord William Howard had been two of the canopy-bearers at Elizabeth's christening.[26] There are no surviving portraits of Howard, but we know he was a poetic young man with a taste for Geoffrey Chaucer.[27]

Like any early modern noblewoman, Margaret would have known that her reputation depended on being virtuous, obedient and chaste. She would also have known that her marriage was a matter to be decided not by her but by her guardians – in this case, the king. But she was nearly twenty, with no parents at hand to give her advice or instruction – only fellow young romantics, steeped in the tradition of courtly love. Perhaps it was this that made it so easy for her to ignore the consequences of falling in love without the king's permission.

In the summer of 1535, Margaret and Thomas Howard began an affair. Soon, they were exchanging tokens. He gave her a cramp ring, a charm meant to ward off illness, while she had her portrait painted and gave him the picture, along with a diamond. Margaret was playing the princess, bestowing lavish, personal gifts on her suitor, but she was falling deeply in love and it was making her reckless.

Both Margaret and Howard had enough sense to know that it was not a suitable match. Howard, though a scion of one of the greatest families in England – Anne Boleyn was a Howard and so was Mary Fitzroy – was not in line to be Duke of Norfolk. A leading noble might marry a royal woman but it was rare for a minor one to aim so high. Knowing this, Margaret put aside whatever gratitude she felt to the king and queen and kept the affair as secret as she could manage. Margaret and Howard took care that Anne, in particular, did not suspect them. If Margaret had to attend on the queen, Howard would loiter in the corridors, waiting to see Anne leave before coming to visit Margaret.[28]

Her affair was one of many that reached a crisis in 1536. In the early afternoon of 7 January 1536, Katherine of Aragon died. Cromwell assured Chapuys that there would be a solemn funeral with hundreds of mourners, but the court itself was not in a grieving mood. The day after the news arrived, the ladies of the court spent their afternoon dancing. King Henry, dressed all in jubilant yellow with a white feather in his hat, joined them, eventually sending for Elizabeth so that he could promenade her about the room.[29] He also took up his old hobby of jousting, galloping through the lists at Greenwich. On 24 January, the Eve of the Conversion of St Paul, he fell from his horse, and for two hours was stunned, unmoving. At last, he managed to regain consciousness, but the fall had lasting consequences for him and for Anne.

On 29 January, Katherine was buried in Peterborough Cathedral, going to her grave as Arthur Tudor's widow – not Henry's wife. Another royal niece – Eleanor Brandon, second daughter of the Duke of Suffolk and Mary Tudor – was the chief mourner. Margaret was not present. Instead, she was probably at court, where, on the same day, Anne suffered another miscarriage, this time of a son.[30]

Her women wept. Anne apparently did her best to console them, saying that this only meant that her next child would be conceived after Katherine's death and that there could therefore be no doubt about his – always his – legitimacy.[31] But she could not take the same line with the king, who told her that it was clear God did not want to give him sons. Henry returned to London, leaving Anne at Greenwich – a marked change, observed Chapuys, 'when formerly he could not leave her for an hour'.[32] The king's affections were already turning towards another woman: Jane Seymour.

It was in this anxious, uncertain atmosphere, away from the eyes of the lovestruck king, that Thomas Howard proposed marriage at Easter 1536. Margaret agreed. Did the nervous tension of the court make them rash? Margaret could not tell the king or the beleaguered queen, but neither could she keep the news to herself, and the day after she accepted Howard's suit, she confided in Margaret Howard, wife of Thomas's elder brother William and her soon-to-be sister-in-law.

There were still more important secrets at court. Anne had enemies and rivals, but none of their efforts to dislodge her or to reduce her influence had worked. Until the spring of 1536, Anne had – at least outwardly – the king's favour and Cromwell's backing. Her foes, however, now found the pretext, if not the evidence, that they needed to destroy her: adultery.

It was the queen's prerogative to be the object of courtly love for aristocratic men, just as it was the king's to flirt with whomever he liked, but whereas the king could take a mistress, the queen had to make clear that the pseudo-chivalric poems and declarations made to her were a construct and a game. By April 1536 both the queen and her admirers were having conversations that were incautious to the point of foolhardiness, broaching the forbidden subject of what would happen to Anne if the king died. When word of such talk spread beyond the queen's chambers, repeated by eager rumour-mongers, it demanded investigation at the highest level.

On 30 April, Mark Smeaton, a musician in Anne's service, was arrested and interrogated at Cromwell's house. After hours of brutal questioning, he confessed to adultery with the queen. He was sent to the Tower the next day, and more arrests and incarcerations followed: William Brereton; Henry Norris; Francis Weston; Anne's brother George, Viscount Rochford, and Anne herself.

Old friends and allies turned away, their loyalty to the king trumping their friendship for the queen. All of the accused maintained their innocence, and apart from Smeaton's confession, there was little evidence against them. Even Chapuys, who was far from being a friend to Anne, wrote that Brereton, Norris and Weston 'were condemned upon presumption and certain indications, without valid proof or confession', and reported that Rochford 'replied so well that several of those present wagered ten to one that he would be acquitted, especially as no witnesses were produced against either him or [Anne], as it is usual to do'.[33] Nonetheless, they were found guilty of treason, on the grounds of having imagined the death of the king and committing adultery against him. On 17 May 1536 all five men were executed on Tower Hill. Henry, in what was macabrely if rightly seen as an act of mercy, allowed them to die under the headsman's axe rather than be hanged, drawn and quartered.[34]

On the day the men died, Cranmer annulled Henry's marriage to Anne. Elizabeth was now as much a bastard as Mary, a fact later confirmed by the Second Act of Succession, passed by parliament in July 1536. Two days after the annulment Anne was beheaded by a swordsman brought specially from Calais – put to death for adultery against a man to whom she had, according to the terms of the annulment, never been married. Henry did not wait long to take a new wife. On 30 May he wed Jane Seymour.

We do not know what Margaret thought of her uncle's ruthlessness, or the horrific end of the queen she had served. For Margaret, Howard and the rest of the young people who had flourished in Anne's household, the wisest course was to adapt. On 15 June, less than a month after Anne's execution, she went with Henry and Jane from York Place to Westminster Abbey to hear Mass. As they entered the church in elaborate procession, Margaret picked up the queen's train. With choristers and clergy leading, the king and his attendants walked forward; Jane and Margaret followed them in together, at the head of the ladies and maids. Each reinforced the position of the other: here was England's new queen, attended by the king's own niece, and here was Henry's obedient niece, high in favour, kept at court, serving the king's third wife.[35]

Only one of the Devonshire Manuscript set put his grief and foreboding into words: Thomas Wyatt, whose poems Margaret had transcribed so faithfully. He had been imprisoned along with Anne's accused lovers, and though he was released around the time that Margaret accompanied Jane into Westminster Abbey, he had watched the five men lose their heads on 17 May. 'These bloody days have broken my heart,' he wrote. 'The fall is grievous from aloft/And sure, *circa regna tonat*' – about the kingdoms, thunder rolls.[36]

For all the break with Rome, the birth of Elizabeth and the deaths of two wives, the English succession was no clearer in the summer of 1536 than it had been at the Greenwich Christmas of 1530. For the first time in more than twenty years, Henry had neither a pregnant wife nor a legitimate heir. He had three children, all legally bastards. This seemed to augur well for the Duke of Richmond: an illegitimate son was a likelier successor than an illegitimate daughter, and Richmond, nearly of age and already involved in affairs of state, was close to his father.[37] But at his moment of great possibility, Richmond suddenly fell ill. By the beginning of July it was whispered that his consumption would prove fatal – and he did not survive the month.

Henry's heir presumptive, then, must be one of his eldest sister's children – but which? The year before, the king had made James V a Knight of the Garter, inducting him into England's highest order of chivalry.[38] Yet James, though the elder and a man, ruled a foreign country and had not been born in England. These two facts had long been thought his stumbling blocks. With certain exceptions, common law held that those born abroad could not inherit property in England. Children of English monarchs could succeed to the crown regardless of their place of birth, but whether or not this privilege extended to the ruler's nieces, nephews and other relatives was unclear.[39] Chapuys, reporting the death of a young son of the Duke of Suffolk and Mary Tudor in March 1534, noted that although the boy had been 'son of the younger sister, his being a native would have made him a formidable competitor for the Scotch king'.[40] Margaret Douglas, though the younger child and a woman, was English-born and had made England her home. Being the king's niece suddenly meant much more than it had five years ago: if Henry did not have another child, Margaret might become his heir.

Yet she had also promised to marry an Englishman. Margaret's secret, imperfectly kept from the start, was too significant to be kept any longer. Someone grew careless, or perhaps Cromwell or the king, conscious of the sudden dearth of heirs, grew investigative. Whatever the case, the engagement was discovered, and her dangerous secret was out.

By 7 July, Margaret knew that their servants were going to be examined. Some of them knew about the affair, but nobody, apparently, knew about the planned marriage. She explained the matter to Howard's servant Thomas Smyth, warning him that he would soon be questioned. Howard, interrogated on 8 July, was not ready to give her up, and she, it seems, did not plan to abandon him.[41] All her life, Margaret had gone where she was bid, by her mother, then by her father, and lately, by her uncle. This time, she resolved to stand her ground.

Henry was in a fury. No Tudor woman, much less his heir presumptive, had the right to defy him so. For five years Margaret had been able to navigate the waters of a changeable court, but a summer storm was set to break.

4

So High a Blood

On the morning of 18 July, England's leading clergy and nobility assembled at the Palace of Westminster for the last day of the 1536 parliament. It had been a brief, exhausting session, and they had already dealt with the vital matter of excluding the young Elizabeth from the succession. That morning, they began their work by introducing an Act of Attainder against Thomas Howard. The bill passed its first, second and third reading, so the Lords sent it to the Commons, who likewise gave their approval. By early afternoon it was settled, proclaimed without a trial: Lord Thomas Howard was a convicted traitor.

The wording of the bill left little room for forgiveness. Howard had been 'led and seduced by the Devil', forsaking his duty to God and the king. Acting with malice and treachery, he had tried to alter the course of the succession. His attentions to Margaret were mere 'crafty fair and flattering words', a tactic in a plot to seize the crown through her:

> . . . the said Lord Thomas falsely, craftily, and traitorously hath imagined and compassed, that in case our said Sovereign Lord should die without heirs of his body (which God defend), that then the said Lord Thomas by reason of marriage in so high a blood . . . should aspire by her to the dignity of the said imperial crown of this realm . . .

In punishment for his 'most contemptuous and traitorous offence', Howard was sentenced to death for high treason – which became the new crime of any man who married a woman of the royal family without the king's permission.[1]

There was an unintentional echo of a verse, attributed to Wyatt, mourning another man who had overstepped the bounds of courtly love with a royal woman. It was an epitaph for Mark Smeaton, the musician accused of adultery with Anne Boleyn: 'A time thou hadst above thy poor degree,/The fall whereof they friends may well bemoan:/A rotten twig upon so high a tree/Hath slipped thy hold, and thou art dead and gone.'[2]

The bill was scarcely more careful with Margaret's reputation. It did not go so far as to call her a bastard, but it impugned her legitimacy: her parents had 'been long divorced by the laws of the Church' and she was 'one such which pretendeth [claims] to be lawful daughter to the said queen of Scots'. Nonetheless, the bill's drafters were remarkably forthright about Thomas Howard's imagined ambitions, and about Margaret's claim to the throne. Howard's hope, they wrote, was that the people of England would reject James V, a foreign prince, and favour his sister, the English-born Lady Margaret.

Margaret now understood what it meant to face Henry's anger. He banished her from court and sent her to the Tower. On the eastern edge of London, separated from the city by a silty moat, the Tower was already more than four centuries old. It was at once a palace – home to the royal menagerie as well as the royal mint – a fortress and a prison. As the king's niece, Margaret was not about to be thrown into a dungeon: she had a well-furnished set of rooms, attendants, including her old chaplain, and the freedom to receive at least some visitors. When she fell ill, she was allowed a doctor and medicines. But all the same, she was a prisoner and Thomas Howard was under a death sentence.

Somehow, Howard found the means to write to her, and she found a way to reply. The Devonshire Manuscript contains a series of poems which, while not written in the hand of either Margaret or Howard, suggest that the two were able to exchange messages during their captivity and to preserve their words for some friend to record into the manuscript. Although it is not certain that they were written while Margaret was still in the Tower itself, as she was later moved to a new prison, they have nonetheless become known as the 'Tower lyrics'.[3]

Paradoxically, in this strictly metered, rhyming verse, Howard and Margaret found the freedom to express their loneliness and love, and to affirm their constancy towards each other. He urged Margaret to keep up her spirits: 'I pray you be of right good cheer/And think on me that loves you best.'[4] Difference in status had brought them to the Tower: 'Since ye descend from your degree/Take ye this unto your part/My faithful, true, and loving heart.' In spite of this, their love was real and holy: she was his 'sweet wife', the one 'to whom forever my heart is plight'; he was her 'loving husband now to be', and it was their 'intent/In God's laws for to be bound'.[5]

Even in summer, the Tower was cold at night, and the stench from the river was inescapable. Before long, Margaret became sick, and an apothecary had to make several visits to her prison, as her health remained fragile even after the crisis was over.[6] But Howard's poems gave her courage in the face of this added misery. She took pride in his steadfastness and swore that she would match him, at first praising him in the third person before addressing him directly as 'my heart's desire':

I may well say with joyful heart
As never woman might say before
That I have taken to my part
The faithfullest lover that ever was born

Great pains he suffereth for my sake
Continually both night and day
For all the pains that he doth take
From me his love will not decay

With threatenings great he hath been said
Of pain and yke [as well] of punishment
That all fear aside he hath laid
To love me best was his intent

Who shall let me then of right
Unto myself him to retain
And love him best both day and night
In recompense of his great pain

If I had more, more he should have
And that I know he knows full well
To love him best unto my grave
Of that he may both buy and sell

And thus farewell my heart's desire
The only stay of me and mine
Unto god daily I make my prayer
To bring us shortly both in one line.[7]

Labouring over the scansion, selecting the most powerful words, not only filled the quiet days but also let Margaret speak to Howard and, briefly, forget her fear for him and for herself. Her own fate was still uncertain: there were reports she had been condemned to death as well.

Would Henry really have sent his niece – and possible heir presumptive – to the block? Some observers doubted it. Her cousin Reginald Pole, for one, thought that Henry had only taken such dramatic steps so that he could make an even more dramatic show of clemency to two attractive, aristocratic young lovers: 'I rather think that in these cases the King wishes an opportunity of showing mercy, and this is why judgement has been passed on them; for their deaths would be so unjust as to create intolerable hatred . . . being condemned only on an *ex post facto* law.'[8]

Margaret's mother, in contrast, believed her daughter was in real danger. Interestingly, the Act of Attainder had suggested that the Queen of Scots herself had some connection to the case, giving legislative permanence to a rumour that she planned to return to England, reconcile with Angus, and 'advance the said Lord Thomas and the said Lady Margaret her daughter into the favour of the people of this realm'. This was nearly pure invention: it is true that the Queen of Scots had mentioned being tired of Scotland and wanting to come home to England, but there is no evidence that she had ever forgiven Angus for his many infidelities or that she wanted to leave her new husband.[9]

Margaret Tudor, apparently unaware of the slight to her own loyalty, wrote to her brother King Henry, asking him 'to have compassion and pity of us, your own sister, and of our natural daughter and sister to the king our only son', and offering to receive Margaret in Scotland 'so that in time coming she shall never come in your grace's presence'. That offer seemed to come from her rather than from James, but she assured Henry that her son 'will not believe that your grace will do such extremity upon your own, ours, and his, being so tender to us all three, as our natural daughter is'. Although she kept up a carefully regal tone throughout the letter, always referring to herself in the royal plural, she made one panicked slip into the singular, writing that Henry wanted 'to punish my daughter and your near cousin to extreme rigour'.[10]

To modern eyes, it seems shocking that a sister should have to make such a plea to a brother, but Margaret Tudor's fears were understandable. Henry took great pride in the women he loved and expected total obedience in return. When he did not get it, his reactions were volcanic: he raged when his younger sister remarried without his permission, banished Katherine of Aragon from court and refused to speak with her or even allow her to see their child, turned his eldest daughter into a servant for his youngest, and had Anne Boleyn put to death. His temper was ferocious and his behaviour increasingly cruel.

Yet he was also unpredictable. As it transpired, Henry did not intend to have Margaret Douglas executed, and told her mother as much – in fact, he was not even going to keep her in the Tower, but send her to a monastery. The dissolution of abbeys and nunneries, seen as hotbeds of loyalty to the papacy, had already begun, but only just. Hearing the news, Margaret Tudor thanked him for 'the great nobleness ye have shown to my daughter', writing that 'she shall never have my blessing an [if] she do not all that ye command her, nor no good that I may do for her'.[11] Henry bent somewhat, and wrote that young Margaret had 'lightly used herself . . . both to our dishonour and her own great hindrance', but assured his sister that 'if she will conform herself to that thing that shall be convenient, we shall, for your sake, extend such goodness towards her as you and she shall have cause to be thereunto satisfied'.[12]

On Henry's behalf, Cromwell wrote to the abbess of Syon, Agnes Jordan, who replied on 6 November 1536 that she would be ready to give Margaret such shelter 'as be or may be to her comfort and our prince's pleasure', adding that 'what service and pleasure shall be in us to do unto her we shall be ever ready to do'.[13] Soon afterwards, Margaret made the long boat trip upriver from the Tower to her new prison, just weeks before the biting December cold froze the Thames solid.[14]

Syon was a vast abbey on the banks of the Thames at Isleworth, west along the river from the centre of Tudor London. Founded in the fifteenth century, it was the only monastery to follow the rule of St Bridget, and it was run as a double foundation of monks and nuns under the overall supervision of the abbess. It was a unique place, and if any abbey seemed capable of withstanding the anti-monastic tide, it was Syon: it had ties to royalty, a tradition of reform and scholarship, and more money than any other nunnery in England.

Yet even Syon had suffered. The abbess and all the nuns had accepted the royal supremacy, as had the confessor of the brothers, but some of the brethren had not.[15] In April 1535, Richard Reynolds, one of the community's thirteen priests and 'a man with the countenance and spirit of an angel', had been imprisoned, tried and convicted for refusing to acknowledge Henry's supremacy.[16] On 4 May, still wearing his monk's habit, he suffered the full penalty for high treason. He was drawn from the Tower to Tyburn, where he was hanged, disembowelled and beheaded. Afterwards, his body was hacked into quarters and the parts were spitted on spears and displayed publicly.[17] Not trusting in the power of even this horrific display, Cromwell forbade Reynolds's brothers from preaching in the abbey church, lest they make a similar show of resistance.

For nearly a year Margaret lived within the bounds of Syon Abbey, a world away from the Tower. While many non-religious were part of the community, the dominant figures were the Bridgettine nuns, dressed all in white and wearing linen crowns emblazoned with five blood-red drops of fabric in the shape of a cross. Margaret cut an incongruous figure, with her royally appointed clothes and furniture – including a chair upholstered in dark red velvet, trimmed with silk fringe in crimson and Venetian silver, and held together with two thousand gilt nails.[18] Although she wrote that she was 'very well treated', she found it hard to adjust to the gentle rhythms of monastic life: the constant reading, writing and praying.

Removed from court and alone responsible for her attendants' needs, she was soon living beyond her means – evidence, perhaps, that the childhood lessons in household management had not quite stuck. Margaret had two more attendants with her than she had had at court. In addition to her gentleman, a groom each for her clothes and her chamber and her longtime chaplain, she had two of Howard's servants – invited into her entourage, she wrote, 'for the poverty that I saw them in'. But her generosity extended further than her purse: she could not afford to pay them all and soon they had no credit locally. Her servants wrote to Cromwell, decreeing that 'they had never more need, for there is no man that will trust them for such meat and drink as they must take, and money have they none, or can tell where to borrow any'.[19]

Syon was intended to keep her in dull, maidenly isolation, but it was a busy, connected place, directly across the river from Richmond Palace and the Sheen Priory. Whether it arrived as gossip, a spy's report, or an update from the abbess, word soon reached the court that Margaret was receiving visitors, both men and women, with the implication that some of them were rather more exciting than appropriate for a penitent young woman. Cromwell wrote her a letter warning that she risked incurring Henry's displeasure again. She kept more servants than she could afford or that Syon could easily house, and she could start by getting rid of all Howard's old retainers.

Margaret knew what she had to say. She defended herself, assuring Cromwell that her infatuation with Howard was over, and asking him 'not to think that any fancy doth remain in me touching him . . . all my study and care is how to please the king's grace'. She was less sure-footed on the matter of her servants – 'I trust ye will think that I can have no fewer than I have . . . I beseech you to be so good as to get my poor servants their wages' – but she did agree to release Howard's old attendants. As for visitors, she wrote, 'I promise you I have none, except it be gentlewomen that come to Sheen, nor never had since I came hither.' Gentlemen guests, she insisted, were out of the question for a chaste, unmarried woman: 'It should neither become me to have seen them nor yet to have kept them company, being a maid as I am now.'[20]

Margaret had not forgotten Howard, but she had good reason to be worried about her reputation and to insist on her propriety. Her physical relationship with Thomas Howard had become a subject of frank court chatter and speculation, with Chapuys writing to Charles V that she had 'been pardoned her life considering that copulation had not taken place'. Still, for all that Henry thought Margaret had disgraced herself and him, others were more sympathetic. Chapuys, who may have remembered Margaret from her time in Mary's household, drily observed that such behaviour was only to be expected in the English court: '[I]f she had done much worse she deserved pardon, seeing the number of domestic examples she has seen and sees daily' – and falling in love was understandable in a woman who 'has been for eight years of age and capacity to marry'.[21]

The story of her ill-fated romance had spread beyond the court and it did not wholly drop out of memory. The previous autumn had seen tremendous disorder in northern England – the great rebellions in defence of the old religion, dubbed the Pilgrimage of Grace. Sir Francis Bigod, arrested for his role in the Pilgrimage, declared that he and his allies thought Margaret and Howard the innocent victims of Cromwell's ambition. The only reason they had been separated, Bigod wrote, was the chief minister's wish for a young, royal bride, 'because the lord Cromwell should have had the lady Margaret himself he procured the statute'.[22]

Beyond Syon's walls, tremendous change was under way. Anne Boleyn's death had given hope to many religious traditionalists that the old faith would be resurrected, but reform continued apace. More and greater monasteries were being dissolved. Saints' days vanished from calendars, images from churches. For a generation, the only means by which most English people could read even a portion of the Bible in their own language had been the pages of William Caxton's *Golden Legend*, which included Old Testament stories embellished with long passages of scripture: now, there were plans to have the entire Bible made available in English.[23] Change bred dissent, but dissent was met with determined opposition. Those who refused to acknowledge the royal supremacy were named traitors; the Pilgrimage was suppressed; and even nobles like the Earl of Kildare, who had led a Catholic uprising in Ireland, might find themselves on the scaffold.

It was not enough, however, to crush open rebellion. Henry and Cromwell had to see evidence that their reforms were put in place in each of the thousands of parishes in the kingdom. Sensitive to jokes and criticism, the regime was hungry for information and skilled in obtaining it. Commissioners were dispatched to determine that the new laws were being followed, reporting any heel-draggers, while spies listened for gossip and disloyal tavern talk. In consequence, people became used to compliance and self-policing: they swore oaths of loyalty, stopped donating money for statues and stained-glass windows, and made handwritten alterations to their service books to keep in line with the ever-changing laws.

Just like the English Church, the English succession remained unsettled. The queen, Jane Seymour, was pregnant early in the New Year of 1537, but by then Margaret's brother James V had made himself much more formidable. After years of talks, he at last succeeded in winning his French bride, marrying Francis I's eldest daughter Madeleine of Valois, a slight and sickly sixteen-year-old. The English knight Sir John Wallop patronisingly observed that he thought 'the king of Scots never saw such a sight' as his own marriage banquet, casting James as a provincial Scot awestruck by the splendour of the French court.

Wallop's condescension could not conceal the obvious truth that James had pulled off a diplomatic coup, confirming the Auld Alliance in the most spectacular manner possible. Soon thereafter, Paul III sent him a papal hat and sword. Even Madeleine's death soon after her arrival in Scotland was treated as only a temporary setback: James immediately started making plans for remarriage in France. He also continued to exact revenge upon the Douglases for having kept him under their control. Margaret's aunt Janet Douglas, Lady Glamis – her father's younger sister – was convicted of plotting to kill James and of conspiring with her brothers Angus and Sir George Douglas. She was burnt alive on Edinburgh's Castle Hill.[24]

While James acquired international honours and prestige, Henry was left to speculate on diplomatic alliances for his now-bastardised daughters and to fear for the succession – until 12 October 1537, when Jane Seymour gave birth to a boy at Hampton Court. In an instant it mattered far less whether the uncontrollable Scottish nephew or the disgraced English niece had the better claim. Jane's child was the king's first legitimate son to be born alive since Prince Henry, who had lived for seven short weeks twenty-six years before. The infant's birthday was the eve of the feast of St Edward the Confessor and the baby took the name of the medieval king-saint. Heedless of the plague, Londoners rushed into the streets to light celebratory bonfires, the city ringing with joyous cannon blasts and thundering renditions of *Te Deum Laudamus*. Prince Edward was christened and confirmed three days later, with both his half-sisters playing prominent roles in the ceremony. Elizabeth, still a toddler, carried the chrism, while Mary served as godmother. Lord and Lady Lisle heard that the 'birth has more rejoiced all true hearts than anything done this forty years'. Hugh Latimer, going even further, declared to Cromwell that 'here is no less rejoicing at the birth of our prince, whom we hungered for so long, than there was at the birth of John the Baptist'.[25] But amidst the near-hysterical joy, Queen Jane, who had seemed to come through her son's birth in good health, sickened and died just twelve days later.

While London celebrated the prince's birth and mourned the queen's death, few people would have heard or cared that Thomas Howard fell ill with an ague and died on 31 October, still shuttered in the Tower. The Earl of Hertford broke the news to Henry immediately, and obtained permission that Howard's mother Agnes, dowager Duchess of Norfolk, should have his body. She had him buried alongside his Howard kin in Thetford Abbey, where the king's son, Henry Fitzroy, also lay. It was, by royal direction, a funeral with little ceremony – though altogether more than a condemned traitor could expect.[26]

In the same week, Margaret was set free, but liberty came with the awful knowledge that she would never see Howard again. She had not been honest with Cromwell when she denied her feelings. For more than a year, she had been kept apart from Howard, compelled to swear that she did not regret the separation. Now, she blamed his death upon herself. It was her royal blood that had made their marriage such a perilous impossibility. She could not keep up the show any longer: her grief was far too powerful.[27]

After she was freed from prison, Margaret acquired the Devonshire Manuscript once again. There is a poem near the end of the book that tells the story of a young woman locked in a tower, summoning her friends and her father to hear her final words before she dies of grief and reunites with her lost love. The poem is in Margaret's hand, and it is tempting to think that she wrote it herself just after Howard's death – the situations correspond, and the tragic heroine's declaration that she would not live a day longer 'to be queen of all Italy' may be a scornful allusion to Henry's marital schemes for Margaret. At the same time, it is possible that the poem was already there and that Margaret had acted as the scribe. But whether she wrote it, or simply reread it, horribly conscious that the metaphors of courtly love could lead to concrete disasters, the poem reads as Thomas Howard's epitaph:

Now that ye be assembled here
All ye my friends at my request
Especially you, my father dear,
That of my blood is the nearest
This unto you is my request
That ye will patiently hear
By these my last words expressed
My testament entire.

And think not to interrupt me
For such ways provided have I
That though ye would it will not be
This tower ye see is strong and high
And the doors fast barred have I
That no wight my purpose let should
For to be queen of all Italy
Not one day longer live I would.

Wherefore sweet father I you pray
Bear this my death with patience
And torment not your hairs grey
But freely pardon mine offence
Sith [Since] it proceedeth of love's fervence
And of my heart's constancy

Let me not from the sweet presence
Of him that I have caused to die.[28]

But Margaret was only twenty-two and more resilient than she realised. Newly provided with an heir, Henry was ready to be magnanimous to his niece as he had not been to Howard, and her brief moment as possible Queen of England seemed over – though the king still had only one male child of his own, and an infant at that. When the summons came, Margaret's underpaid attendants packed up her clothes and furniture for the journey back to court.

5

These Worldly Storms

When Henry and his train removed to the palace of Hampton Court, Margaret had a double lodging in the second court at the foot of the king's staircase.[1] In 1540, Henry had an elaborate Astronomical Clock built and installed in the tower. From her window, she could watch its assembly. It is an enormously complicated piece of clockwork, telling observers not only the time of day but the sign of the zodiac, the phases of the moon, the tides of the Thames. In later life, Margaret was an avid collector of timepieces, both watches and clocks. What did she make of them as a young woman, seeing the mechanism of the Astronomical Clock take shape – simultaneously reassuring and inexorable?

In late 1537, Margaret had come back to a changed court. There was suddenly no queen, and Henry was no longer the same king and uncle who had jovially welcomed her to Greenwich seven years before. She had seen him in and out of love, and now she saw him grieving for Jane: the court remained in mourning until February 1538.[2] Henry's health had grown unpredictable, his mood even more so. Seeing the once-active king putting on weight and suffering from debilitating leg pain, Chapuys thought that he had 'lost much of his old buoyancy of spirits', and the French ambassador remarked that courtiers had become paranoid and secretive, saying 'so little what they think that I only know things by halves'.[3] Margaret's home had become a more dangerous, uncertain place.

She had changed as well, experiencing love and grief and finding her own capacity for defiance. In one essential thing, however, she was constant. She had watched Henry strip her cousin Mary of her household and title, condemn her mistress, Queen Anne, to beheading, and sentence her own lover Thomas Howard to death. She had spent a year in prison on the king's orders. But she still loved her uncle and he, she believed, loved her. He saw to it that she was well-dressed and that her servants were paid, that she received some of Jane Seymour's beads, and that she, at the age of twenty-two, was one of the pre-eminent noblewomen of his court.[4]

There was still gossip about her marriage prospects – including at least one rumour that she was to wed Anne Boleyn's recently widowed father, the Earl of Wiltshire. But there was no longer any gossip about her behaviour. While in Syon she had told Cromwell 'all my study and care is how to please the king's grace and to continue in his favour', and she seemed to mean it.[5]

It was an unspoken truth that Margaret was still very close to the throne. In the New Year's Gift Roll of 1539, she was grouped with the king's own children: Henry gave her a gilt cup made by his own goldsmith.[6] Henry had his heir apparent but he was himself a second son and did not want to stake his dynasty on the survival of one baby. He decided to marry again, this time to a European bride. He made a bid for Mary of Guise, the striking and recently widowed daughter of one of the most powerful nobles in France. She, however, was already engaged to Henry's nephew James V, and Henry's efforts to shake the Auld Alliance failed. Mary wed James and moved to Scotland, where, it was reported, she remained as obstinately papist as her new mother-in-law, Margaret Tudor.[7]

Margaret again found herself drawn into Henry's diplomatic games. Disappointed in France, Henry pondered a series of marriage alliances with the Empire: his daughter Mary would wed the Infant Don Ludovic of Portugal while Elizabeth, Margaret and Mary Fitzroy would marry 'such of the princes of Italy as shall be thought convenient', but this plan was dismissed before Henry's messenger had even departed.[8] If it was frustrating for Henry, it was equally frustrating for Margaret. She was now in her mid-twenties, more than a decade older than her mother had been when she wed James IV. She was capable of deep love and had expected to be married long ago, and she found it hard to keep her promise to avoid romantic entanglements.

When the Emperor Charles and King Francis formed their own alliance, Henry abandoned his imperial marriage schemes and turned elsewhere. At Thomas Cromwell's suggestion, he agreed to marry Anne, the sister of the Duke of Cleves, establishing ties with German Protestant princes.

Henry's new wife planned to arrive in England before Christmas 1539, but poor weather conditions in the Channel kept her trapped in Calais for two weeks. At Greenwich, the court observed the season in its usual fashion, with plays, music and gift-giving at the New Year. By now, Margaret's cousin Mary had sworn the oath attesting to Henry's supremacy over the Church of England and was on rather better terms with her father than she had been when Margaret was imprisoned. The two women renewed their old friendship and Mary was generous at Christmas, giving gifts not just to Margaret herself but also to her chaplain, her gentleman servants and her two grooms.[9]

On the morning of 3 January 1540, Margaret rose early and rode the short distance from Greenwich to Blackheath, a barren but impressive nearby field that had long served English monarchs as a site for meeting important visitors.[10] Margaret, her friend Mary Fitzroy and her cousin Frances Brandon were at the head of a company of thirty women appointed to greet Anne of Cleves. All around them, servants readied the plain, setting up pavilions, lighting fires and clearing trees so that spectators could observe the ceremony. The nobles, with less to do, waited, their eyes turning towards the peak of the hill by which Anne would arrive, shivering but curious.

At noon, Anne of Cleves came down Shooter's Hill and met her chamberlain, chancellor and counsellors. After her newly appointed almoner finished a Latin sermon, Margaret and the rest of the women came forward to meet their new queen for the first time. What Margaret made of Anne at that meeting is unknown. The new queen's looks divided opinion: she was tall and carried herself well, but whereas many called her attractive, the French ambassador Marillac dismissed her as 'not as young as expected or as beautiful as people said', which the French queen took to mean that she was 'old and ugly'.[11] They could not have had a real conversation: Margaret had no German and Anne neither English nor French, so they had no language in common. Nonetheless, the new queen left her chariot, thanked Margaret and the ladies for her welcome, and having kissed them all, led them into the tents, where they recovered from the January cold.[12]

While Anne's arrival set off a social scramble to get sisters, daughters and nieces into her service, Margaret could take her place for granted.[13] There were ladies and gentlewomen of the Privy Chamber, ladies and gentlewomen attendant, maids and Anne's own ladies from Cleves, but Margaret was first of the 'Great Ladies'. She attended the queen and she seems to have played a role in staffing: an account of the Queen's Household notes that an avener, that is, senior officer of the stable, by the name of Thomas Hungate, was 'sent with my lady Margaret'.[14]

When she was not with Anne, Margaret was often with Mary, and the two of them gambled together. On one occasion, Mary lost a wager and had to give Margaret an extravagant frontlet – an ornamental accessory worn on the forehead.[15] Margaret again became a part of the intellectual life at court: she guarded the Devonshire Manuscript and became, in a small way, a literary patron. John Drummond dedicated his translation of Arnold de Villanova's *The Defence of Age and Recovery of Youth* to her, apologising for offering so small a book and promising that a larger one would follow.[16] The work contained advice on how to restore a dull complexion and avoid an excess of phlegm – take warm baths and avoid fruit, fish and dairy – and noted that 'nothing doth cause a man to look old as far as desperation . . . that is the cause that many being tossed, and turmoiled, and vexed with these worldly storms, suddenly their hair waxes hoar, or white'.[17]

Worldly storms, however, were gathering about the court. Henry had found Anne deeply unattractive from the start, and their marriage lasted only seven months. The king determined to punish Cromwell for this disaster, stripping him of his offices and imprisoning him. Come July 1540, Anne accepted a demotion from Henry's wife to his 'sister', Cromwell was put to death, and the king married for a fifth time. He had found his new bride among the ladies of Anne's household. She was a cousin of Anne Boleyn, and her name was Katherine Howard.

Katherine had grown up in the household of her step-grandmother Agnes, dowager Duchess of Norfolk – the mother of Margaret's dead lover, Thomas Howard. Her music tutor, Henry Mannox, pursued her when she was barely a teenager and was furiously jealous when she later fell in love with a young kinsman named Francis Dereham. In 1539, however, Katherine came to court to serve Anne of Cleves and Dereham left England for Ireland. While in Anne's service, Katherine's name was linked with Thomas Culpepper, another distant relative. At court, Culpepper was a gentleman of the Privy Chamber with a house in Greenwich and lucrative lands and offices from his royal patron; away from court, he had a dark reputation involving sexual violence and murder, though he had escaped punishment through Henry's intervention. The connection came to nothing, and none of Katherine's history seems to have been common knowledge when she married the king. In the account of the French ambassador, she comes across as doll-like: small, poised, fashionable, with the motto '*Non autre volonté que la sienne*' – 'No other wish but his'.[18]

For the first time Margaret found herself serving a queen who was younger than she was, but Katherine was a charming mistress. She seemed to be adapting well to her unexpected role, and she treated her niece-by-marriage generously, giving her small gifts of jewellery, including a pair of earrings.[19] Her ascent brought Margaret into contact with another attractive young Howard: the queen's brother, Charles. He had not profited much by his sister's rise. The king had given him gifts of clothing and five shops in Cheapside – which he promptly sold to a leather-seller – and he may have had a role in the Privy Chamber, but he had not been showered with titles or honours. He was just as unsuitable as his dead uncle Lord Thomas Howard had been, and though Margaret was attracted to him, she flirted without falling in love.

Whether or not Katherine knew about Margaret and Charles, there is no evidence that Margaret knew anything about the queen's own romantic life. Francis Dereham returned from Ireland and obtained a post in her service, though he always denied that they resumed their old affair.[20] Culpepper, however, was a different matter. One of Katherine's letters to him survives, extravagant in language: 'I heard you were sick, and never longed so much for anything as to see you. It makes my heart die to think I cannot be always in your company . . .' What little evidence there is suggests that they were in love now, if they had not been before her wedding, and they were soon taking extraordinary risks.[21]

In the summer of 1541, Margaret almost certainly accompanied Henry, Katherine and the rest of the court on a great progress to the north of England. It was a change of pace: Margaret was often outdoors and spending a good deal of time on horseback, revisiting places she had not seen since 1530.[22] This otherwise triumphant tour was marred by an incident involving Margaret's half-brother, James V. A proposed summit between the two kings at York never took place, even though Henry VIII waited there for weeks, making preparations for this meeting with the nephew whom he had never met. The King of Scots sent a gift of 'certain falcons of good kind' but did not come in person, much to Henry's anger.[23] Meanwhile, the queen was meeting in secret with Culpepper. As he would later testify, Katherine would acquaint herself with the geography of each new house, '[seeking] for the back doors and back stairs herself', finding places for furtive assignations in the middle of the night.[24]

The brilliant summer gave way to some of the darkest weeks of Margaret's life. On 18 October 1541 her mother died at Methven Castle. Margaret Tudor suffered a 'palsy' – probably a stroke. She expected to recover and did not rush to make a will, but it soon became clear that she would not get better, and the King of Scots was sent for. Henry Ray, Berwick Pursuivant at Arms, informed the English Privy Council that as Margaret Tudor lay dying, waiting for her son to come to her, the old queen's thoughts turned to Angus and Margaret Douglas. She asked her confessors to tell James to be 'good and gracious unto the earl of Angus and did extremely lament . . . that she had offended unto the said earl'. They were also to ask him 'to be good unto the Lady Margaret Douglas her daughter . . . that she might have of her goods'. She qualified the request with the rueful explanation that her daughter ought to have the gift 'forasmuch she never had nothing of her before'.[25]

The account was second-hand and stretches credulity. Margaret Tudor had been glad to get rid of Angus, while James remained implacably opposed to the Douglases. The charge to her son to take some care of his half-sister, though, is slightly more plausible. The queen had never been close to her daughter – they had not seen each other in well over a decade – but in 1536, when she thought Margaret's life was in danger, she had sworn to Henry that her daughter would have a home in Scotland with her and with James. Given she was facing death herself, perhaps she hoped that her two living children would be reconciled.

As this was the version of events that reached the English court, it is almost certainly the one that Margaret received – a bittersweet acknowledgement that although her mother loved her, they had not had and would never have a relationship as adults. She did eventually own her mother's prayer book, the same illuminated Book of Hours that Henry VII had given to Margaret Tudor at Collyweston thirty-eight years before, but when she came to inherit it is unclear.[26] Margaret was not given the chance to grieve her long-unseen mother or to attend her burial at Charterhouse Kirk in Perth, the 'fairest abbey . . . of any within the realm of Scotland'.[27] Much worse was still to come.

By the beginning of November 1541, Katherine Howard's household was under investigation. At first, it seemed that the queen's only crime was to have had a romantic life before her marriage to Henry, but Archbishop Cranmer, charged with investigating the matter, soon found that she had been unfaithful to the king – if not with Dereham, then with Culpepper.[28]

It was as if the entire court had been infected with some fierce and scandalous disease. The young women of the royal family had to be removed from the seat of contamination: Mary was to go to her brother Prince Edward, while Margaret and Mary Fitzroy, Duchess of Richmond, were to be sent to Kenninghall Lodge, home of the duchess's father, the Duke of Norfolk, who had the unfortunate distinction of being uncle to both Anne Boleyn and Katherine Howard.[29] Before Margaret could depart, however, Cranmer took her aside and, on Henry's instructions, gave her a thorough dressing down. Her affair with the queen's brother had not been as clandestine as she thought. The king, speaking through the archbishop, reproached Margaret for her 'much lightness' and told her to remember 'how indiscreetly she hath demeaned herself', first with Thomas Howard and now with Charles. He gave her warning 'to beware the third time, and wholly apply herself to please the king's majesty'.[30]

This time, there were no poems and no declarations of undying constancy. Charles Howard kept his freedom. The French ambassador reported that Katherine's brothers and those of Culpepper took to riding out in public, writing '[i]t is the custom and must be done to show that they did not share the crimes of their relatives'.[31] Charles eventually went to Venice, keeping a house and five armed servants.[32] Margaret took her chastisement, no doubt shaken but thinking herself lucky, and left the court for Kenninghall Lodge, a grand house in the East Anglian countryside, some sixty miles from London.

Although she and Charles Howard escaped punishment, Margaret heard only dark news from court. The Duke of Norfolk, fearing arrest and imprisonment, joined her and his daughter at Kenninghall. Desperate at the scandal, the head of the Howards was reduced to writing to the king that 'the most abominable deeds done by two of my nieces' had left him in 'the greatest perplexity that ever poor wretch was in' and hoping for Henry's mercy. The entire Howard family had come under scrutiny and it seemed that some of Margaret's oldest friends would be dragged down with the queen. Lord William Howard,

Thomas's older brother, was shut up in the Tower, along with his wife, the woman to whom Margaret had confided news of her secret engagement back in the Easter of 1536.[33] Although Margaret later wrote to her father of 'the goodness that [Norfolk] showed' her, Kenninghall was not a happy place.[34]

Word reached Margaret that Katherine Howard and a handful of attendants had been sent to her own prison, Syon Abbey, which was by now suppressed and empty of its old religious community. In London, Katherine's lovers went to trial, and her own name was utterly destroyed along with theirs. They were convicted, condemned and executed, Culpepper by beheading and Dereham by hanging, drawing and quartering – no royal mercy on this occasion. Soon after the New Year of 1542, a parliament met and condemned Katherine by Act of Attainder. In a grim reversal of Margaret's own cold river journey, Katherine was taken from Syon to the Tower, gliding past the ruins of abandoned abbeys all along the riverbank, crossing under London Bridge, where the severed heads of Dereham and Culpepper stood boiled and spitted, coming to her final prison. Within weeks, she too lost her head.

Once again, Margaret came back to a court where a wifeless, self-pitying king presided. Over the course of 1542 the years-old tension between her uncle Henry and her brother James worsened. Events in Europe spurred on the decline: France and Spain were in arms against each other, with Henry taking the Spanish side. James, for his part, would not abjure Scotland's Auld Alliance with France. In standing with the French, James had re-emerged as a serious threat to Henry's northern border. Now, just as her mother had once done, Margaret saw England and Scotland ready for war.

6

Lennox

The half-Scottish girl from the fortress of Tantallon had grown into a thoroughly English woman of the court. James V was her half-brother, but Henry VIII and his children were her family. With them, she had become a woman who could run a queen's household, talk poetry with the leading writers of the day and expect to make a brilliant diplomatic marriage. Few looking at the richly dressed lady with the fine skin, pale eyes and coppery Tudor hair would recall the lonely, frightened child who had fled Scotland in secret fourteen years before. On 10 August 1542, however, Margaret almost certainly did.

On that morning, just as they did every day, Margaret's attendants came to her closet to help her into her clothes. She wore several layers even in the summer heat, so dressing took some time. Although we cannot know what she thought as her ladies arrayed her in her shift, farthingale and kirtle before fastening her into one of her many hand-fashioned silk gowns, it easy to imagine that her mind was no longer in England.

Her father, Angus, was riding northwards to wage war on James in Henry's name. She had little reason to feel kindly towards her half-brother: she had not seen him in more than a decade and James had already seized both her parents' estates, apparently quite ready to see her left with no inheritance at all.[1] Although she had seen little enough of Angus since 1530 – he had kept away from court and made himself useful on the borders – she sent him letters before he headed away to war.[2] If she felt any fear for James, she probably felt far more for her father.

Unlike English-born Margaret, Angus was a Scot, but for the moment, he was Henry's man and would fight for him. He correctly calculated that James V would never restore him to his lands and estates, whereas Henry might, 'if it pleased the king's majesty to remember this small matter among his great affairs'.[3] Angus's journey north marked the beginning of a turbulent two years that would draw Margaret back into Scottish politics and force her to declare her own allegiances.

The campaign in the autumn of 1542 proved disastrous for the Scottish king. In October the Duke of Norfolk led a week-long raid into Scotland, torching border towns and leaving the countryside devastated. The Scots retaliated with an incursion into Cumbria the next month. They crossed the river Esk and found themselves facing a small English force on the marshy ground of Solway Moss. The English, though outnumbered at least five to one, trapped the Scots in an indefensible position and triumphed handily. The English were eager to see it as a second Flodden – Henry's commissioners told him 'that the Scots were never so far out of courage since [James IV] was killed'.[4] They were overstating the case, but it was an ugly, demoralising defeat. Hundreds of soldiers drowned in the frigid waters of the Esk while the English captured two earls and many nobles besides.

For Scotland, setback soon worsened into crisis. James V was already sick and retreated to Falkland Palace amidst the forests of Fife. Falkland had been his passion, a medieval castle that he had transformed into a Renaissance palace to rank with the great houses of France – but it had once been his prison, a fortress in which his stepfather, Angus, had kept him captive and from which he had scarcely managed to escape. This time, he was dying, and would never leave, though he did live long enough to hear that his pregnant wife had given birth to a sickly, premature girl. In the brief time that James had ruled his kingdom as an adult, he had been a patron of writers and architects, moved on Europe's diplomatic stage, and done his utmost to make the Stewarts' vaunted 'imperial kingship' a reality. Now he was dead at thirty, and his only legitimate heir was an infant daughter. Once again, Scotland's crown passed to a child: the six-day-old girl, Mary, Queen of Scots. Word of James's death reached the English court two days before Christmas 1542. Nobody seemed to have quite the same intelligence: ambassador Chapuys, for one, spent some three weeks uncertain whether James's baby daughter was dying, dead or stubbornly alive.[5] It was clear, though, that the situation had changed.

When Margaret heard the news, she did not mourn her brother publicly. It was nearly the New Year, an occasion for dancing, feasting and trading gifts with friends and relatives, and she put herself in the thick of the court's celebrations. That year, knowing her cousin Mary's love for clothes, Margaret gave her a gown 'of Carnation Satin, of the Venice fashion', probably meaning that it was made of luxurious Venetian silk; Mary, for her part, gave Margaret a golden brooch.[6] It is possible Margaret was doing what she had done when Cromwell questioned her about her behaviour at Syon, hiding her feelings to keep up her standing with the king. But she may not have mourned at all. It had so far gone untapped, but Margaret was capable of bitter, lasting rage against her family's enemies, even when those enemies were also kin.

Henry's thoughts are better documented: they turned – inevitably – to dynastic possibilities. He had a son; James had a daughter. Diplomacy might achieve what warfare had so far failed to do. Henry invited several of the Scots lords captured at Solway Moss to Hampton Court, and revealed a plan that would, among its many unintended consequences, shape the rest of Margaret's life.

Nearly twenty years earlier, Henry had considered marrying his daughter Mary to his nephew James V. That plan had come to nothing, but the events of 1542 presented the prospect of an even better match: this time, he had a son and heir to offer a queen, rather than a daughter to offer a king. For Henry, with his conviction that he was, in fact, feudal lord to the monarchs of Scotland, it was far better that England should supply the husband and Scotland the wife. With one marriage, he could secure his northern border, assert his imagined rights in Scotland, and subsume Mary Stewart's claim to the English throne beneath his son's.

The point was not lost on the Scots. To some, especially persecuted Protestants, the match seemed to herald reform and the hope of liberty to practise true, godly religion. John Elder, a Scottish clergyman exiled to England for his Protestant beliefs, wrote to Henry that this was a chance to put aside the 'Devil's convocation' of bishops, along 'with Beelzebub's fleshmongers, the abbots and all their adherents, being quite expulsed and driven away, both the realms of England and of Scotland may be joined in one, and so your noble majesty for to be superior and king'.[7] Others were less sanguine, certain that any such match would mean the end of independent Scotland and the loss of its monarchy. For many Scots, the feeling was 'that if the two realms were made one Scotland would be undone . . . the mind of Scotland was to have a king among themselves as they have always had'.[8]

Persuaded by Henry and his promise of freedom, the Scots captured at Solway Moss agreed to the scheme, swearing to see that the infant queen Mary was raised in England and married to Edward. Had the plan worked, and had Edward VI fulfilled the promise of his youth and lived to adulthood, Margaret would have led a very different life. She would have been among the greatest ladies of Edward and Mary's British court, first cousin to the king and aunt to the queen, doubtless the wife to some nobleman of political or diplomatic significance. With time, she might even have become a Protestant. In this alternative history, she would have stayed, at best, a distant heir to the throne. Instead, Henry's plots failed, and Margaret was caught up in her parents' perilous world of cross-border British politics.

As Henry laid out his dynastic vision, events were under way in Scotland that would present Margaret with an unexpected marriage proposal. Just as it had during the minority of James V, a power struggle followed the accession of the infant Mary, Queen of Scots. The vital question of this contest was whether Scotland should remain allied to Catholic France or seek new ties to Protestant England. Complicating this problem were the spread of Protestantism in Scotland and the personal rivalries among the country's leaders. The young queen's mother, Mary of Guise, naturally favoured strengthening the Auld Alliance with France and maintaining Scotland's traditional Catholic faith. So did David, Cardinal Beaton, the most powerful clergyman in the land. James Hamilton, Earl of Arran, was Mary's heir presumptive, and seemed more open to persuasion in matters religious and political.[9]

David Beaton was Scotland's only cardinal, named to the office with a mandate to keep Scotland clean of Protestantism, that 'contagion [that] infected the whole of the neighbouring country and corrupted its faith'.[10] He was a steadfast opponent of the reformers – for John Elder, he was 'the father of mischief', and for English diplomat Ralph Sadler, he was 'a wily fox'.[11] Beaton, though, was more than a hammer of the heretics. He was an urbane, cosmopolitan veteran of Scottish and French politics; the father of eight children by his devoted mistress, Marion Ogilvy; and – so he swore – one of four men named by James V in a deathbed will to be Regents for Mary, Queen of Scots.

Beaton seemed more than a match for James Hamilton, Earl of Arran. But the dark-haired, dark-eyed earl, with his open, guileless face, was the sort of man whom it was easy to catch off guard but almost impossible to actually defeat. Still in his early twenties in 1542, Arran had grown up having to deal with crises before he seemed quite ready to face them. He inherited his title at the age of ten and was married off soon after, becoming a father while he was little more than a child himself. By now, he had all the trappings of a great noble, and had been close to the late king, but he also had a reputation as a man bereft of political instinct. Margaret's uncle Sir George Douglas dismissed him as 'but a simple man' and Ambassador Chapuys had the impression that he was 'half-witted'. But Arran was not a fool: he was simply young, and he was about to surprise everybody.[12]

During the tumultuous weeks that followed the king's death, Arran utterly outmanoeuvred Beaton. The sources are incomplete, but it appears Beaton told an assembly of the Scottish nobility that James had named four Regents for the new queen, excluding the Hamiltons from power. Arran convinced them otherwise and was proclaimed governor. He knew that only a sickly infant stood between him and the throne of Scotland.

Now wholly in control of Scotland's finances, parliament and council, Arran stripped Beaton of his role as lord chancellor. Looking to consolidate his grip on power, he began to act the part of Protestant reformer, and declared himself ready to listen to Henry's proposals.[13] Agents of England and France made swift journeys to press their respective kings' policies, even though Arran had pushed the Scottish leaders of pro-French feeling to the political sidelines. Sent by Henry, Angus and his brother George swept back into Scotland with the Solway Moss lords following in their wake. France dispatched Matthew Stewart,

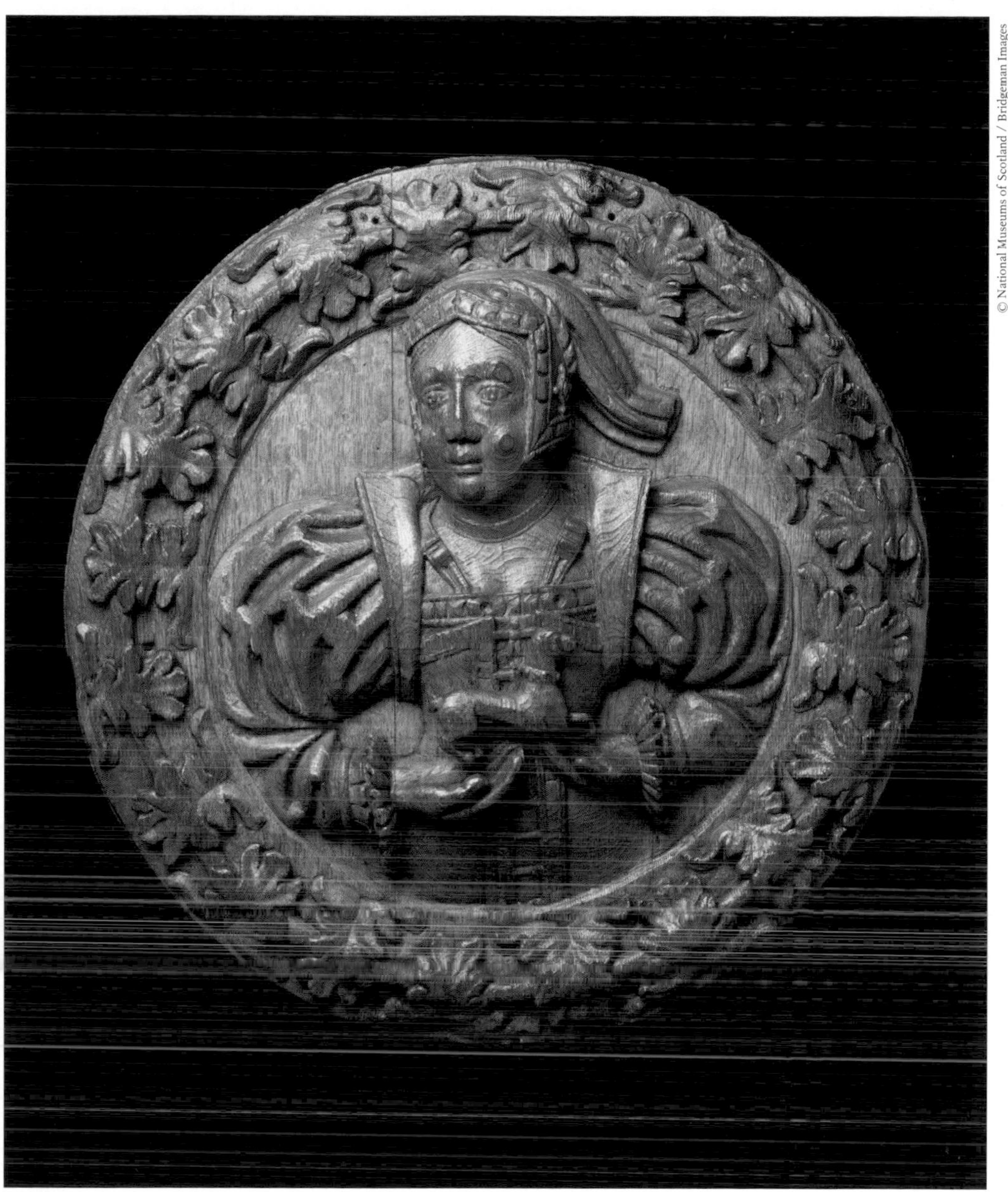

This oak medallion is one of a series commissioned by James V. It is thought to show his mother, Margaret Tudor, holding a greyhound – a Beaufort family symbol. Originally brightly painted, the 'Stirling Heads' were displayed on the ceiling of the King's Presence Chamber at Stirling Castle.

Margaret Douglas's father Archibald, 6th Earl of Angus. He is shown wearing a piece of jewellery in the shape of a heart, the Douglas family emblem.

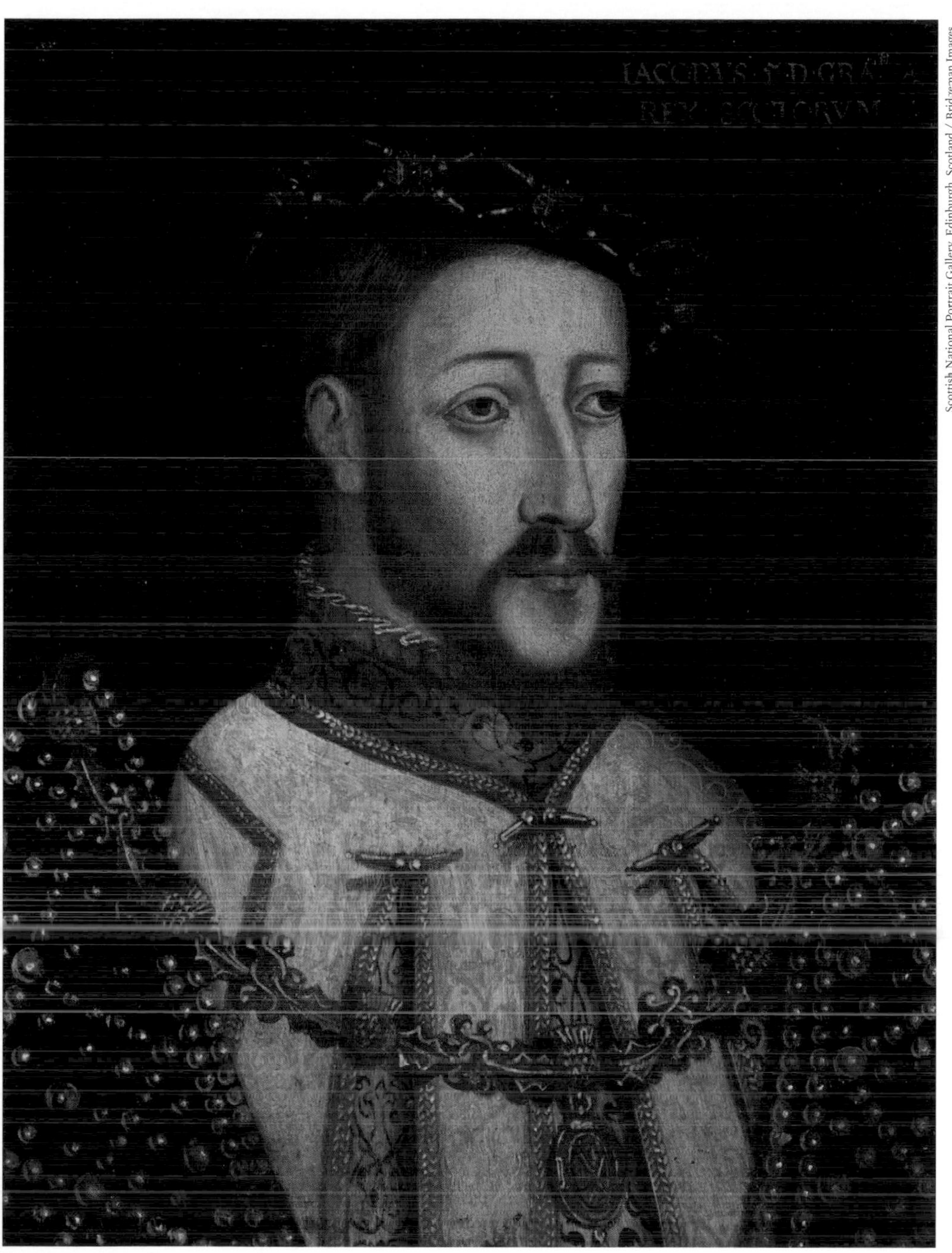

In this late sixteenth-century portrait of Margaret's half-brother James V, the king is wearing the collar of the Order of the Thistle.

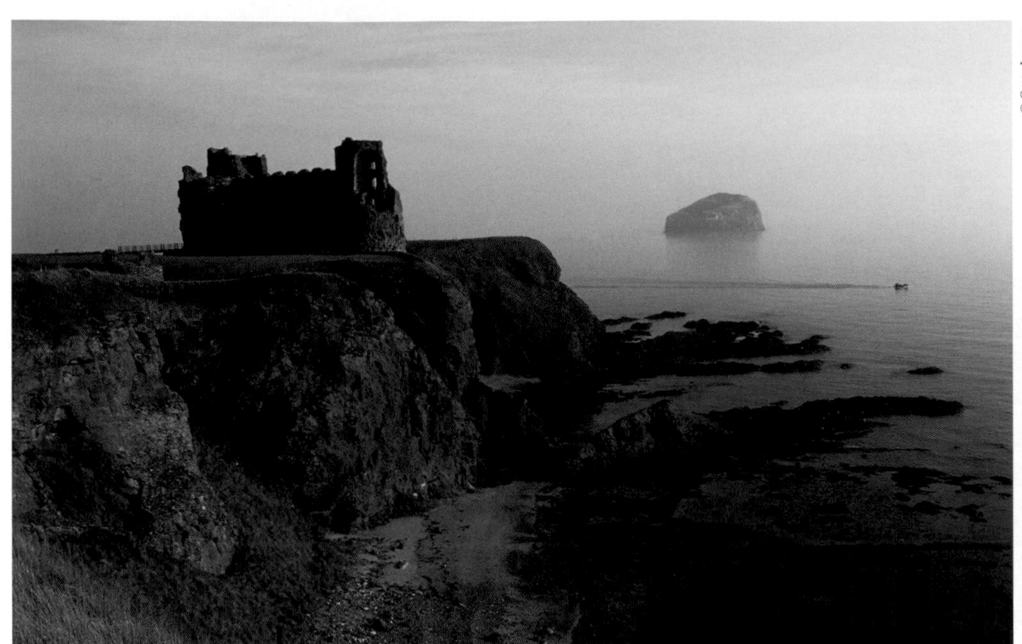

Tantallon, seat of the Douglas earls of Angus. Located near North Berwick, the castle looks out over the Firth of Forth and the Bass Rock.

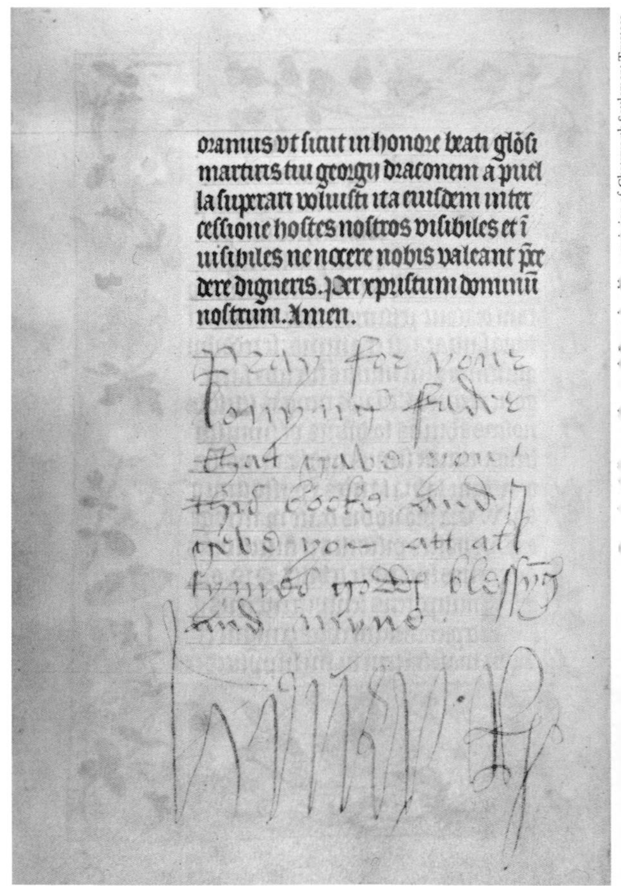

oramus ut sicut in honore beati glo[ri]o[s]i
martiris tui georgii draconem a puel
la superari voluisti ita eiusdem inter
cessione hostes nostros visibiles et i
nvisibiles ne nocere nobis valeant p[re]c
cere digneris. Per xpristum dominum
nostrum. Amen.

Pray for your
lovyng fader
that gave you
thys booke and
gyve you att all
tymes godds blessyng
and myne
Henry R

A leaf from the Book of Hours given to Margaret Tudor by Henry VII on her departure from England to marry James IV. The annotation (in modern spelling) reads 'Pray for your loving father that gave you this book and give you at all times God's blessing and mine. Henry R.' It was later owned by Margaret Douglas.

Margaret was a contributor to, as well as a scribe and owner of, the Devonshire Manuscript. This leaf is one of several she annotated with the note 'and this' (upper right hand corner), suggesting that the poem was one which she set herself to 'learn but to sing it'.

Margaret has been proposed as the subject of several portraits of unidentified Tudor noblewomen, including this dramatic painting attributed to William Scrots and likely dating from the mid-1540s. Although the sitter's identity is still uncertain, the features, clothes and cost of a full-length portrait all make Margaret a plausible candidate.

Henry VIII gave the manor of Temple Newsam to Margaret and Lennox. As this oil painting suggests, relatively little of the medieval and early modern house remained by the mid-eighteenth century.

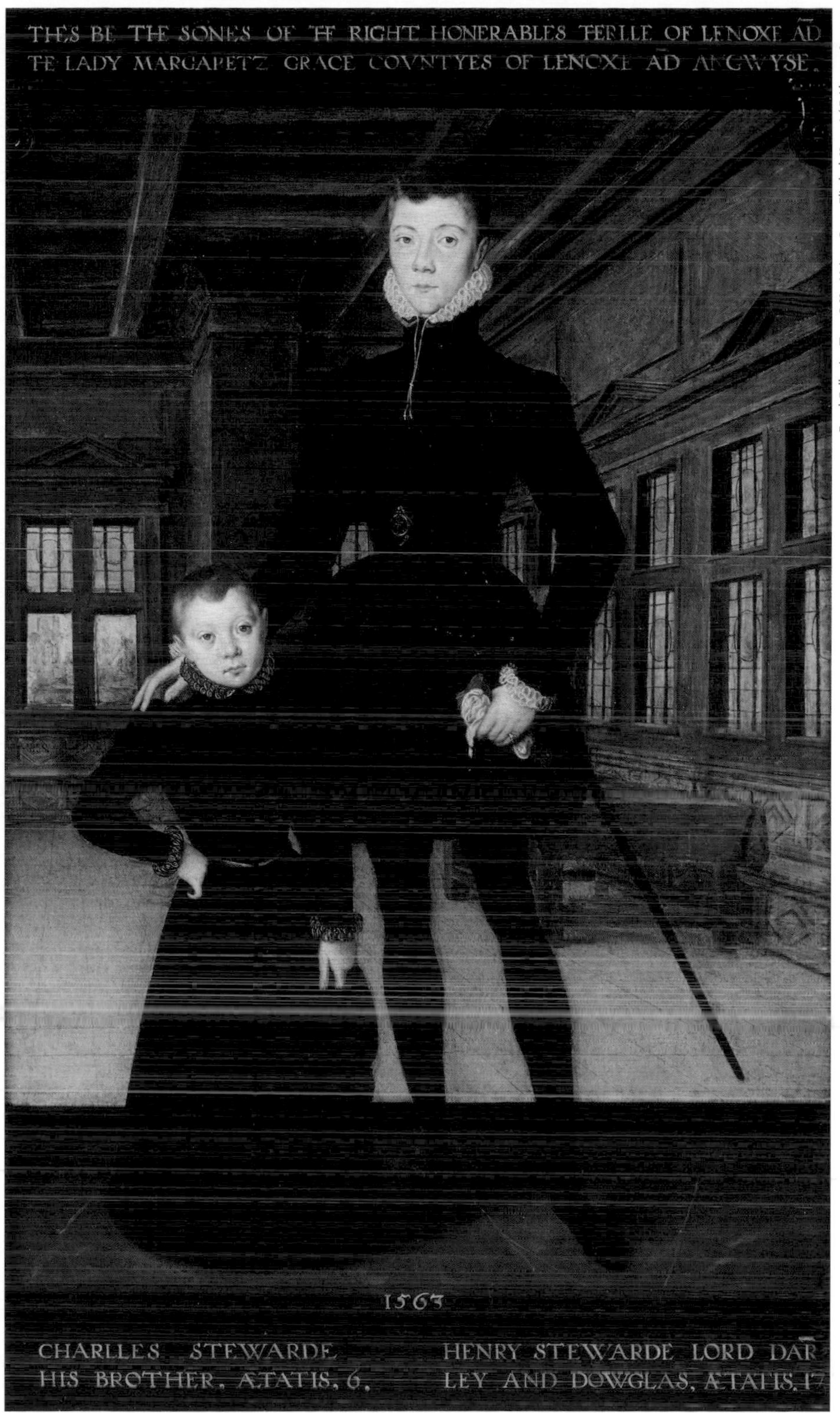

Painted by Hans Eworth, this double portrait depicts Henry, Lord Darnley and Charles, 5th Earl of Lennox, the two of Margaret and Lennox's four sons who survived to adulthood.

The sitter in this rather dark and sober portrait is usually identified as Margaret. It dates from the early 1560s, likely at some point between Francis II's death and Darnley's marriage to the Queen of Scots.

fourth Earl of Lennox: its own prodigal Scot and Arran's greatest dynastic rival.[14]

For Arran, this was unwelcome news. Like the Hamilton earls of Arran, the Stewart earls of Lennox were close relatives of the Scottish royal family. While both families claimed descent from James II's daughter Mary, the Hamiltons were her heirs in the male line and had the stronger right to be called 'second persons of the realm'. But there were whispers of bastardy to consider. Arran's father had gone through a protracted divorce from his first wife in order to marry his second, Janet Beaton. Arran was the eldest son of this second marriage, but there was doubt that he and his siblings were legitimate. If Janet Beaton was, as Lennox would later say, a 'concubine', then Arran was a bastard and the earls of Lennox were the nearest heirs to the Scottish crown.[15]

To men like Angus, who aimed for power and money rather than the crown itself, enemies and allies were never fixed. Arran and Lennox, by contrast, always knew who their ultimate opponents were: one of the few constants of Scottish politics was that these two men would always find their way onto opposite sides, bringing their families with them.

Lennox already bore the scars of the decades-old rivalry. In 1526 his father John had died in a duel at the hands of Sir James Hamilton of Finnart, Arran's brutal, bastard-born half-brother. Matthew inherited the earldom of Lennox before he was ten years old. The two families staged a ceremony of reconciliation in 1531, dividing up forgivenesses, lands and offices, but the Hamiltons got the better end of the deal. Knowing that this was no lasting peace and that he was not yet a political match for the Hamiltons, young Lennox removed himself to France in 1532.

While Arran married young and came into his duties as a Scottish earl, Lennox spent his adolescence in the glittering court of King Francis I. By 1542 he had become a young man 'of a strong Body, well proportionate, of a sweet and manly Visage, straight in Stature, and pleasant in Behaviour'.[16] Good-looking, with blue eyes, auburn hair, and his family's characteristic long nose, he was an experienced soldier and courtier, restlessly ambitious and a ruthless enemy.

When Francis decided to send an ambassador to Scotland with the task of upholding the Auld Alliance, Lennox was the natural choice, even though he had not set foot in the country for ten years. He came home in March 1543 with the aim of confounding Arran's pro-English strategy and made common cause with Cardinal Beaton. Almost immediately they were faced with a crisis. On 1 July 1543, England and Scotland concluded the Treaty of Greenwich, which held that Scotland would stay independent and that Mary would grow up in her own realm, but that she would eventually marry Edward.

In response to the treaty, Lennox, Beaton and their allies swore a formal bond opposing the match with Edward. They rallied their forces at Linlithgow, the picturesque but ill-fortified palace where the young queen had lived since her birth eight months before, and demanded that she be moved to the fortress-like Stirling Castle, where, as Ralph Sadler observed, she would be almost impossible to abduct.[17] Arran, quite outnumbered, had to agree, and it was Lennox who had the honour of accompanying Mary and her mother to their new home.

Arran was the governor, but Lennox held Mary. How, in the face of such opposition, could Arran retain his grasp on power? In the five weeks that followed Mary's removal to Stirling, it seemed that he would honour his alliance with Henry, and he did ratify the Treaty of Greenwich at the end of August. In private, though, he could see that he would have to change his strategy and make peace with those nearest the queen if he wanted to keep his role and his title. This meant making overtures to Beaton. The cardinal, given the chance to look magnanimous and to deal a blow to Henry, was prepared to hear Arran's proposals, and in the first week of September, the two men made a public show of reconciliation. Arran recanted his Protestantism, owning up to his errors and promising penance, and Beaton welcomed him back into the Catholic Church. The earl's 'godly fit' was over.

For a brief moment, Scotland's queen dowager, senior cleric and greatest nobles were all united against Henry's British schemes. Mary of Guise, Beaton, Arran and Lennox agreed that the time had come to crown the queen. On 9 September 1543, thirty years after the Scottish nobility had been hewn down at Flodden, the heirs of Flodden's dead gathered in the Chapel Royal at Stirling for the coronation of the nine-month-old Mary, Queen of Scots. Ralph Sadler sent Henry a sniffy report that 'the young Queen was crowned . . . with such solemnity as they do use in this country, which is not very costly'.[18] But there was no dismissing the power of that day.

Together for an instant in a long lifetime of rivalry, Arran and Lennox carried the regalia to the altar. Arran had the imperial crown, fashioned of Scottish gold and emblazoned with pearls and ancient gemstones, while Lennox bore the silver-gilt sceptre, capped by a glowing rock crystal and the figures of Christ, the Virgin, St James and St Andrew, Scotland's patron saint. Beaton performed the sacred ritual, holding the crown over Mary's head. When he was through, Scotland had an anointed sovereign once more. Three months later, the Scots formally rejected the Treaty of Greenwich.

With the pro French Beaton now working with Arran, Lennox might have expected a place in the highest levels of Scotland's government. There were rumours that Lennox might marry Mary of Guise, or even the infant queen herself. In reality, though, the new understanding between Arran and Beaton left no room for Lennox. The cardinal did not need them both – and Arran's young son seemed a likelier suitor for Mary's hand than Lennox did.

Lennox was impatient, ambitious, and incapable of working with his detested rival Arran for long – three qualities that proved stronger than his loyalty to France. He played both sides, holding quiet negotiations with the English ambassadors and their Scottish allies while continuing to act as France's official representative, even though he was hoarding away the money and military supplies intended to bolster France's position in Scotland. As 1543 ended and 1544 began, his double-dealing cost him his place on the governor's council. Liberated, he took the French supplies over to England and openly allied with the pro-Henry lords – led by Archibald Douglas, Earl of Angus.

It had been a remarkable twelve months: Arran, once apparently Protestant and pro-English, had rejoined the Catholic Church and abandoned Henry, whereas Lennox, who had come back to Scotland as the ambassador of Catholic France, was now looking for an alliance with the Protestant English king. There was, however, a logic to Lennox's behaviour: he would never be able to become the leading figure in Mary's minority unless he could find a way to replace Arran as governor and be recognised as second person of the realm.

Together, Lennox and the pro-English lords gathered their troops and made an effort to bring Arran back to the English cause, but the governor overcame their forces, taking some of them hostage and forcing the rest home to their own strongholds. Still harried by Arran, Lennox redoubled his efforts to reach a deal with Henry VIII. Lennox's hope, he made clear, was that he would become Henry's greatest ally in Scotland, and in return, would marry the king's half-Scottish niece, the lady Margaret Douglas.

He had this match in mind less than two weeks after Mary's coronation and quickly grew determined to bring it about.[19]

Why was he set on Margaret? There were compelling political reasons. As Angus's daughter and Henry's niece, she would bind him to the party favouring the union of Mary and Edward, and even for a man who had aimed at marriage into Scotland's royal family, winning the King of England's niece would be a triumph. There is also the tantalising, more romantic chance that they already knew each other. In October 1543 the English Privy Council wrote to Ralph Sadler that Lennox declared his 'fervent love and affection to his highness's niece the Lady Margaret Douglas'.[20] While this may well have been a bit of courtly *politesse*, Lennox and Margaret had both spent the 1520s in Scotland, and their fathers had been close allies for much of that decade. It may be that they had met as children, and that although they had not seen each other for some fifteen years, Lennox was summoning up distant memories of the girl from Tantallon.

By now, though, Margaret was one of the most prominent women at court, ranked only behind the king's own daughters in the order of precedence. Even the Howard family, who had lost a son because of her, cultivated her and sought her patronage. She became godmother to the eldest daughter of William and Margaret Howard – brother and sister-in-law to her own dead lover, Lord Thomas. It was traditional for a girl to be christened with her godmother's name, so in a wry and bittersweet twist, Margaret's goddaughter received the peculiarly masculine moniker of Douglas Howard. Women of her rank were valuable allies to have, able to recommend a friend's young daughter to some great noblewoman in need of a lady-in waiting. With a dozen years' experience of Henry's court, Margaret was a woman who could do favours.

Above all, she was part of the royal family. On 12 July 1543, while the furore over the Treaty of Greenwich raged in Scotland, Henry married Katherine Parr, his sixth and final wife. It was a quiet, intimate ceremony, held partly in English and partly in Latin. The bare handful of invited guests was still enough to crowd the confines of the Queen's Holy Day Closet, a small room above the star-studded ceiling of the Chapel Royal at Hampton Court. Few women were present to hear Katherine swear 'to be bonny and buxom in bed and at board', but Margaret and the king's daughters were at the forefront.[21]

Like Margaret, Queen Katherine had belonged to Mary Tudor's household, and all three women were of similar ages. Now that Katherine was Henry's wife, they became something of a trio. They had thoughtfulness and curiosity in common: Katherine was easily the most cerebral of the three and a theologian in her own right, but Mary was also a keen scholar – she and Katherine worked together on a translation of Erasmus's *Paraphrase* on the New Testament – and Margaret, though she had neither Latin nor Greek, was a poet.[22] As in her teens, when she had been caught up in the brilliant circle of the Devonshire Manuscript, she was part of the intellectual life of Henry's court. The new queen probably gave them both copies of her book *Psalms or Prayers*. They all penned brief, charming poems of friendship to Jane Wriothesley, Countess of Southampton, in the pages of her private prayer book. Margaret, for one, declared that 'As I have said ye shall me find/In word and deed, I you assure/Which is to be your earnest friend/As long as my life doth endure.'[23] It had been years since Margaret had seen Mary as happy as she was in Katherine's company.

The three women also shared a love of dancing, which was both 'a noble and virtuous past-time' and an energetic, flirtatious way to spend an evening. On one occasion the Duke de Najera made a diplomatic visit from Navarre to England and visited the queen's chamber, where he and his nobles joined Katherine, Mary and Margaret for a revel: 'The Queen danced first with her brother, very gracefully; then the Princess Mary and the Princess of Scotland danced with other gentlemen, and many other ladies did the same.'[24] There was some confusion about Margaret's title – she was not a Princess of Scotland – but whether processing through a graceful Spanish pavane or stepping lightly through a fast-moving galliard, she was at the very centre of court life. The historian George Buchanan would later observe that she was 'a princess in the flower of her age, celebrated for exquisite loveliness of shape, and elegance of form'.[25]

In this happy period Margaret's place in the line of succession, so much a source of concern in the late 1530s, lost some of its importance. This was due, at least in part, to the influence of Katherine, who encouraged Henry to restore his daughters to their rightful place in the order of succession. The Third Act of Succession, passed by the 1543–4 parliament in July 1543, decreed that if Edward died without lawful issue, the crown would go to Mary and then to Elizabeth, 'with such conditions as by his highness shall be limited by his letters patents under his Great Seal, or by his majesty's last will in writing signed with his gracious hand'.[26]

In the 1530s, Elizabeth and Mary had been bastardised and declared the children of invalid marriages by parliamentary statute. Now, they were restored to the line of succession. The Third Act also clarified their places in that line: when families had no sons, their daughters inherited jointly, which was clearly impossible when the inheritance in question was the crown – Henry was no King Lear. He made it explicit that his eldest daughter would succeed before her younger sister. With Mary and Elizabeth restored, Margaret dropped two places in the order of succession, but she was still a favourite with Henry: it was not that his niece fell from his good graces, but that his daughters returned to them. Moreover, while Henry, himself a second son, was preoccupied with what might happen if his heir did not survive, Prince Edward was a healthy young boy. There seemed little reason to worry that any Tudor woman would find herself heir to the throne.

The court could see that Margaret was high in favour with the king. Henry gave her the means to dress as well as his own daughters. Like Mary and Elizabeth, she drew the cloth for her wardrobe from the great silk store at Whitehall, and in the final five years of Henry's life, Margaret claimed nearly as much cloth as her cousins: Mary received 1,500 yards of cloth, Elizabeth 1,300, and Margaret just over 1,000. She wore shifts made from the finest white cambric. Stiff hoops, known as farthingales, supported her skirts. Over her undergarments went kirtles and gowns, all crafted from different woven silks, often lined with soft sarsenet – she was especially fond of satin and velvet, favouring expensive black-dyed fabrics as well as vibrant crimsons. Along with these went sleeves in a range of styles, partlets to raise the low necklines of her gowns, and headdresses trimmed with precious stones or delicate embroidery. Margaret already had the passion for jewellery and metalwork that would last throughout her life, and her necklaces, brooches and earrings sparkled against the rich blacks of her gowns and hoods. For Henry, and to any observant courtier, she was a Tudor princess.[27]

Still, the question of marriage must have been on her mind and the court's. It was unusual for a queen's daughter to make it to her late twenties and remain unmarried. Margaret's foreign matches had come to nothing, her rumoured English suitors were dead, and her two love affairs had each ended in disaster. Henry, though, made his niece a remarkable promise: he would 'never cause her to marry with any but whom she shall find in her own heart to love'.[28]

Few sixteenth-century noblewomen were free to reject arranged matches – especially those so close to the throne. Even Henry's favourite sister, the beautiful Mary Tudor, had found herself the third wife of Louis XII of France, a man more than thirty years her senior. It so happened that Louis died within three months of his wedding and that Mary was therefore able to marry her beloved Charles Brandon, Duke of Suffolk, but she had to do it in secret. When Suffolk presented Wolsey with this *fait accompli*, it fell to the cardinal to inform Henry. Writing back to the anxious duke, the cardinal told him of the king's dreadful rage that Suffolk had broken faith and married his sister: 'You put yourself in the greatest danger that ever man was in.'[29] When the same King Henry gave his niece his word that she could reject the suit of a man she did not love, it constituted a show of deep affection.

This promise was part of the backdrop to Henry's talks with Lennox. Commissioners for the king and the earl, empowered to bargain for their masters, held long negotiating sessions, trying to work out a deal that would last. The earl's commissioner was his secretary, Thomas Bishop, a native of the ancient Ayrshire village of Ochiltree.[30] Bishop was a fierce, unpredictable man with dreadful handwriting. He would soon come to detest Margaret and regret the role he played in marrying her to his master, but for the moment he was an old friend and loyal servant to the earl, and he would not compromise on Lennox's demands.[31]

In May 1544 the commissioners came to terms. Under the Treaty of Carlisle, Lennox promised to ally himself with Henry and his Scottish policy, uphold the Protestant faith, and keep Mary in Scotland. In return, the king promised him wealth, English estates and the office of governor, though only as an English appointee, rather than as second person of the realm of Scotland. He also offered him Margaret's hand, but that offer was still conditional – she would have to agree to marry Lennox.[32]

Why was Henry so insistent that Margaret have the freedom to reject the suit of any man she thought she could not love? Did he, perhaps, feel that Lennox was a less than glorious match for a granddaughter of Henry VII, and hope that Margaret would not want him?[33] Did he want to avoid another matrimonial scandal, like the one she had caused in 1536? Or did he simply honour a promise to a much-loved niece? It is impossible to be sure, though all three motives may have played their parts. As Lennox came south to pay formal court, ten months of intense diplomatic negotiations now hinged on Margaret. It was her choice alone.

There is no record of their meeting: what day it took place, or where, or whether they spoke in the presence of others or alone. But it is plain that Margaret, upon hearing Lennox's suit, had no doubts. They had both been shaped by the same powerful forces and they understood each other. They had grown up amidst the uncertainty of James V's minority and knew what it meant to be dispossessed; they had had more than their share of romances; they stood close to the thrones of their native countries. Behind the good looks, Lennox was prone to melancholy, needed companionship, and was something of a pessimist. It is unsurprising that Margaret, resilient, hopeful and practised at being in her own company, inspired his devotion. Better matched than anybody could have expected, Margaret and Lennox agreed to wed, embarking on what was one of the happiest marriages of the entire Tudor dynasty.

On the morning of 29 June 1544, Henry, Katherine, family and guests gathered in the new Chapel Royal of St James's Palace. Light streamed through the great north window. The air was full of the clean, sharp smell of polished oak and the polyphonic melodies of the gentlemen and boys who made up the choir. Beneath Hans Holbein's ceiling, its intricate mass of gilded Tudor roses shining in the candles' flames, Margaret and Lennox took hands and swore their marriage vows. It was a brief ceremony, but a potent one: it bound them together for the next twenty-seven years.

The newly married couple and their guests filled the rest of the wedding day with celebrations. Guests feasted at flower-strewn banquet tables, drank wine by the gobletful and danced through the afternoon and evening. Margaret's family welcomed Lennox into their number with generous gifts: Henry gave them both cloth of silver from the silk store, along with money, houses and lands in Yorkshire. More privately, Mary presented the bride with a balas, or pale ruby, glad for Margaret even though she knew that their relationship would have to change. For her cousin now had a new name and role: Margaret, Countess of Lennox.[34]

Throughout her teenage years and her twenties, Margaret had embraced her life as an English princess, throwing herself into the glamour, scandal and intellectual ferment of Henry's court. Events outside her control brought Scotland back into her life: not only the niece of the King of England, she was now the aunt of the Queen of Scots and the daughter of Henry's greatest Scottish ally. But the marriage to Lennox had been within her control: she chose her part as Lennox's wife, knowing that it meant re-entering her childhood world of Scottish politics. She had decided to enter fully into the quest for Anglo-Scottish union.

On that summer day, with the bells of St James ringing out, everything seemed in order. Margaret was married to a man she would come to adore and who might soon become governor of Scotland. She, her new husband and her father were all in high standing with Henry, whose plans for Scotland included an important role for each of them. This happy state of affairs, however, was not to last. Over the next two and a half years, Angus, Lennox and Margaret would all lose Henry's favour, with spectacular consequences.

7

The Third Time

Newly married, Margaret divided her time between court and a house in the village of Stepney, just to the east of the city of London. It was a town of 2,000 people, largely millers and farmers as well as growing numbers of courtiers and gentry who wanted comfortable country estates.[1] She was still high in the king's favour and her match was working well: she was Lennox's 'good Meg', he was her 'own most loving husband'.[2] She became pregnant almost at once and gave birth to a son early in 1545. They named him Henry, in honour of his great-uncle, the king.

This was prudence as much as love. Shortly after her wedding, Margaret's father abandoned Henry. English raids on the Scottish borders and coasts damaged lands belonging to the Douglases, and there was a limit even to the loyalty of Angus, Henry's erstwhile brother-in-law and most dependable Scottish ally. The rift between Angus and Henry opened even wider when Sir Ralph Evers subjected Melrose Abbey to brutal attack. As trembling Cistercian monks looked on, appalled, the English soldiers ransacked the monastery's medieval tombs. Melrose was not just the resting place of the heart of Robert the Bruce, symbol of the Douglas family, but the burial ground of the Douglases themselves. Once again, Margaret's male relatives arranged themselves on opposing political sides, and Lennox was calling Angus 'a detestable enemy'.[3]

Angus soon proved himself a valuable and politically visible asset to the Scottish cause. Reconciling with his new son-in-law's great rival Arran, he secured a major victory over an English force at Ancrum Moor on 27 February 1545. The day won, Arran embraced Angus and welcomed him back to the Scottish fold. Francis I invested him with France's highest chivalric honour for his success: he was named to the Order of St Michael, given the right to wear a collar of gold cockleshells hung with the badge of the warrior-angel. Angus had put Margaret in a difficult position, which she handled with all the grace she could muster. She stayed on civil terms with her father, but there was no questioning her loyalty. When it came to the future of Scotland, both she and her husband were squarely on the side of Henry VIII.

Marriage brought new responsibilities, and Margaret was now mistress of considerable estates in the north of England, gifts from Henry VIII in recompense for the French lands Lennox had forfeited to come over to the English side.[4] There were two impressive manor houses. One was Settrington, some twenty miles from the coastal town of Scarborough, with a great chamber hung with black and white tapestries and a stable full of cattle, oxen, swine, sheep and horses.[5] The other was Temple Newsam, a short distance from Leeds. It owes its name to the Knights Templar, who owned the land from the late twelfth century until their suppression in the early fourteenth.[6] Today, the estate bears the marks of extensive remodelling in the eighteenth century, with few traces of the old medieval manor: the house, with its columned neoclassical facade, sits amidst gardens laid out by Capability Brown. An inventory taken in the 1560s, however, gives some insight into what it looked like when owned by the Lennox-Stewarts. In the Tudor century it was one of the most splendid houses in England.

Having spent years in the households of Mary and of Henry's wives, Margaret was now in charge of her own estates and of a grand, welcoming house, and bought the goods and furniture needed to make it into the family seat.[7] Quiet since the forfeiture of its old owners, the Darcys, Temple Newsam was suddenly filled with conversation, worship and music – and the chattering of the Lennox-Stewarts' expensive family pet, a monkey fed on a diet of treacle.[8] At the centre was the Great Chamber, a large room with seating for the family and for guests – a space in which Margaret and Lennox could indulge their hobbies, like playing bowls on a gleg table, an antecedent of the modern billiard table, and listening to or playing the virginals.

Such a house required constant management, so Margaret supervised a substantial team of retainers and servants. Behind the scenes, the house had its cellar, buttery, pantry, kitchen, wet larder and dry larder, as well as a brewhouse, with its mash-vat or malt-tub, and a room for making pastry, with a bolting-table for sifting flour and a dedicated kneading trough. There were rooms for all the members of the household, including a musicians' chamber complete with a music stand and two bedsteads. Beyond the house itself, there was a barn for stowing oats and hay, and the park where the family's many horses roamed.[9]

Margaret conceived again soon after Henry's birth, and she was already heavily pregnant by the autumn of 1545. She was almost certainly in Yorkshire rather than in Stepney, opening up the house and awaiting the birth of her second child, when the news came from London that her first-born son had suddenly died.[10] Losing young children was common, but that did not mean that she did not feel the loss: she and Lennox already thought of him as their 'son and heir'. He was buried in the parish church at Stepney with a simple prayer: 'Here lieth Henry Steward . . . whose soul Jesus pardon.'[11] But nine days after her first child's death, she gave birth to another son. This boy survived. He was probably born and baptised in Temple Newsam, carried to the chapel wearing an ermine-trimmed mantle of crimson cloth. Like his dead brother, he was named after the king and known as Henry, Lord Darnley.[12]

Margaret had loved court life and she brought some of the trappings with her: she still owned the Devonshire Manuscript.[13] But coming north also meant forming new ties. There were tenants who were owed patronage, local institutions like parish churches and chantries to support, fellow northern nobles to befriend. She was a frequent visitor to Wressle, the home of the Percy earls of Northumberland.[14] Lennox, though often absent, wrote whenever he could, relying on messengers to take his letters back to Margaret in Yorkshire.[15]

In the early years of their marriage, Lennox was often in Scotland, where he was a devoted, if ultimately ineffective, servant of Henry's Scottish policy – which was dubbed, some centuries later, the 'Rough Wooing'. In the spring of 1546, as Lennox made one of a series of unsuccessful efforts to secure Dumbarton Castle on the Clyde, events in Scotland and in Europe were moving rapidly. Cardinal Beaton was assassinated by a gang of reform-minded conspirators seeking revenge for his part in the trial and burning of the Protestant George Wishart. Arran and Mary of Guise, united in their anti-English sympathies, were left in an uneasy truce. Meanwhile, France had provided valuable help to the Scots throughout 1545, but Henry had captured Boulogne in September 1544 and now England and France were ensconced in diplomatic negotiations over its fate. For all that Henry wanted to be Scotland's acknowledged overlord, he wanted even more to emulate his Plantagenet forebears and rebuild the English crown's holdings in France. On 6 June 1546, just one week after Beaton's death, the Treaty of Camp brought a temporary halt to the Rough Wooing. England and France agreed that the English would keep Boulogne for eight years, after which the French would be able to reclaim it at the cost of two million crowns. They also compromised over Scotland, agreeing that Henry would not go to war without 'new occasion'. Lennox could return to Margaret and Darnley.

Like his mother, young Darnley was English by birth and upbringing, but British by inheritance. He had a claim to be one of Scotland's most senior nobles, as heir to the earldoms of Lennox and Angus. At his birth, though, there were obstacles in the way of both of these Scottish claims, and he was instead positioned as an important English nobleman. He was the first Tudor boy to be born since Prince Edward nearly ten years before, and he was also Henry's first great-nephew. As a child, his father had been styled 'Master of Lennox', indicating, in Scottish fashion, that he would one day inherit his father's earldom; young Henry, however, was known as Lord Darnley, in the English manner that referred to eldest sons by their fathers' subsidiary titles.

Margaret adored her son and was with him constantly. In his earliest years she was responsible for his education, especially in matters of religion. Later, he had male schoolmasters, who were highly trusted members of the household and who gave him instruction in languages, music and the art of composition. After his death, chroniclers would call Darnley spoiled, and it is true that Margaret protected him from the storm of politics that she and Lennox had both faced while growing up. She had spent her own childhood at the mercy of her parents' personal and political feuds, and she saw to it that Darnley grew up where he was born, that he was cherished, and that he had schooling befitting his rank. She also did not let him forget that he was not only heir to two great earldoms, but cousin to the rulers of both England and Scotland. None of this, though, should be unexpected; it was usual for aristocratic mothers to indulge their children and raise them to be conscious of their status.

In the two years after her marriage, Margaret remained on good terms with Henry. In September 1544, for instance, the king added a handwritten postscript to the end of a letter to Katherine Parr, sending 'blessings to all his children and recommendations to his cousin Margaret and the rest of the ladies and gentlewomen and to his Council'.[16] But by the time Henry came to write his will in December 1546, it was apparent that something had gone terribly wrong in his relationship with the Lennox-Stewarts.

Under the terms of the Second and Third Acts of Succession, already passed by the 1536 and 1543–4 parliaments, Henry had the authority to change the order of succession in his will, and he used it. While the Third Act had designated an order of inheritance among the royal children, Henry's will went much further. First, it mandated that any children he might have with Katherine Parr would succeed Edward, taking precedence over Mary and Elizabeth. Second, it dealt with the reality that there might never be 'issue and heirs of the several bodies of us and of our said son Prince Edward and of our said daughters Mary and Elizabeth'.[17]

Henry had spent much of his reign trying to ensure his dynasty's future. Now, he steeled himself to decree what would happen if all of his children died without heirs. His will laid out a new order of succession in which the heirs of his younger sister, Mary, took precedence over those of his elder sister, Margaret. Under its terms, Henry's own children would succeed, to be followed by their Brandon cousins, Frances and Eleanor. Only if Edward, Mary, Elizabeth, Frances and Eleanor all died without legitimate issue would the crown descend 'to the next rightful heirs'. It might be inferred that he meant the three living descendants of his eldest sister – Mary, Queen of Scots, Margaret Douglas and Henry, lord Darnley – but Henry did not mention a single one of them by name. Henry's will indicated a clear demotion of Margaret Tudor's line.

Why? What was Henry trying to achieve by demoting his sister's heirs? The answer has been a Tudor mystery. There were compelling reasons for not wanting Mary Stewart to inherit the English throne. If she were to wed a Scot or a Frenchman, it was possible that through her, the English crown might come into foreign hands. These reasons, though, did not extend to the loyal, Anglicised Lennox-Stewarts. Were they victims of Henry's desire to exclude the Scottish queen? Perhaps, but it would have been simple to demote Mary while leaving the Lennox-Stewarts in their rightful place. Had they instead done something themselves to merit demotion?

For some time there has been only one insight into the matter. In a 1561 letter to William Cecil, Lennox's former secretary Thomas Bishop gave an account of the 'special services' he had done for Henry and his successors and the favours he had received in return. One paragraph mentions a gift of land from Henry 'a little before his death and after the breach with my lady Lennox'.[18] In his account, Bishop suggests that Margaret argued with Henry shortly before his death, with the implication that this quarrel led him to exclude her and her family from the will.

Bishop was an unsympathetic observer, writing some fifteen years after the fact. But he mentioned the quarrel casually while explaining his financial affairs, and the lack of detail offered suggests that Cecil already knew everything he needed to know about the dispute. In this instance, Bishop can probably be taken at his word.

What might have led Henry and Margaret to quarrel? Religion is not a satisfying explanation. Lennox and Margaret were committed to the policy of matching Edward with Mary, Queen of Scots, both before and after Henry's death, suggesting that they adopted Henry's Scottish vision, Protestantism and all. They held many traditionally Catholic beliefs – they upheld the efficacy of prayers for the dead in Purgatory and paid stipends to local chantry priests – but the king was no evangelical and they were in step with him.[19] Other evidence, recently re-examined, offers further details. While Bishop's 1561 note has long been thought to be the sole contemporary reference to Margaret's quarrel with the king, he mentioned it at least twice, and the second manuscript explicitly links the quarrel to the Lennox-Stewarts' exclusion from the line of succession.

For most of her life, Margaret had lived on others' sufferance, dependent first on her parents, then on Wolsey, and then on Henry for virtually everything. The qualities most evident in her words and actions were her patience and adaptability. But she had already shown that she could be both stubborn and defiant, sure that she was acting for the right. That confidence in her own judgement became more apparent now that she had her own money, household and independence. When crossed, she fought back, and like her half-brother, she did not forgive easily.

Not long after Darnley's birth, Margaret got into a fight with Bishop. She had never warmed to him: he was a man of 'accustomed ill demeanour' and 'dogged nature', unpleasant to be around, and an inveterate womaniser besides.[20] Pregnancy and childbirth had left her unwell and perhaps short-tempered.[21] Before long, Margaret threatened to throw Bishop out of Lennox's service. Facing the loss of his livelihood, Bishop turned to Henry for help, and the king reacted ferociously:

> The king's majesty, worthily my complaint hearing thereof, sent two of his Council, declaring how good he had been to her father and herself, who to requite him, having but one servant in the house put him away, and besides sought to have the rule of her husband . . .

Margaret went down on her knees to swear that Bishop was a liar, while Lennox called him a thief, but there was no reconciliation: 'She for ever after lost a part of his [the king's] house, as appeared at his death.'[22] This letter suggests it was not religion that led Henry to consign the Lennox-Stewarts to the dynastic rubbish heap. It was a toxic combination of family resentment and British politics.

To Bishop's mind, there were three elements to Henry's anger with Margaret. First, some of it was directed at her father, Angus, who had spent a comfortable exile in England and appeared a loyal ally until he rejected Henry's policy and joined the anti-marriage party. Having been unable to vent his anger on Angus, Henry turned on Angus's daughter. In the final years of his life, Henry's temper was fierce and unpredictable, so even though he and Margaret had been on good terms, it is credible that the slightest provocation could lead him to link her to her disloyal father rather than her loyal husband.

Second, Bishop painted himself as a valued subject of Henry VIII, one whose interests the king would defend at the expense of his own niece. There is no doubt that Bishop had played a critical role in securing Lennox's allegiance to England and that Henry had rewarded him for his role. In addition to an annuity of £25, he gave Bishop the manor of Pocklington in Yorkshire, with lands worth nearly £60 per annum.[23] To Henry, Margaret's distaste for Bishop and her efforts to get rid of him seemed a show of impudence and disloyalty. Again, this suggests that Margaret's dispute with Henry was a family quarrel complicated by the question of her allegiance to Henry's Scottish policies – and it is worth noting that Angus had no love for Bishop and that Henry had been told as much.[24]

This is borne out by the third theme, the charge that Margaret sought 'the rule of her husband'. These accounts date from the early 1560s, by which point both Margaret's allies and enemies alike had come to portray her as the dominant character in her marriage, so it may have been that Bishop was overlaying his memory of the quarrel with then-contemporary views of Margaret. Moreover, though no correspondence from this period of their relationship survives, the Lennox-Stewarts' later letters to each other show that their marriage was a partnership of equals. Still, Bishop believed that his own role – a royally sanctioned role – as Lennox's counsellor had been usurped. He did not imply that Margaret was trying to achieve some political aim, like getting Lennox to rejoin Angus's party. Rather, she was trying to instruct her husband in the conduct of affairs, which was enough to undermine the mandated order within a marriage. Bishop, long a loyal servant of Lennox the courtier, commander and diplomat, was saddened to see him led by a woman, and if his account is to be believed, so was the king. What good was a soldier who could be commanded by his wife?

All these disparate threads – and the fact that they are so disparate – suggest that this was a family dispute, gathering unconnected slights into a major quarrel. It was serious: Henry did not send his counsellors on such missions lightly, and he rewrote his will to demote the Lennox-Stewarts. Still, it appeared much less serious than the fight over Thomas Howard back in 1536. The matter remained fairly private and nobody went to prison. Margaret's relationship with Henry could turn stormy, but she had always been able to win back his favour.

This time, though, she would not have the chance. Henry was ill, and on 28 January 1547 he died at Whitehall, unreconciled to his niece. The will stood. Margaret's reaction to Henry's death and to his new will further the idea that this was a personal fight she bitterly regretted rather than some grave ideological dispute. She stayed loyal to Henry after his death, speaking warmly of him to her family, friends and servants. Angus, apparently one of the causes of the quarrel, received a sharp reminder from Margaret that Henry 'had been so good and liberal a prince to you, which ought never to be forgotten'. In 1562 her retainer

Ralph Lacy testified that he 'heard her say that King Henry VIII would call her his niece and make much of her'.[25] She kept Henry's portrait in the great chamber at Temple Newsam, alongside that of her much-loved cousin Mary, and had a 'tablet with the picture of King Henry VIII therein' at the time of her death.[26] For all his temper had cost her, Margaret had loved the old king as a young woman, and did so until the end of her life.

In the cold winter of 1547 the Lennox-Stewarts were in a bleak position. Margaret had lost her place in the order of succession and a whole other family now stood between her and the throne. Of course, her chances of succeeding would have been remote even without the will, but to not even be named in the list of heirs was a terrible humiliation. The fate of the young Scottish queen, and with it, the fate of Margaret's family, remained unsettled. England itself now had a child for a monarch: a precocious young boy too young to rule himself but too old not to be reckoned with.

Margaret, though, was resilient. She had reason to hope for advancement and she would not hide away in Yorkshire. Now, she had new aims: to adapt to the political reality, to preserve the rights she had, and to position her family for the future. Lennox's old colleague, Edward Seymour, was to be the leading figure in the young king's minority. The Scottish queen was still unmarried and the Rough Wooing was about to recommence in earnest: the new king needed the prospect of a male heir. Whatever the statutes or Henry VIII's will might say, no woman had ever sat upon the English throne. Apart from the newly crowned King Edward VI, there was just one boy living who could claim legitimate descent from Henry VII: Henry, Lord Darnley. How high could the Countess of Lennox aim for her son, the only other Tudor prince?

Part Two

THIS WOMAN AND HER SON

8

Rough Wooing

Torches lit the wintry night as a vast procession bore the dead king's body out of Westminster. The king's porters, black staves in their hands, led a great column of mourners: 250 poor men in black hoods and gowns, each one proudly wearing on his left shoulder the badge of a red and white cross set in a burning sun, servants, clergy, gentlemen, knights, ambassadors, peers, on foot and on horseback, bearing the symbols of Tudor England. The flames illuminated banners setting out Henry's place in a long line of kings and saints. Picked out in silk were Henry's arms, along with those of Katherine Parr and Jane Seymour; the heraldry of his father and grandfather; the great English saints Edmund, Edward the Confessor and George. When at last they reached Windsor, Henry was buried next to Jane Seymour, to the sound of the ancient words of the Mass.[1] It was an elaborate show of continuity, of the enduring strength and grace of royal blood: kings begot sons of their own bodies to uphold order and religion.

Margaret knew that in spite of the show of sameness, Henry had left England deeply changed. Its affairs were unsettled at home, in Europe, and especially in Scotland. For her, Douglas by birth, Tudor by upbringing, Stewart by marriage, this was a moment for swift transformation from charming courtier to independent political actor.

Her cousin Edward, suddenly king, showed promise. He had a passion for athletics and military affairs and he was both devout and scholarly, making rapid progress in Latin and Greek under the humanist watch of his tutors.[2] But he was only nine, old enough to take an interest in affairs of state but too young to direct them himself. Power passed into the hands of his uncle Edward Seymour, Earl of Hertford, Jane Seymour's elder brother. Hertford quickly assumed the dukedom of Somerset and the title of Protector.

In 1547, the Duke of Somerset was in his late forties and had been in royal service for more than three decades, though he had only achieved real prominence after his sister's brief marriage to Henry. He had played a part in both of Henry's final military adventures, serving at Boulogne and in the war with Scotland. In appearance he was respectable, even dour – the imperial ambassador wrote that he tended 'to parsimony in everything'.[3] In spirit, however, Somerset was a fiery Protestant, determined to finish the work that the old king had started, and that included bringing about the godly union of England and Scotland through the marriage of Edward and Mary.

In Somerset's Protestant imperialism Margaret saw opportunity. Privately, she may well have regretted her quarrel with the dead king and her political demotion – years later, one of her servants said she lamented the misfortune of Henry's will and its impact on her claim to the throne.[4] To the world, however, she and her husband were both wholehearted supporters of the new regime. Lennox had secured his place in England by swearing to uphold Henry's Scottish policy, and his only hope of wielding power in Scotland's government was to see his rival, the Earl of Arran, overthrown. Margaret was determined to help him do it, even though it meant conflict with her own Scottish family.

In the heady first months of the new reign matters went well for Somerset and for the Lennox-Stewarts. The English invaded

Scotland in the summer, bent on a double policy of capturing Scottish strongholds and of winning or 'assuring' Scots to their side. On 10 September 1547, English forces under Somerset and John Dudley, Earl of Warwick, met a Scottish army under Arran and Angus at Pinkie Cleugh. Margaret's father, always fearless, distinguished himself: at one point, it looked as though his troops might force the English to a draw, and even when it became clear that they could not, he stayed in his saddle and galloped up and down the field, shouting encouragement at the men.[5] But Somerset triumphed all the same, and the day cost thousands of Scottish lives.

Away in the south-west, Lennox and Thomas Wharton did not manage such a dramatic triumph, but they did not let Somerset down. Working steadily, they seized garrison after garrison and convinced thousands of Scots to give their word – and often their hostages – that they would support the English invaders. Lennox seemed to be proving his worth. Even Angus, victor of Ancrum Moor, was running out of patience with the governor, the Earl of Arran, and holding secret talks with England.[6]

Margaret remained in Yorkshire, managing the Lennox-Stewart estates and missing her husband, who was just as lonely for her as she was for him. At the end of the autumn campaigning season, he returned to England, thanking Somerset for the permission to go back to Margaret: 'For your grace's gentle consideration and license for my repair to . . . my wife I most humbly thank your grace.'[7] That Christmas, they could reflect that they were recovering well from the blow of Henry's will: their Scottish enemies were in a desperate position, the new regime had use for their services, and their son had survived the dangers of infancy.

But the New Year of 1548 brought dramatic reverses. Arran had already opened talks with France; he reached terms in January. The English saw they would soon be facing French as well as Scottish troops.[8] Angus, his flirtation with the English set aside, routed Lennox's partner Wharton at Drumlanrig – aided by the once-assured Maxwells, who turned upon the English mid-battle.[9] Just as quickly as Lennox and Wharton had won the south-west, they lost it again. Lennox's service had been loyal, but in the end, inglorious: his active role in the Rough Wooing was over.[10]

Margaret was furious with her father. On 20 June 1548, Angus wrote to her with word that Dalkeith, where her mother had first met James IV thirty-five years ago, had been destroyed. A host of Douglas cousins suddenly found themselves homeless. He asked that Margaret and Lennox see them 'put in friends' hands and gently treated', noting that one of the affected was the Laird of Glenbarvie – 'a sickly tender man', wrote Angus, with 'nine motherless bairns'.[11]

She could not believe the brazen effort to manipulate her. Angus had not only undone Lennox's works in south-west Scotland but also remarried and had a son who might disinherit Margaret, so his messenger's urgent demand that she and Lennox speak to Somerset on behalf of the discomfited Douglases struck them both as brazen presumption.[12] Lennox replied that Angus and Douglas would have done better to ask somebody else for help: 'We have received no such benefit at neither of their hands.' He wrote to Somerset immediately, asking what he ought to do. As Lennox finished and dated the letter, Margaret told him to add a note before signing it: 'My wife hath desired me to make humble recommendations unto your grace and saith that she will make answer neither to father nor uncle until she knows your grace's pleasure herein.'[13] She was creating a new role for herself, conveying information between her Scottish relatives and the English court.

If Lennox was unable to be of much use in Scotland, neither was anybody else. Arran had reached an agreement with France by which Henry II would send French troops to assist the Scots. In return, six-year-old Queen Mary would become engaged to the four-year-old Dauphin Francis, his eldest son and heir. In return, Arran would receive a French dukedom and his son a French bride. The French king's troops were soon in Scotland, a Scottish parliament confirmed the treaty between the two countries, and on 7 August 1548, Queen Mary left Scotland for France. She would not return for thirteen years.[14]

Margaret had spent four years devoted to the idea of the Anglo-Scottish royal marriage. It took her some time to accept that it would never take place and that Mary would not come back. In March 1549, seven months after the queen set sail, she decided to make her own foray into politics, trying to win Angus back to the English side and reproaching him for his unfaithfulness to Henry VIII: 'If ye call to remembrance your being here in England, albeit your deeds showeth the forgetfulness thereof, insomuch as ye are so contrary to the king's majesty's affairs that now is, his father being so good and so liberal a prince to you, which ought never to be forgotten.' The English case was a weak one, but she put it as strongly as she could. Angus was a reformer, and she used the language of godliness in her efforts to persuade him:

> I hear say that ye have professed never to agree with England forasmuch as the most part of your friends are slain, but whom can you blame for that but only your self wills, for if ye would agree to this godly marriage, there needed no Christian blood to be shed. For God's sake, remember yourself now in your old age and seek to have an honourable peace, which cannot be without this marriage. And what a memorial should that be to you forever if ye could be an instrument for that!

But there was more at stake than her loyalty to the dead king Henry.

Margaret knew that if she and her father remained on opposite sides, she might never succeed him as head of the house of Douglas. Angus's brother, George Douglas, was ambitious, clever, and had a dedicated following in Scotland, while Margaret was confined to England. She did her best to divide the two brothers. Many Scots, she warned her father, had told her that George aimed at Angus's title: '[He] I know would be glad to see you in your grave . . . My uncle George hath said . . . that though you had sons he would be heir and make them all bastards.' But Margaret had no intention of letting the earldom of Angus pass to George Douglas's line without a struggle: 'My Lord, if God send you no more sons and I live after you, he shall have [the] least part thereof or else many a man shall smart for it.'

Margaret often struggled to keep her temper from overriding her strategic instincts. She was merciless in her upbraiding of her father: 'If I should write so long a letter as I could find matter with the wrong of your part and the right of mine it were too tedious for you to read.'[15] But she was coming into her own as a political actor. She was certain of her rights and of her loyalties, her anger was colder and better aimed than when she had turned it on Lennox's old secretary, Thomas Bishop, and she was realising how she could play one rival off against another for her own ends.

With Lennox back in England, the two of them focused their attentions on their cherished son Henry, Lord Darnley. She would later say that her eldest boy had his 'education and bringing up . . . only at home with his father and me', benefiting from 'that help of the father's company' as well as her own.[16] There is a hint from Thomas Bishop that she and her husband were already entertaining tremendous ambitions for their son.

Bishop had not prospered in the wake of the quarrel and the Lennox-Stewarts, with remarkable forbearance, allowed him to remain in their service.[17] According to Bishop, he 'had the conference of marriages both with the Dowager [Mary of Guise] and a contract written with my hand, remaining privily with himself, by me aired for the consent of the marriage of this Scottish queen' – that is, the marriage of Mary, Queen of Scots. Bishop had been Lennox's 'commissioner for his own marriage . . . and since . . . agreed with the duke of Somerset for the marriage of my lord Darnley his son'.[18] The Lennox-Stewarts were suggesting, in short, that their son should be King of Scots, and that his children would be the heirs to the English crown if Edward died without issue. If Bishop really did make such a proposal to Somerset on Darnley's behalf, there is no record of it, and even if Somerset had agreed to such a plan, it would have been impossible to achieve after Mary's departure into France. It does, however, raise the possibility that Lennox and Margaret already saw their son as a potential king.

But if her ambitions were wide-ranging, Margaret's political orbit was narrowing. Her new friends were the other noble families of northern England.[19] Meanwhile, her ties with her old circle at court weakened. Katherine Parr had remarried shortly after Henry's death, choosing Somerset's younger brother, Sir Thomas Seymour, and dying in childbirth in September 1548. Margaret's cousin Mary Tudor had left London for East Anglia. Mary was a Catholic, and it was only a matter of time before she came into conflict with Somerset's regime over religion.

Reformers had walked a difficult line in the last years of Henry's reign. The dead king had cast off papal authority and made himself head of the Church, but also held fast to doctrines that were anathema to Protestants. For Henry, communion bread and wine became the body and blood of Christ during the Mass; salvation came not only through the grace of God, but also through the works of men; the souls of the dead could be consigned to Purgatory where the prayers of the living might help them on their way to Heaven. He wavered on the English-language Bible, allowing it briefly but retreating in 1543, declaring that only the elite could be trusted to read the Bible in their own tongue. It was hardly the vision of English Bible-reading conjured up by the translator William Tyndale when he told a learned man 'I will cause a boy that driveth the plough shall know more of the scripture than thou dost.'[20]

There had been space for the 'new learning', even in the conservative decade of the 1540s. Katherine Parr, for one, had managed to maintain it at the very centre of the court. But the demands of tradition had imposed limits. Reformers could argue that they were returning to the roots of Christianity, stripping away centuries of human errors that had no basis in scripture, but it was easy to see how such radical acts could look less like a return to lost essentials than the invention of a wholly new religion. Protestants faced the mocking question 'Where was your Church before Luther?', and it was not for nothing that Henry always thought of himself as a Catholic.

With Henry's death, however, Somerset set to the work of serious reform. The printers and booksellers flooded London with Protestant works, from European theology to the English Bible.[21] Priests read from a book of homilies meant to ensure that ordinary Christians in every parish of the country would hear sound learning, whether their local priest could write an orthodox sermon or not. Scouring iconoclasm cleared parish churches of their holy paintings and statues: some images still stood, the gouges on the painted faces testament to the true faith's triumph over idolatry, but far more vanished altogether.

Many embraced the new religion, and still more were prepared to go along with it. Others resisted, sometimes within their homes, sometimes openly. In 1549 thousands of people in western England joined together in the religious revolt known as the Prayer Book Rebellion, while in East Anglia, even committed Protestants rose, unhappy with the state of Somerset's government.[22] Struggling to quell the disorder in the country, the Protector soon faced an uprising within the Privy Council itself. He was forced to resign, and government came into the hands of John Dudley, Earl of Warwick, the other victor of Pinkie Cleugh. Warwick was a long-standing associate of Somerset, Katherine Parr and Thomas Cranmer. He had been a convinced Protestant and an ally of Thomas Cromwell as early as the 1530s. He had ten children, decades of court experience, and no Scottish ambitions to distract him from the government of England – especially from its religious reform.

Throughout Somerset's Protectorate, Margaret had done everything she was expected to do. Politically, she proved unshakeably loyal to her husband and to England while also establishing a small role for herself in cross-border politics, preserving ties with the Douglases in the hope of either gathering intelligence or winning them back to their old English side. Personally, she was the model landed noblewoman, mother to a precocious young son, prominent link in the network of the northern nobility, an orthodox religious example to her tenants. But, as she was about to realise, her loyalty had its limits.[23]

9

Idols and Images

One day, early in Edward's reign, Margaret caught her servant John Hume saying that Christ was not present in the consecrated bread and wine of Holy Communion. Worse, he refused to hear the Mass, saying that 'he should be damned' if he did. As the mistress of her estates, Margaret held herself bound to keep Settrington and Temple Newsam in decent spiritual order, and the souls of her servants and tenants mattered like those of her own husband and children. Hume had gone beyond Henricianism, even beyond Lutheranism: his was radical Protestant theology, and to Margaret it was heresy. Her duty was plain. She had to stop the infection from spreading and she had to correct the man's errors if she could. Together, she and Lennox sent the unrepentant Hume to the Archbishop of Canterbury, hoping he could be brought back to orthodoxy.[1]

But by 1550 it was Margaret's position, and not that of her Protestant servant, that seemed out of step. Thomas Cranmer, the very archbishop to whom she had turned for help, had been moving towards a new theology of the Eucharist for some time and now he articulated it: transubstantiation was 'abominable heresy'.[2] More change was soon to come and prove impossible to countenance. Over the course of her life in England, Margaret had adapted to constant but incremental alterations in religion. At some point in the latter half of Edward's reign, she found that she could no longer make such compromises.

Margaret was twenty-two years older than Edward VI. She had grown up in a world of universal Catholicism; he had not. Edward embraced the Protestantism of his tutors: the Catholic-inflected traditions tolerated and even cherished by many of his older subjects had no emotional hold over him.[3] From the start of his reign, Edward had been identified with Josiah, the Old Testament king who had come to the throne as an eight-year-old boy and grown into a great reformer and iconoclast: 'the workers with familiar spirits, and the wizards, and the images, and the idols, and all the abominations that were spied in the land of Judah and in Jerusalem, did Josiah put away . . .'[4] Under the Earl of Northumberland and an increasingly involved Edward, reforms came swiftly and without equivocation. In parish churches throughout the country old images and service books were defaced and destroyed; priestly vestments abolished; altars stripped, torn down and replaced with simple communion tables.

Alongside this destruction came the release of enormous creativity. The year 1552 saw a new Book of Common Prayer, the banning of feast days of most saints and doing away with the old understanding of the Mass. By the 1549 communion rite, priests had distributed the Host with the words 'The body of our Lord Jesus Christ, which was given for thee, preserve thy body and soul unto everlasting life.' After 1552, plainly dressed men in bare-walled churches gave their parishioners new spiritual assurance: 'Take and eat this, in remembrance that Christ died for thee, and feed on him in thy heart by faith, with thanksgiving.'[5]

Margaret had adhered to Henry VIII's capricious religious policy, which sometimes looked like a true reform movement and sometimes like a vandalised Catholicism. By marrying Lennox, she had agreed to Henry's Protestant – or at the very least anti-papal – ambitions for Scotland. Some of her closest associates were reformers, including both Mary Fitzroy, her fellow Devonshire Manuscript scribe, and Katherine Parr. Her husband was nominally a Protestant and so were her Scottish relatives. Even her cousin Mary Tudor, defiant in the 1530s, had made her peace with Henry.

The climate of Henry's last years had allowed Margaret to associate with reformers while holding on to doctrines that were fundamentally not Protestant. She and Lennox gave money to chantries, paying clerics to say Masses for the souls of the dead in Purgatory. In this they were in line with Henry, who endowed chantries to pray for his own soul. To most Protestants, however, this was heretical superstition. Purgatory was not mentioned in the Bible and man was justified by faith and saved by the grace of God alone, not by the endlessly repeated prayers of fellow Christians.

For Margaret, faith informed everything from the books she read to the prayers she memorised to how she understood her relationships with her king, family and tenants. It shaped time itself: each day, there were hours set aside for prayer; each week, there were the rituals of Friday fasting and the keeping of the Sabbath; each year, the body of Christendom moved through the great emotional cycle of Christian time – the yearning of Advent and joy of Christmas; the penitence of Lent; the meditation and mourning of Holy Week; the indomitable, triumphant hope of Easter. Even so, most people, even deeply spiritual people, were willing to adapt to new religious practices. Despite the quickening pace of reform under Somerset, Margaret stayed within the official Church during his Protectorate, calling the proposed union of her niece Mary and cousin Edward a 'godly marriage'.[6] Although Margaret undoubtedly found Edward's alterations jarring – they changed the habits of a lifetime – there is no evidence that she opposed them until the latter half of his reign.

In the absence of written sources, it is impossible to say whether or not there was one change that drove Margaret out of the state Church, though for many Catholics it was the Mass, a rite for which she had real respect and devotion. We can, however, say roughly when the change happened: when she wrote to Angus in 1549, she was still advocating Somerset's religious policy, but by November 1553, others were describing her as a Catholic.[7] Her moment of conversion seems to have taken place during the second half of Edward's short reign.[8]

She had fewer and fewer reasons to keep adapting. The Lennox-Stewarts were worth much less to Northumberland than they had been to Henry VIII or to Somerset: the new Protector did not share their passion for the Anglo-Scottish project. Northumberland made his peace with France in the Treaty of Boulogne in March 1550, bringing the Rough Wooing to a halt, and with Scotland in June 1551, withdrawing English troops. Mary, Queen of Scots, was gone to France and Arran, now known by his promised French title as the Duke of Châtelherault, was her Regent. It was not an auspicious moment for Lennox or his family: his great dynastic rival held power in Scotland, where he had been declared a traitor, and the government of England had no obvious use for him.

At the same time, Margaret had new reasons to care profoundly about doctrine. Over the course of her life, she gave birth to eight children – four boys and four girls. Given that she and Lennox married when they were nearing thirty, they had a remarkably fertile marriage.[9] Two of the boys were born before 1547 and the other two after 1553; she probably had her four daughters during Edward's reign.[10] Six of her eight children died at birth or shortly afterwards, and it seems likely that Margaret had her children baptised and laid to rest by Catholic rites, turning to familiar rituals at those moments of celebration and grieving. Moreover, Darnley was still a young child but he was old enough to begin his education, and perhaps Margaret found it impossible to instruct her son in this new faith. She brought him up as she had been raised – a Catholic.[11]

Margaret transformed her house into a place where she and her family could practise the old religion. She brought the sensuous world of Catholicism into Settrington and Temple Newsam: beads for repeating the prayers and meditating on the mysteries of the Rosary, and statues and icons of Christ, the Virgin and the saints to focus the mind during worship. Priests came – quietly – to hear confessions, grant absolution, and perform the act that lay at the heart of the Mass: the transformation of the eucharistic bread and wine into the body and blood of Christ.

One occasion on which Margaret did leave Yorkshire for London was the visit of Mary of Guise in the autumn of 1551. Guise's arrival created a delicate diplomatic situation for Margaret and for Lennox.[12] He had once been a suitor both to Guise herself and to her daughter, and she had been partly responsible for his forfeiture. But Margaret, though she had never met Guise, was her sister-in-law, so when a tempest forced Guise's ship to land at Portsmouth on 22 October, Margaret headed south. Although Lennox did not go with her, the rest of the nobility turned out in force.[13]

Margaret arrived at court and was reunited with friends and relatives she had not seen in years: her cousin Frances Brandon and her husband the Duke of Suffolk; their eldest daughter, the Lady Jane Grey; her old friend Mary Fitzroy, Duchess of Richmond, a companion from the Devonshire Manuscript days and the woman with whom she had retreated to Kenninghall in the wake of Katherine Howard's arrest. On 4 November, Margaret and more than a hundred nobles, ladies and gentlewomen rode sedately through the streets of London to greet the dowager Queen of Scots and bring her to Westminster.

Margaret met Guise at the Bishop of London's palace, near St Paul's Cathedral. Her sister-in-law had been holding court for two days and the palace was full of gifts from local worthies: meat, quail, fish, wine, spices.[14] They would have had little chance to speak in the crowd of retainers before the now-enormous procession left the palace and headed for the gates of Westminster. The king and his council were waiting and servants were hard at work in every room, preparing for the evening's banquet – when Margaret would be able to speak at greater length with the dowager queen.

The evening feast recalled the luxury and ostentatious consumption of Margaret's first arrival at court. The boy king and the dowager queen sat under one cloth of estate, with two separate sets of servants to attend them and table settings in both gold and silver. But while most of the ladies took their meal in a separate room, it was Frances and Margaret who sat at the dowager's left hand.

Two days later, they were together again at the Bishop of London's palace, this time to convey Guise out of London and back towards Scotland. It was another enormous procession: the Protector, Northumberland, alone brought a hundred men, forty of them dressed in distinctive black velvet with black-and-white sleeves. They rode through Cheapside and Cornhill to Shoreditch, where they said their farewells.[15]

What did Margaret make of it all? She had always loved court life – it brought out the wit and charm in her character, and it must have been a pleasure to see old friends. Yet there were real disappointments as well. Although we do not know what she and Mary Fitzroy, Duchess of Richmond, said to each other, they never regained their old close companionship: they found themselves on opposite sides of the Reformation and the duchess died not long after their meeting. On a more concrete level, if Margaret was entertaining hopes that a good impression on

Guise would get the dowager to welcome the Lennox-Stewarts back into Scotland, she was to be disappointed. Worse, she had incurred the suspicion of the zealous men surrounding Edward. That suspicion would prevent her from ever reconciling with her father.

In the spring of 1550, Lennox had sent his servant William Patterson into Scotland with a message to Angus: he hoped that Angus was in good health and that he would prove friendlier than he had been in the recent past. His children by his second wife had died and when Patterson arrived at Douglas Castle Angus was eager for news of Margaret, Lennox and Darnley. Together, they walked up and down the green, and the earl became confidential: 'Well, seeing [Lennox] hath sent nothing else to me, I will break a little of my mind to thee.'

He was in a reflective mood, giving Patterson a long message to carry back to Yorkshire. 'Thou shall declare my daughter this thing in the world I love best, and my lord her husband, and that young boy their [son], for my children are dead that thou saw, and if they be at heaven, well then I am in comfort, and yet I am als [as] strange to their doings and proceedings, or when they intend to pass over the world, as any enemy they have, which breaks my heart.' Darnley had a good claim to be his heir as well as Lennox's, and Angus wanted to be part of his grandson's upbringing: 'I shall wear these old bones of mine but I shall make him a man yet. The world is very strange: I have seen many things. It hath been said in old times that an earl of Lennox and Angus could have ruled something upon this side Forth . . .' He said that he would be glad to speak with Lennox and Margaret, so that he could see Margaret 'ere I die' and give Lennox advice 'for the weal of both the realms . . . There was bands betwixt us afore this, but now there is greater bands of flesh and blood.' As for any fears that he was ruled by his younger brother George, Lennox should put those away: the Douglases should not 'go any way or do anything but as I will'.[16]

If Angus's message had any effect on Margaret, it went unrecorded. She and Lennox were turning away from Scottish politics: the next year, a Scottish man was accused of trying to assassinate the young Mary, Queen of Scots, by means of poisoned pears. He tried to implicate both Lennox and his brother John, Lord d'Aubigny, causing Lennox to swear that not only was he innocent, but he did not want a Scotsman so much as to enter his house.[17]

But by 1552, Margaret found herself longing for her father's advice and comfort. Like Angus, she had just lost children, and finding herself pregnant again in her late thirties, she wanted his blessing. Reconciliation might also help her claim to succeed him and become Countess of Angus in her own right. She despatched a servant to court asking for permission to go back to Tantallon for the first time in decades, explaining that she wanted to visit Angus and get 'the surer knowledge of his favour'. Lennox, she promised, would remain in England.[18]

The Earl of Northumberland took up the matter with William Cecil, an indefatigable young man of firm Protestant convictions who had survived Somerset's downfall and become one of his successor's most valued confidants.[19] The two of them came to the same conclusion: despite Margaret's promise that Lennox would remain in England, they thought it almost certain that he would try to return to Scotland with her.[20] The next day, the Privy Council met and sent a letter to Margaret.[21] It has not survived, but she did not get permission to go into Scotland. Bitterly disappointed, Margaret stayed in Yorkshire and gave birth before the end of the year, losing yet another child to either stillbirth or infant death.

Seven months later, Margaret petitioned again, and Northumberland reconsidered. He told Cecil that he now understood that Lennox 'dare not come within the realm of Scotland for an old grudge . . . and feud between the governor's blood and him', as he claimed to be Mary's heir presumptive and had said that the governor came 'of the base line'. Northumberland reasoned that Lennox would not risk going over the border. Margaret, for her part, was unlikely to cause trouble in Scotland while her husband and child remained in England: 'I cannot think of much danger in her going to her father as I did when you and I did commune of it.' He was even optimistic that Angus might 'open some matter to her worthy the hearing'. Confident that the Lennox-Stewarts had no political levers to pull, Northumberland could afford to find the business odd: 'It amuses me to think what . . . moveth her father to seek to have her to come so far only to speak with him but some mystery there must needs be in it.'[22] The refusal and suspicion revealed just how much her ties to court had withered.

She might well have stayed in Yorkshire for years, her connections to kin and old friends severed and her ambitions for Darnley kept small and unthreatening, had Edward not suddenly become sick. He declined over the early months of 1553, and his physicians and courtiers had to confront the horrifying fact that their active young king was going to die before he attained his majority. But like his father, Edward was determined to direct the future of his kingdom from his deathbed: he wanted a male, Protestant heir, even if that meant overturning Henry's will and an Act of Parliament. He drew up what he termed his 'devise for the succession', a document that declared the crown would go to the male heirs of Frances Brandon or, failing that, to the male heirs of Jane Grey, Frances's eldest daughter. This meant leaping over not only Margaret Tudor's line but also those who had a place in Henry's order of succession: his daughters Mary and Elizabeth, Frances Brandon and Jane Grey herself. As Edward's health worsened, he had to recognise that neither Frances nor Jane was about to have a son. In a new draft, he declared that the crown would go to Jane and her male heirs.

Edward was not bound by old ideas of dynastic right: he would supplant Mary and Elizabeth and have Jane Grey inherit instead of her still-living mother. Why, then, did he ignore Darnley, a living male Tudor with a claim to the throne that was arguably better than that of Jane – he was descended from Henry VII's eldest daughter, not his youngest? There is a simple twofold answer: Jane Grey was married to Northumberland's son Guilford Dudley, so the duke naturally had an interest in seeing Jane succeed. At the same time, Darnley's exclusion reinforces the surmise that for the evangelical Edward, the Lennox-Stewarts were not to be trusted with the godly reformation.

On 6 July 1553, Edward died. The Protestant polity rushed to proclaim Jane queen, but they had not counted on Mary Tudor: the dying king had misjudged his sister and his people. Mary was a demure and pious person but she was convinced of her own claim to the throne. As a teenager, her certainty had given her the courage to defy Henry VIII, even when he broke up her household and kept her separated from her mother. She was the heir by right, by parliamentary statute, and by Henry's will, and now she demanded the crown. When Jane's council refused to acknowledge her, alleging that she would undo the Reformation and bring foreign soldiers into England, Mary raised a force of English supporters. Catholics rallied to her, and so did many who believed she was queen and usurpers had no right to the throne. By 19 July, Edward's plan had failed completely. The citizens of London acclaimed Mary as queen and Jane Grey was imprisoned in the Tower. Not even a king, it seemed, had the right to tamper so obviously with the succession.[23]

Neither Margaret nor anybody else had had any way of guessing that Edward would only reign for six years. She had yoked herself to the Catholic cause knowing that England might stay an officially Protestant realm for decades, even if it meant placing herself and her son further than ever from the seat of power. But with her cousin and oldest friend suddenly queen, her faith was vindicated, and Margaret resolved to quit Yorkshire for London.

10

Best Suited to Succeed

On the evening of Tuesday, 17 October 1553, the new queen gave a banquet in honour of the departing Spanish ambassadors. Mary had planned a fairly informal occasion. At her right hand sat the four envoys, guests of honour at this small gathering. Not everybody was happy to be there, and while 'the music of hautboys, cornets, flutes, harps, and dulcimers ceased not to play', there was tension. Edward Courtenay, Earl of Devon, a Catholic descendant of the house of York, was not getting along with the Spanish ambassadors and refused to acknowledge them. Mary's half-sister Elizabeth, lurking in a window, had quarrelled with Courtenay and was making ready, she told imperial ambassador Simon Renard, to leave her sister's court. But for Margaret, waiting at the window with her aggrieved young cousin, it was a triumphant return.[1]

Margaret had been in Yorkshire while Mary was fighting for her crown, missing both the drama of Jane's nine days and the victory of her cousin's coronation. As soon as she was able, she hurried towards London and found that Mary forgave her the absence. On her journey south Margaret paused near Oxford, and as she rested, messengers arrived with a gift from the queen: '[F]or good look's sake, a fair diamond'. Soon afterwards, Mary presented her with ten fine gowns, ten embroidered kirtles, and clothes and gems worth £500.[2] It was sudden largesse on a scale even Margaret, whom Henry VIII had dressed like a king's daughter, had not known before. But what was she to make of it? Was Mary's lavish liberality wholly personal, a debt owed to an old friend and close relation, or did it augur a new political role for Margaret's children and for Margaret herself?

Before the banquet, Renard had already presented Mary with a Spanish marriage proposal. For Mary, there was no question of remaining single: she wanted a husband's support and she knew it was her duty to have children. In her youth she had been bruited as a prospective bride for most of the leading princes of Europe, including her mother's nephew, the emperor Charles V. Now, the suitor on offer was Charles's son Philip, more than ten years Mary's junior. By accepting him, she could revive England's old alliance with Spain, rebuild broken ties with Catholic Europe, and, she prayed, produce an heir.

The men around her saw the matter differently. On 16 November a parliamentary delegation beseeched her not to marry Philip, lest he assume control of her government. Mary listened to their arguments, at first with impatience and then with anger. It was not the business of parliament to tell her whom she could or could not wed and, as she pointed out, they would never have tried such methods of persuasion on a male monarch: 'Histories and chronicles would show that such words had never been spoken.'[3]

But in spite of her determination to marry Philip and have children of her own, she knew that she needed another plan in reserve. Nine days after her contest with the parliamentarians, she met with her confidants William Paget and Simon Renard to discuss the matter of her heir. All of the obvious candidates were women: the queen's half-sister Elizabeth, next in line according to the Third Act of Succession and to Henry's will; Mary, Queen of Scots, demoted by the will but descended from Henry's eldest sister; and Jane Grey's mother Frances, Duchess of Suffolk, next in line to Elizabeth under the terms of the will and, unlike the Queen of Scots, English.

The Spanish Renard thought that Mary would never allow her half-sister to succeed, given she was a Protestant, a bastard and Anne Boleyn's daughter: 'as her mother had caused great trouble in the kingdom, the Queen feared that Elizabeth might do the same'. There seemed to him no grounds for favouring Frances – Mary Stewart had the strongest right. For his part, the English Paget thought that no parliament would repeal Henry's last Act of Succession and that the wisest course would be to marry Elizabeth off to the Catholic Courtenay. But Mary, though she listened patiently to both men, told them she had her own candidate in mind: 'if God were to call her without giving her heirs of her body, the Lady Margaret Douglas . . . would be the person best suited to succeed'.[4]

Renard's is the only account of this conversation, but there seems no reason to doubt him. He was one of Mary's closest advisors, and he was clear that he preferred the Scottish queen's claim to Margaret's.[5] Neither is there any call to think Mary unduly sentimental. It was true that she and Margaret had nearly twenty-five years of history and had shared defining experiences: they had survived the collapse of their parents' respective marriages, been called bastards, and had kings of England do their utmost to disinherit them. More important, however, were the questions of religion and right. Elizabeth and Mary Stewart had both better claims and greater liabilities. Elizabeth was a bastard and Mary was not English – birth abroad had never kept a rightful monarch off England's throne, but Mary was also Queen of Scots and engaged to the French Dauphin. If Elizabeth and Mary were discounted, either Margaret or Frances was next in line. And Margaret had a son – the Tudor line would endure for at least another generation.

Margaret could not have known what went on in the meeting with Renard and Paget, but she knew how open-handed Mary was towards her, and so did the rest of the court. The Lennox-Stewarts had new sources of income: Mary gave Margaret licence to buy 1,200 sacks of wool and to sell them anywhere in England or Europe, and – in what must have struck Margaret as an ironic gesture – the queen also granted her the revenues of the old Syon lands.[6] Lennox had a sudden rise: the queen gave him the late King Edward's best horse and the office of Master of Hawks, as well as a brooch with England's patron, St George, crafted in diamonds – in Mary's eyes, the Scottish Lennox was an Englishman. For the first time since Henry's reign, Margaret had a permanent place at court, with private access to Mary herself. She lived in a set of richly decorated rooms, with warrants from the Tower for ten beds and twenty-one tapestries, and she and her servants took their food from the queen's own kitchens. Mary's Christmas gift to Margaret was a golden girdle studded with diamonds and rubies and worth some £500: the days of exchanging single gowns or jewels were gone.

Part of Margaret still longed to go to Scotland and talk to her father, but Mary wanted her nearby. It was impossible to leave. Margaret took precedence over Elizabeth in court ceremonials: the French ambassador reported that where the queen had once taken her sister by the hand and showed her 'honour and favour' on grand occasions, she now consigned her to walk behind Margaret and Frances Brandon.[7] Mary made the court's new hierarchy physical with a pointed room allocation: Elizabeth had rooms directly beneath Margaret's own, and had to listen to continual 'crashing [and] casting down of logs, pots, and vessels unreproved'. It was, said Lennox's secretary Thomas Bishop, much to Elizabeth's 'dispirit'.[8]

Until now, Margaret had given no sign that she did not get along with Elizabeth, and unlike Mary, she had cherished memories of time spent in Anne Boleyn's household. But Margaret and Elizabeth now could see that they were rivals in the succession and they no longer shared a common religion: Elizabeth was a reformer, Margaret a Catholic. Margaret's thoughts in 1553 went unrecorded, but five years later she declared in secret that she thought her claim to the throne was stronger than Elizabeth's.[9] Was she already allowing herself to hope that she, and not her cousin, would be England's next queen?

Whatever her hopes for herself, Margaret turned her newfound prominence to her son's benefit. Coming to court meant leaving Darnley in Yorkshire, but he was now eight years of age and old enough for Margaret to show him off to both sides of the family. For this, she involved his tutor, John Elder. He was the same man who had encouraged Henry VIII to drive the monks – 'Beelzebub's fleshmongers' – out of Scotland back in the 1540s.[10] He had unexpectedly parted ways with the reforming movement, probably at some point in Edward's reign.[11] On New Year's Day 1555 he sent Margaret's brother-in-law Robert, Bishop of Caithness, some of Darnley's verse exercises, along with an account of his progress. The boy spoke good Latin and French, and was 'endowed with a good wit, gentleness, beauty and favour'. Elder was confident that Darnley would 'prove a witty, virtuous, and an active well-learned gentleman', a worthy son to his 'noble parents . . . my singular good patrons'.[12]

Even more critical was cultivating Darnley's relationship with Queen Mary. In March 1554, Darnley sent her 'a little plot of my simple penning, which I termed *Utopia Nova*' – a clever invocation of the Catholic martyr Thomas More, author of *Utopia*, and by extension of the Catholicism Mary shared with the Lennox-Stewarts. The queen, in return, gave Darnley 'a rich chain of gold'. Thanking her for the gift, the boy wrote that he set his mind 'to virtuous learning and study', spurred not only by the promise of rewards but by the hope, 'even now, my tender age notwithstanding, to be serving Your Grace, wishing every hair in my head for to be a worthy soldier'.[13] Darnley became rather a pet for the queen: she sent him not only several Venetian lutes, including one worth a hundred crowns, but 'the bravest of King Edward's apparel' as well.[14]

But although Margaret was high in favour in London and Darnley was scampering about Temple Newsam in the late king's clothes, it would have taken at least a parliamentary statute to transform Margaret into Mary's heir. Mary would rather have seen her cousin succeed her than her sister, but what she wanted far more was a child of her own. She and her council concluded a marriage treaty with Spain, crafted to allay English fears about Spanish influence on government. England would not join in Spanish conflicts, and if Mary died childless, Philip would go back to Spain.

The treaty did not reassure Mary's subjects, and rebellion broke out in January. Some of the disorder was easily put down – Jane Grey's father, the Duke of Suffolk, raised only a handful of men and was promptly imprisoned. In Kent, however, Sir Thomas Wyatt – namesake son of Margaret's friend the poet – conjured up a real force of men who gave the queen an ultimatum: renounce the Spanish alliance or be overthrown in favour of Elizabeth. Once again, Mary defeated her rebels, and this time felt compelled to deal harshly with them. Suffolk and Wyatt were put to death, and so were Lady Jane Grey and her husband. Elizabeth was imprisoned in the Tower.

But just as her fellow contenders for the English crown seemed weaker than ever, Margaret had to turn her attention back to Scotland. The dowager Queen Mary of Guise, with French assistance, was engineering a quiet coup against Lennox's old enemy the Duke of Châtelherault, formerly the Earl of Arran. On 3 April, Spanish ambassador Renard wrote another letter about the Lennox-Stewarts to Charles V, this time from Brussels.

According to Paget, the dowager had written to Lennox 'that if he wishes to return to Scotland she will have his property restored to him and show him treatment befitting his rank', a tantalising offer for one with 'some chance of succeeding to the Scottish crown'. The letter was discussed in London and Mary Tudor's advisors came up with a plan. Lennox would head to the borders and further unsettle the case: he would tell the Scots that he wanted to come home, enter Scotland, and then ally with the Hamiltons against the dowager, 'with a view not only to driving her from the country, but to making himself King if possible and throwing Scottish affairs into confusion'. The English would try to fund the expedition, but Spanish support would be invaluable, as Mary did not want to go to parliament until after she had been married. Paget asked Renard to tell Charles that 'no money that was ever raised would have been so well spent' on Spain's behalf as well as England's.[15]

The scheme was nonsense, bordering on absurdity – not least because it hinged on Lennox working with his Hamilton rivals – but if it had come to anything, Margaret would have been queen consort of Scotland, in line to the English throne, and Darnley would have had a strong claim to both crowns in his own right. It was a dizzying moment, but it was very brief. Within ten days, the Duke of Châtelherault had given up the regency and the dowager had assumed it. Back in England, Mary was preparing to wed Philip. Margaret had entertained new ambitions, for her son and for herself, but it would soon become clear to her that being a monarch's favourite was not the same thing as being a monarch's heir.

11

Countess of Angus

Philip arrived in England on 20 July 1554 and met Mary at Winchester three days later. Ignoring the driving rain, he presented himself at her lodgings dressed in a gold-embroidered coat and with a white feather in his hat. The two were married in Winchester Cathedral on 25 July, feast of St James the Apostle, patron saint of Spain. Charles V had given his son Philip the kingdoms of Naples and Jerusalem so that Mary, a queen in her own right, could wed a king rather than a prince. For all the splendour of the occasion – the tapestry-decked cathedral, parades of English and Spanish nobles, the massed voices of the queen's choir and the cathedral's – there were moments of conscious simplicity: at her request, Mary's wedding ring was a plain golden band with no stone, 'because maidens were so married in old times'.[1] The next month they were in London, welcomed with a deafening peal of cannon-fire from the guns of the White Tower. They took up residence in Whitehall, with Mary living in the apartments on the King's Side and Philip on the Queen's.[2]

Margaret missed the wedding, probably because she was once again pregnant. She did, however, cultivate ties with the new king and his Spanish retinue.[3] When Margaret gave birth to a son, she had him christened Philip, and the queen celebrated the baptism with gifts of plate and jewels.[4] Margaret also made friends with Jane Dormer, one of Mary's closest attendants, who became the Countess de Feria through her marriage to

Gomez Suárez de Figueroa.[5] Philip would later call the Lennox-Stewarts 'good Catholics and our affectionate servitors'.[6] But the queen's chief concerns were now a religious settlement and having a child of her own – thoughts of altering the succession, or even trying to alter it, were far from her mind. Margaret had to realise that her exalted expectations for her family were only a chimera.

Mary's marriage slowly proved a humiliating failure. By autumn, the entire court believed that the queen was pregnant: she was regularly being sick and her clothes no longer fitted.[7] In November she was convinced that she had felt the child quicken and move.[8] But spring came and went and there was still no heir: rumours began circulating that she was not pregnant at all. Philip left England after only a year of marriage, to the queen's grief and Margaret's chagrin. If Mary died without issue, Spain was already making plans to preserve the Anglo-Spanish alliance by marrying Elizabeth to a Spanish ally, and the Lennox-Stewarts did not come into the picture.[9]

Amid the frustration, there was joy. Margaret and Mary were both forty, nearing the end of their childbearing years. Margaret's own son Philip died while still an infant. But while Mary was enduring her phantom pregnancy, Margaret really was pregnant, albeit for the final time.[10] In 1555 she gave birth to a son and named him Charles, perhaps in honour of Philip's father. After losing six children, she would have found it hard to imagine that the boy would live, but Charles survived – first days, then months, then infancy entirely, and she could let herself hope that he really would grow up. From the start, Margaret had been fiercely ambitious for Darnley, who was her heir as well as Lennox's. Charles got away with rather more and she never aimed so high for him, possibly too glad of his survival to spend time imagining him a king.[11]

Margaret could have her sons Philip and Charles christened openly by the rites of the Catholic Church, something she could not have done during Edward's reign: Mary's Counter-Reformation was under way. Reginald Pole, papal legate, arrived at Dover on 20 November 1554. English and a Plantagenet, Pole was the son of Mary's old governess, and the man her mother, Katherine of Aragon, had once wanted Mary to wed, but Pole had foregone marriage for a brilliant Vatican career. A cardinal of nearly twenty years' experience and a theologian who combined reforming zeal with profound orthodoxy, Pole was an uncompromising defender of Church unity and papal authority. On 28 November he addressed parliament, thanked them for allowing him back to his own country, and absolved them of the sin of schism: England was returned to Rome.

Between them, Mary and Pole set out not only to restore the Catholic Church but to remake it. Parish churches either brought old communion vessels out of hiding or rushed to acquire new ones; priests spoke the words of the Latin Mass once more. England's printers produced volume upon volume of Catholic books liturgical, devotional and polemical. Sermons delivered in person and in print celebrated England's return to the Catholic fold.

It was not enough that Catholicism should be restored; Protestantism had to be routed, and the hunt for obstinate reformers began. The ostensible goal of persecuting heretics was not to put them to death but rather to reclaim them for the true faith and stop the spread of their pernicious ideas. Almost without exception, accused heretics were given opportunities to save themselves. Most took that chance: they could serve their cause without dying for it.[12]

But there were nearly 300 Protestants who refused to recant or, in the case of Archbishop Cranmer, found that even recantation would not save them. These 300 were excommunicated and burned alive. The immediate impact of these deaths is debatable: public displays of sympathy and unrest were rare, and had Mary lived longer, she might have completed her reformation. Yet the effects of the burning campaign proved catastrophic for English Catholicism. Friends recorded the victims' steadfast courage, in their written accounts and in their own memories. When the time came, they would have the stories of 300 Protestant martyrs to tell, and Mary Tudor would be branded 'Bloody Mary'.[13]

Margaret had remained devoted to the Mass and to the practices of traditional religion – to rosaries and devotional statues and long-remembered prayers. As her old servant John Hume could testify, she believed religious dissent required corrective punishment – the idea of 'charitable hatred'.[14] Speaking of Protestants in the abstract, she could be bigoted, labelling them heretics.[15] The Protestant controversialist John Jewel would later say that she was 'a woman hostile beyond measure to religion, beyond even the Marian madness'.[16] In her role as mistress of the Lennox-Stewart estates, she had to correspond and work with the men charged with refurbishing the parish churches for Catholic worship.[17] But what Margaret thought, as she watched her old friend and cousin become an ardent persecutor of England's Protestants, she did not record.

Mary's marriage had not given her an heir, and it was soon to provide her with yet more political trouble. Philip's father, Charles V, had inherited his titles as a teenager and had been ruling for forty years. In 1556 he abdicated the Spanish crown in favour of his son and lived out his final two years in a monastery. As the drafters of the Anglo-Spanish marriage treaty had feared, Philip drew England into Spain's foreign-policy sphere, asking for English help when he went to war with France in 1557. Aid was not automatic: Mary's Privy Council opposed the idea, but the queen was determined to share her husband's cause, and in June, England entered the war on the Spanish side.

Margaret had good reason to rue Mary's decision. She was being drawn into Scottish affairs again, and Scotland was bound to France. Her father, Angus, had been ill since the previous year, apparently with erysipelas, a painful reddening of the skin known as St Antony's Fire. By January 1557 he was on his deathbed at Tantallon, the Douglas fortress he had once lost to James V but had since reclaimed in triumph. One account of Angus's death reports that Margaret sent her secretary in her stead. This man, a priest by the name of Sir John Dixon, was with the earl when he finally died.[18] Another version holds that one of Angus's servants made the melancholy joke that he was surprised to see Angus die in bed: 'I thought to have seen you die leading the vanguard, and I with many others fighting under your standard.' The old man rallied: 'You say well; and now see me here willing and ready to die in the vanguard of my Saviour Christ, whose standard I bear here before my eyes.' Raising a crucifix, he kissed it: 'Lo, here is the standard under which I shall die.'[19]

France mourned Angus; Margaret's feelings were undoubtedly more complex.[20] They had been on opposite political sides for a decade and he could infuriate her, but she had never given up hope that they would be reconciled. Her father had left his lands to his male heirs, so his successor was Margaret's cousin David, son of her uncle George Douglas. Margaret did not recognise his right. She had sworn to Angus that she, not George Douglas's descendants, would be his heir if he died without sons, and she immediately began using the title Countess of Angus. The tussle soon took on a new aspect: David Douglas died in 1558 and the title passed to his young son Archibald, whose uncle James Douglas, Earl of Morton, assumed guardianship.

For Margaret, nobody would ever be as dangerous and persistent an antagonist as her cousin Morton, and even the moments when they found themselves in common cause were uneasy and brief. He was roughly Margaret's age and they almost certainly knew each other as children in the court of her half-brother, James V. Young James Douglas had grown into a thick-set, yellow-haired man who spoke slowly and with traces of an English accent, the result of years spent south of the border. He and Margaret had nothing in common politically: like the rest of the Douglases, he had abandoned the English cause during the Rough Wooing, and he was quietly a Protestant in still-Catholic Scotland.

Morton's private life was profoundly unhappy. He got his title by marrying Elizabeth, youngest daughter of the previous earl.[21] A strain of mental illness ran in her family and affected both Elizabeth and her elder sister Margaret, the wife of Lennox's rival, the Duke of Châtelherault, formerly the Earl of Arran. Elizabeth became ill in the late 1550s and was eventually declared insane, and the couple lost at least seven children. In public affairs, Morton was sharp-witted and courageous, but also unscrupulous, hypocritical and eager for power, and being guardian and tutor to the Earl of Angus was power.[22]

Margaret had a dependable ally in her cousin Mary Tudor, who did her best to help Margaret claim her father's title. She sent an envoy to meet with Mary of Guise and negotiate for the earldoms of Lennox and Angus. The dowager, however, sidestepped the matter of Lennox's lands. It was not within her power, she said, to set aside the judgements against the 'sometime earl of Lennox . . . for that is a matter of special grace which we are always accustomed to refer to our dearest daughter herself'. As for the Countess of Lennox, the dowager offered little hope of success, noting that Margaret lived in England and stood 'in some cases far different from the privileges that are given to subjects of this realm'.[23] Whatever impression Margaret had made on her sister-in-law during the visit to Edward's court, it was not enough to override Mary of Guise's own political sense.

Guise had no reason to favour Margaret's cause. As one French observer noted, Margaret was an Englishwoman married to a Scottish traitor. He thought Mary Tudor's support for her claim was nothing more than evidence of the English royal family's 'ancient hate and rancour . . . between the house and race of Douglas for the great service done by them to our sovereign prince': in other words, petty revenge by England on Morton and the Douglases for their support of Mary of Guise and of France. In spite of her Scottish father and husband, Margaret was – and was perceived as – an Englishwoman, not a Scot. She would not have disputed the point, but in some French and Scottish eyes she did not seem to count as a Douglas at all, and that she would never concede: she was not just the Countess of Lennox, but the Countess of Angus in her own right.[24]

Mary Tudor, however, was struggling against France on all fronts and could not hope for even a minor victory on Margaret's behalf. Going to war at Philip's request cost her Calais, England's last continental possession. Compounding the disaster was the fact that it was Mary Stewart's uncle, the Duke of Guise, who carried the field against the English. On 24 April 1558 the Guise family finally achieved their ambition of the previous ten years: the fifteen-year-old Mary, Queen of Scots, wed the Dauphin, Francis, at Notre Dame Cathedral in Paris. At the wedding celebrations, the French political elite celebrated the newlyweds as monarchs of Scotland and heirs to the thrones of France and England.[25]

While Margaret took to signing herself 'countess of Lennox and Angus', she seemed to have no chance of recovering her father's earldom: with the marriage of Mary and the Dauphin, the Auld Alliance was stronger and more dangerous than ever.

Worse, Mary Tudor's health was collapsing. The succession was still unsettled, but the ailing queen refused to admit as much. On 28 October 1558 she added a codicil to her will which noted that 'the next heir by the laws of the realm' would succeed only 'if it should please God not to give me issue'.[26] Only at the very end did it become clear to her she would never have children, and by then it was too late to try to change the succession: her half-sister would inherit her crown, and Margaret would see another woman assume the role she had let herself think might be hers.

Mary and Cardinal Pole both died on 17 November 1558. They took with them any hope that England might remain a Catholic country, or that the Lennox-Stewarts might take the place of the Tudors. The throne now descended to brilliant, enigmatic Elizabeth Tudor, who took up the crown and the hopes of England's religious reformers: the persecuted bastard daughter of beheaded Anne Boleyn was Queen of England and Ireland. Like the Psalmist recounting the tale of the rejected rock that became the cornerstone, Elizabeth declared *A Domino factum est istud, et est mirabile in oculis nostris*: 'This is the Lord's doing, and it is marvellous in our eyes.'[27]

Margaret was not bitter with Mary; she had lost her oldest friend and mourned her deeply, both in private and in public. She kept Mary's portrait in the Great Hall of Temple Newsam, a constant memorial to the dead queen.[28] But the previous ten years had tried Margaret sorely. She had gone through eight pregnancies, most of them in her thirties and all tinged with the fear that she or the baby might not survive.[29] She never forgot any of the children: they are all depicted on her tomb, 'four sons and four daughters'. Her father had said that not knowing what his dead children were doing left him heartbroken, and there is no reason to doubt that Margaret felt the same.[30] Like Henry VIII, Angus had died before she could make amends with him, and he had left her without an inheritance. Her eldest son, whom she had tried to position as an English prince, was still only Henry, Lord Darnley – and neither he nor she shared Elizabeth's reformed religion.

Bitter loss, familial ambition and passionate Catholicism: it was small wonder that the men who surrounded the new queen would never see Margaret as the poetic and charming Lady Margaret Douglas. To them, she was the power-hungry, untrustworthy Countess of Lennox. But she would never see herself that way. She was a deprived heir and daughter, determined to defend her right.

12

Spoilt Children of the Devil

As sunset neared on Saturday, 10 December 1558, Margaret was standing in the Privy Chamber of St James's Palace, waiting to begin her role as chief mourner for her dead cousin. For more than three weeks, Queen Mary's coffined body had lain in this black-draped room with her women keeping watch, hearing Mass every day; burying a queen took time. Now, men and women of every estate assembled behind a cross: gentlemen, knights, peers, bishops, all ahead of the body of the monarch. Margaret took up her place of honour behind the corpse, with the Earl of Huntingdon and the Viscount Montagu at her side and Lady Katherine Hastings carrying her train. Behind her, two by two, came the great noblewomen of the realm, followed by a host of ladies and gentlewomen. With the bells tolling three o'clock, the procession moved slowly towards the chapel.

It was the same room in which Margaret had been married fourteen years before, but now black cloth hung from the walls and the altar was covered with purple velvet, the liturgical colour of penitence and prayer for the dead. In the centre of the chapel stood a hearse, lit with forty-six tall candles, each one decorated with crowns and Tudor roses. Margaret watched eight gentlemen place Mary's body within the hearse. Then, kneeling on a black cushion, she prayed. Incense hung in the air while the clergy intoned the service of the dirge.

On Sunday morning the mourners gathered in the chapel to hear the requiem Mass. At the moment of the offering, the company rose and Margaret walked towards the altar with her attendants, where she knelt and presented a symbolic gift before returning to the hearse. There, quite alone save for one officer of arms standing before her, she bowed to Mary's body. When the Mass was over, Margaret ate with the rest of the mourners, and then retreated to her room for a brief moment before returning to the chapel to hear another dirge. More Masses followed the next day and on Tuesday morning.

At last, after dinner on the Tuesday, the corpse was carried to a chariot and covered with a pall. On top of the pall rested Mary's effigy, wearing the robes of state and all her regalia: the orb, the sceptre, the crown. Five horses with black velvet trappers drew the chariot, each one ridden by a hooded page of honour carrying a heraldic banner. At each corner of the chariot rode a herald carrying a pennant: St Mary Magdalene, St George, the Blessed Virgin Mary and the Holy Trinity. Margaret mounted her horse and waited for the long line of mourners to move, some on horseback, some on foot. At last, the horses dragged the chariot forward and she followed after it, leading a train of women on horseback and in carriages from St James to the west door of Westminster Abbey.

The abbey was draped with black; before the altar stood an enormous canopied hearse lit with a thousand burning candles and elaborately decorated with Mary's emblems and figured wax archangels. The Bishop of Worcester blessed Mary's corpse with incense and holy water, and twelve men carried her body and laid it within the hearse. Margaret took up her place before the corpse and the dirge began, recited by three bishops. Over and over the mourners prayed for Mary's soul, running through her long list of titles at every repetition.

The next day, there were yet more Masses, culminating in the great requiem. At the offering, Margaret walked to the altar and kneeled down. That done, she returned to the hearse, and alone once again, bowed to Mary. Nobles, gentlemen, ambassadors followed; the line of mourners seemed to go on forever. But at the end of it all, the twelve men took up Mary's body and laid her in her grave. Her nobles broke their staffs of office and placed them in the tomb with her: the old queen was dead and buried. Straight from the graveside, the men left behind the majesty of the abbey to meet the gathered throng of Londoners. The Garter King at Arms shouted 'God save Queen Elizabeth!' Trumpets sounded, hats were thrown into the wintry air, and for Margaret, everything had changed.[1]

Although she was mourning for Mary and may have been resenting Elizabeth's accession, she was, at least at first, attentive to protocol. At the New Year of 1559, Margaret and Lennox both gave Elizabeth purses full of money and Elizabeth presented them with gilt cups in return – not gifts that revealed any special degree of closeness, but perfectly correct and traditional for nobles of their standing.[2] This cordiality, however, was not to last.

Formidably educated and an accomplished linguist and musician, Elizabeth also had real political nous. She had survived her half-siblings' reigns, despite entanglements with the treacherous Thomas Seymour and with Mary's rebels. At the time of Henry's death in 1547, few would have predicted that she would become queen, but the improbability of her accession only strengthened Elizabeth's belief that it was her destiny to reign. Whenever anybody suggested that she had inherited because she was an exceptional woman, set apart from the rest of her sex, she dismissed the idea: she was queen because she was her father's daughter, and dynastic right was simply the hand of Providence at work.[3]

Soon after she ascended the throne, the newly crowned Elizabeth informed parliament of her intent to stay unmarried. '[A] marble stone,' she said, 'shall declare that a Queen, having reigned such a time, lived and died a virgin.'[4] Whether or not Elizabeth meant it, it was a wise thing to say. It was a profession of constancy at a time when women were seen as the more sensual and lustful sex. Better to marry than to burn, but not to burn at all was a mark of strength befitting a monarch. The late Mary had recognised as much, casting marriage as a matter of duty, not desire, and affirming that she was 'not so *bent* to my will, neither so precise nor affectionate' that she needed a husband: 'I have hitherto lived a Virgin, and doubt nothing, but with God's grace am able so to live still.'[5] For Elizabeth, remaining single was also politically sensible: she was only twenty-five and could afford to wait.

Just as her half-sister Mary had done, Elizabeth saw that marriage for a queen regnant was a perpetual quandary. She remained single, a decision that would shape the political culture of her reign. On the one hand, she would be free to dangle the prospect of marital alliance to the European powers and the chance of a crown to her many would-be successors. On the other, there would always be potential Catholic heirs – and they might not wait for Elizabeth's death before raising a following amongst England's Catholics and restoring the country to Rome.

Elizabeth's new Secretary of State – Master Secretary, to his innumerable correspondents – was William Cecil. Scion of a gentry family with court connections and a long tradition of service, Cecil had studied at Cambridge and had a brief legal career before starting to work for the Seymours. A short-lived marriage in the early 1540s had left him a widower with a son, but for the last thirteen years he had been married to Mildred, a talented scholar and relative by marriage of the Greys, who was as committed to religious reform as he was. He made himself invaluable during Edward's reign and he survived Somerset's fall, but Cecil's Protestant convictions led him away from court during Mary's reign and into Elizabeth's orbit. He was ready to work tirelessly on her behalf.[6]

Cecil and Elizabeth would be a formidable team for forty years, but their disagreements, though rare, were dramatic, and the most significant of these would be over Margaret's niece, Mary Stewart, Queen of Scots. At the behest of her Guise relatives, Mary and Francis began to style themselves the monarchs of Scotland, England and Ireland after Mary Tudor's death. They were not Elizabeth's heirs but the rightful rulers, and she was a usurper. In the short term, there was no way for them to put their claim into practice. France made peace with both England and Spain in 1559, Henry II's own concerns and depleted treasury taking precedence over Guise ambition.[7] But the Scottish queen had inadvertently made herself one of Cecil's worries and stirred up anxiety over the succession. Elizabeth, firm believer in dynastic right, did not disagree in principle with the idea of a Catholic successor, but she did not want to name an heir and standard-bearer for would-be rebels; Cecil objected strongly to the idea of letting another Catholic woman lead England back to Rome. Mary became even more alarming when her father-in-law, Henry II, was killed in a jousting accident, aged only forty. Her fifteen year old husband was suddenly Francis II and she was now Queen of France as well as Scotland.

Within a year of her accession, Elizabeth had made her own religious settlement. Later called a *via media*, it looked to many Catholics less like a compromise than a reversion to heresy. The rood screens and church furnishings, so painstakingly restored under Mary, vanished in a state-sanctioned explosion of iconoclasm. Catholics had to attend services or be fined for recusancy. Every public office-holder in England had to swear an oath to

Elizabeth's supremacy in temporal and spiritual affairs, and every clergyman in England had to preach at least four sermons every year denying all foreign power. Every subject, the priests were to remind their congregations, owed Elizabeth 'loyalty and obedience, afore and above all other potentates in earth'.[8] It was an old idea that religious dissenters were likely to spread dangerous ideas or even provoke riots. But the 1559 settlement made it clear that Catholics were not only a threat to their own country and community; they were seen as potential allies of European Catholic powers.[9]

Margaret could not accept Elizabeth's changes to religion. Once again she found herself outside the established Church – a position made even lonelier by events in Scotland. The country had its own reformers, both outside the Church and within. Provincial councils from 1549 onwards were concerned with stamping out heresy but also with strengthening and purifying the established Church, calling for better, more scripture-focused preaching and introducing a new, semi-vernacular catechism.[10] For some this was not going far enough, and convinced Protestants found themselves forced to meet in secret to discuss more radical ideas.[11]

The years 1559–60 brought a movement towards reform on a far grander scale. One by one a handful of Scottish burghs declared themselves Protestant. The blue-eyed, bearded John Knox, long exiled in England and Europe for his zealous Protestantism, came home to Scotland and did what he did best: he preached a sermon so powerful that it moved the townspeople of Perth to rise and mutiny. They tore down the Charterhouse until only its defaced walls remained, cast out the community of monks and destroyed Margaret's mother's tomb.[12] The Lords of the Congregation raised an army and scored a series of victories in the late spring and early summer of 1559, culminating in their march into Edinburgh in July.

In October they overthrew the ailing Mary of Guise, depriving her of the regency. But the dowager made a strategic retreat to the port of Leith, gathered French troops and forged onwards. By November, Edinburgh was again in Catholic hands, and the Protestant reformers, whose ranks now included the Duke of Châtelherault, were looking to England for support.[13]

For Elizabeth's advisors this was tortuous to watch. They shared the religious convictions of the men struggling for reform and they believed a Protestant Scotland would be far less of a threat to Elizabeth than one ruled by the Catholic Mary of Guise. Elizabeth listened to their arguments, but she had strong convictions of her own. She disliked Knox, who had justified rebellion with a blistering attack on the very idea of female monarchy. Any man who obeyed 'the monstriferous empire of a woman' was a sinner: 'I judge them not only subjects to women, but slaves of Satan, and servants of iniquity.'[14] Having just finished one war with France, Elizabeth had no interest in getting into another, and she was always reluctant to support rebels against their anointed sovereign.

The answer ultimately lay in the concept of amity. Over the winter of 1559–60, William Maitland, representing the Congregation, worked with Elizabeth's advisors to craft an agreement. The English would send help to Scotland, leading to the establishment of a new government in Edinburgh and of a Protestant alliance across mainland Britain, with the promise of Scottish help for the English in Ireland. Elizabeth approved the plan, and come January 1560 an English fleet set sail for Scotland.[15]

Margaret saw that the growing ties between the Protestant rebel lords and Protestant England portended disaster. She and Lennox would face a Scotland dominated by reformers, with the Hamiltons – headed by the Duke of Châtelherault – acknowledged heirs to the absent Mary Stewart. Quietly, Margaret and

Lennox made contact with Scots who still supported the dowager queen: if they supported her against the rebels, they might earn back not only the earldom of Lennox, but also the earldom of Angus.[16]

Margaret's world swelled with spies and counter-spies. Yorkshire was her refuge from court, but the queen's information-gatherers reported from every corner of the realm. In December 1559, Elizabeth gave the Duke of Norfolk, her Lieutenant-General in the north, instructions to spy on Lennox and Margaret, warning that they might be drawn into the Scottish conflict by the French or 'by such others as favour not our proceedings in religion'.[17] To Elizabeth, Margaret and her husband were dangerous, and with every move they made, they earned still greater mistrust.

As Margaret asserted herself in the political sphere, observers began mocking Lennox. The French ambassador Antoine de Noailles wrote that the earl was 'governed by his wife'.[18] Shortly before Christmas, Margaret and Lennox dispatched their servant Lawrence Nesbitt to de Noailles in London, sending with him a large family tree – it took up two sheets of paper – outlining Lennox's claim to be the second person of the realm in Scotland.[19] Nesbitt was arrested and imprisoned in the Tower.[20] William Maitland, in England on behalf of the Congregation, suggested that the entire project was merely 'a crafty fetch of the Queen Dowager' and warned the English against cultivating the Lennox-Stewarts. In the first place, they were not worth the effort, lacking any real political support: if Lennox was a match for Châtelherault, why did he 'suffer himself [to] be driven far off his native country'? In the second, and more damningly, the Catholic Lennox was not likely to win any new supporters: '[H]e and my lady are known enemies to the religion.'[21]

Lennox protested to Cecil that Nesbitt's only task was furthering his affairs in Scotland and that he did not believe Elizabeth could be offended by any efforts he and Margaret might make for 'the recovery of our own in that realm'. He asked that Cecil remind the queen 'how gracious and beneficial her grace's progenitors hath been always unto my wife and me: and again how upright we have kept ourselves from our beginning to this hour, intending with the grace of God so to continue'.[22] When the Privy Council refused to concede the point, Lennox was forced to backtrack, apologising for sending an ignorant servant 'who perhaps hath overshot himself in words more than his knowledge'.[23]

Margaret's own case in Scotland was not proceeding any better than Lennox's. On 6 January 1560, Mary of Guise granted the wardship of the earldom of Angus to her 'trusty cousin' Morton, Margaret's first cousin, James Douglas. In return for promising his obedience and swearing to 'take no part with them that has lately rebelled', Morton gained temporary control of the lands of Margaret's father and all the revenues their rents and resources could raise.[24] Six months later, James Hamilton, Duke of Châtelherault, and his son – now known by his father's old title as the Earl of Arran – swore a bond of manrent to Morton and to young Archibald Douglas, eighth Earl of Angus, with Maitland as the first witness. The Hamiltons had a claim to Morton's title: Châtelherault's wife was the eldest daughter of the previous earl, while Morton's wife was the youngest. They gave it up, swearing to defend Morton's right. This solemn oath also bound Châtelherault and Arran to support Douglas's claim to the earldom against Margaret and her children, 'to the pain of ten thousand pounds to be paid by us to them in case we fail herein'.[25] It was a Douglas-Hamilton pact against Margaret and Lennox. Two weeks later, Mary of Guise was dead, taking with her the Lennox-Stewarts' best hope of a counter-alliance.

The miserable episode drew to a close in the summer when, under the terms of the Treaty of Edinburgh, English and

French troops were to leave Scotland, Mary and Francis were to renounce their claim to be monarchs of England, and Scotland was to be governed by a largely Protestant council of nobles. The Queen of Scots was not consulted and would never accept the treaty, but her illegitimate, Protestant half-brother Lord James Stewart had control of the Privy Council and she was still in France.

Back home, the Lennox-Stewarts' relations with the new English regime were at breaking point. Elizabeth's advisors prepared a memorandum with answers to be given in case either Margaret or Lennox asked for money owed and needed. They were to inform them that '[a]ll covenants concluded for the part of Henry VIII fulfilled, and one hundred thousand crowns more disbursed without fruit for the earl's advancement, by the earl none fulfilled . . . [W]e be not ignorantly advertised from Scotland that you and my lady may dispend more here above the revenues of the Lennox nor both the earls of Angus and Morton may spend if you had them all.' The memorandum decreed that Margaret and Lennox were disloyal and ungrateful, whereas the queen herself was 'most gracious', and indeed 'not so strait as ye have been used of other princes'. They were, in short, to be thoroughly reproached: 'The queen's highness is good lady unto you both to suffer you to enjoy these great livings . . . considering what faint hearts see her goodness.'[26]

By November 1560, Margaret was beside herself. Every step Elizabeth had taken threatened her family's interests on both sides of the border. She now felt justified in doing just what the regime feared disaffected Catholics were liable to do: she turned to the Catholic powers of Europe.

Alvarez de Quadra had once been the Bishop of Aquila, but he had been anxious to leave his ecclesiastical post for new surroundings. Elizabeth's accession gave him the opportunity. Philip, confident of de Quadra's good sense and diplomacy, made him Spain's new ambassador to the English court.[27] Dismayed with what he found, he wrote in May 1559 that 'the state of things here . . . is the most miserable that can be conceived . . . the heretics of our own times have never been such spoilt children of the devil as these are, and the persecutors of the early church were surely not impious enough to dare to pass such unjust acts as these.'[28]

Margaret and Lennox arranged to meet with de Quadra, telling him of their grievances with Elizabeth: '[N]ot only did the Queen treat them as prisoners because they were Catholics, but she was trying to injure their claim to the succession by helping the duke of Châtelherault.' But they wanted more than a chance to vent their frustration. Confident that with Spanish support they and their allies would have the means to restore Catholicism in England, they asked for help from Philip. As Margaret spoke, de Quadra realised that she and her husband were not, as he had first believed, talking in the abstract about what might happen if Elizabeth died suddenly. Rather, they were both nearing the end of their patience with the queen. '[T]hey did not mean it in that way, but to attempt to overthrow her at once.' If that failed, they wanted leave from Philip II to go into the Spanish Netherlands, cutting themselves off from Protestant England.

But just as she was on the point of exile, Margaret's luck turned. On 5 December 1560 sixteen-year-old Francis II of France died, leaving Mary, Queen of Scots, a widow at the age of just eighteen. Some Protestants, not thinking so far ahead as they might have done, rejoiced at the news of the young king's death, celebratory on behalf of their French co-religionists. Thomas Randolph said it was 'a happy relief to so many afflicted and troubled souls as were in danger of death and banishment', a sign of God's grace 'so suddenly unlooked for, unthought of, contrary unto the expectation of all men [in taking] away so great a scourge'.[29]

For Margaret, however, it was the great, unlooked-for opportunity of her life. It did not take much imagination to guess that Mary would soon return to her own throne and country and that she would eventually marry again. She might want another king or prince – certainly kings and princes would court her. But if Margaret could persuade her niece to marry Henry, Lord Darnley, it would unify and strengthen the dynastic claims of Margaret Tudor's heirs. Together, Margaret's son and niece would have the chance to unite the crowns of England, Scotland and Ireland, and restore the British Isles to the Church of Rome.

13

The Bishop and the Hawk

The steeple of St Paul's Cathedral soared over London, the tallest spire in a city crowded with churches.[1] Early in the afternoon of 4 June 1561, London was racked with a devastating thunderstorm and a burst of lightning hit the towering steeple. The fierce winds of the tempest kindled the flames and carried the smells of smoke and brimstone into the city below. While panicked city officials conferred, the interior of the cathedral caught fire, and sizzling debris filled the air. A crowd of gentlemen and commoners alike scrambled to douse the flames before they could spread, and it was only due to the hard work of 500 men and the sudden ebbing of the storm that the blaze was stopped.[2]

Far to the north in Yorkshire, Margaret heard news that six men in the service of Robert Dudley, son of the late Duke of Northumberland, devout Protestant, trusted counsellor and would be lover of Elizabeth, were marching through St James's Park with several of the queen's guards when they were 'stricken with sudden death'. One of her servants, a man by the name of William Forbes, would for ever after connect these disparate events in his mind. The following year he was interrogated by William Cecil. Forbes swore that Darnley's schoolmaster, Arthur Lallart, wrote Margaret a commentary on the predictions of the seer Nostradamus. 'My lady,' said Forbes, read the prophecies and 'looked that the highest should have declined, but it turned to herself and to Paul's steeple'.[3] He was linking together the eerie images of the fiery church, the stricken men and the fortune-telling teacher to insinuate that Margaret trafficked with the supernatural. But which was she: the collapsing steeple or the lightning strike?

Six months before the fire, in the week after Francis II's death, Thomas Stewart, Laird of Galston, arrived in Yorkshire with a message for Lennox. He had been the family's intermediary with Mary of Guise, and Margaret welcomed him out of the December cold to hear his news. Lennox's friends in Scotland urged him to secure Elizabeth's support for both his claims and Margaret's, so that he could take up his place as one of Scotland's leading nobles and she, as 'nearest and lawful heir', could be acknowledged Countess of Angus. There was more: Lennox's friends reproached him with 'great sloth' and urged him to 'be more diligent' in his own affairs, but they also promised that if Elizabeth's aid was not enough to convince Mary, Queen of Scots, to restore them both, they would rally to his cause.[4]

Lennox was spurred to action and dispatched Galston to Westminster immediately. He had the misfortune to reach London just after the court received word of the French king's death, which gave Elizabeth an excellent reason to do nothing to aid Lennox and Margaret in their Scottish causes.[5] Although Elizabeth was, as usual, putting Lennox off with vague promises, there was already growing fear about what the Lennox-Stewarts would do next. The Duke of Châtelherault sensed danger and told the English ambassador Thomas Randolph that he wished both Lennox and Darnley far away from the border and nearer England's court, ideally occupied with some business 'that all occasions of practice and means either to draw him into this country, or conveying of him to any other place, might be taken away'.[6] The queen's delaying tactics gave Galston the chance to get back to Yorkshire and perform another favour for the family, this time at Margaret's urging.

Margaret took to her chamber and began to write. Normally, she dictated her letters to a secretary before adding her spiky signature – *Margaret Lennox and Angus* – after the closing courtesies. But this time she held the pen herself, because a deeply personal message called for her own hand.[7] When she had signed her name, she folded the note, sealed it and handed it to Galston. He left Yorkshire for France with messages from Margaret, Lennox and Darnley, all written with their own pens and all addressed to Mary Stewart, dowager Queen of France and Queen of Scots.

The young queen was arresting, an eighteen-year-old redhead with perfect skin and a famously graceful figure who stood nearly six feet tall. She had lived in France for almost as long as she could remember and loved her adopted country, but she never forgot her responsibilities as Queen of Scotland, even if her absence in France and relative youth meant she had had virtually no role in ruling her own realm. Mary was old enough to have firm opinions on policy. The Treaty of Edinburgh, which had been concluded in her absence, promised that she would give up her claim to the English crown: it infuriated her and she refused to accept it.

Margaret had never met this niece who had already been the unwitting cause of dramatic changes in her life. For her part, Mary had no reason to think kindly of her uncle-by-marriage – Lennox was a traitor – and she probably knew little about her aunt Margaret. Francis's death changed that. It is unlikely that Margaret and Mary ever met: they conducted their entire relationship by letters, gifts and messengers, and it would take years before they developed real affection for each other. Although they would use each other for the next decade, each of them felt a right to the other's loyalty.

Mary had forty days of secluded mourning to plan her next move. She and Francis had had no children, so she had no obvious role at the French court. Worse, her late mother had been a member of the house of Guise, France's most powerful noble family and a threat to the primacy of the royal house of Valois. Catherine de' Medici, her mother-in-law, was now Regent for Francis's younger brother, the newly crowned Charles IX. She had no love for the Guise, who were already trying to get Mary engaged to Don Carlos, Philip II's eldest son and heir to the throne of Spain. Closeted away, and with Spanish talks proving futile, Mary decided she would go back to Scotland. The prospect of her return to her newly reformed realm threw the political classes of England and Scotland into agitation: whatever Mary chose to do in the matters of religion and remarriage would have consequences throughout Britain.

When the queen did emerge from her isolation, Margaret's emissary was there, waiting. Galston was among the first to greet her – and to remind her that in Lord Darnley she had a marriageable, English-born, Catholic cousin. Within a month of Margaret's messengers reaching Mary, people were already discussing the chance of a match. The Spanish ambassador Bishop de Quadra wrote to King Philip II that 'Lady Margaret Lennox is trying to marry her son Lord Darnley to the queen of Scotland, and I understand she is not without hope of succeeding.'[8] Darnley's old tutor, John Elder, was in on the strategy. In a bid to impress Mary with Darnley's precocity, he showed her samples of his former charge's handwriting, which the young lord 'wrote being eight years of age'.[9] Galston was back in Edinburgh by March 1561, in contact with both Lennox and Cecil but especially with Margaret. He told her that although he protested ignorance when others broached the subject, 'the Common bruit of Scotland is that my Lord Darnley is gone in France to be a suitor to the queen's grace of Scotland'. One of the Lennox-Stewarts' retainers, William Forbes, said later that Galston, upon his return from France, remarked that 'all should be well for my Lord Darnley with the queen'.[10]

Margaret was being optimistic but not outlandishly so. On paper, Darnley had much to recommend him. It had been more than a century since a Scottish monarch had married a subject, but Darnley was not a Scot, in spite of his claim to the earldoms of Lennox and Angus – he was an English-born member of England's royal family. Marriage with him might strengthen Mary's claim to the English throne and eventually see them ruling throughout the British Isles, giving her a native-born husband and removing a rival claimant. Although the Rough Wooing had been a Protestant policy, there was nothing intrinsically reformed about the idea of uniting England and Scotland through royal marriage – and the godly, in the winter of 1560–1, were speaking the language of friendship and alliance rather than union. Margaret saw the Anglo-Scottish relationship in different terms: unionist, dynastic, Catholic. Together, her niece and her son could unite the crowns and restore their kingdoms to the old religion.

None of this was going to be easy, but after years of being wrong-footed by events, Margaret began to drive them. The Queen of Scots was enormously eligible and Margaret knew she would have to win over not only Mary but as many allies as she could.

It was lucky for Margaret that Henry VIII had given her estates in Yorkshire. Catholicism had had greater staying power in northern than in southern England. Removed from the centres of reform, people at all levels of society were still loyal to the Mass and the traditions of the old religion. Most of the leading nobles were Catholics – the Lennox-Stewarts prominent among them. John Best, Bishop of Carlisle, lamented to Cecil that 'the rulers and justices of peace wink at all things and look through their fingers', letting blatant violations of the settlement go unpunished. Amongst those not of noble rank, reform had met with even less success. If Cecil could see the state of religion in the north, wrote Best, 'I believe it would cause you weep'.[11]

Far from the febrile court, surrounded by likely allies, Margaret set to work. Wanting to know what her opponents were planning, she ordered her servants to collect and exchange news of anti-Catholic persecution in Yorkshire. She sent spies to Thomas Bishop's house at Pocklington to learn his dealings, and dispatched Hugh Allan to York 'to understand things about my Lord President' – the Protestant Henry Manners, second Earl of Rutland, President of the Council of the North.[12] These men also served as messengers to her friends. Margaret and Lennox had been based in the north for nearly twenty years and had strong ties to their fellow Catholic nobles, both men and women. They corresponded and met in person. Some of them already treated the young Darnley as a sort of prince, giving him the head of the table even when great peers of the realm were present.[13] If Margaret called on them, they were ready to act.

Margaret knew that England was not enough. If Darnley were to woo the Queen of Scots, he would need supporters in Scotland, and not only from Lennox's old network of friends and kin, but beyond it. When it came to religion, the Scottish aristocracy was not wholly reformed; many leading nobles upheld Catholicism, both in their own households and among their tenants.[14] Margaret dispatched loyal Thomas Stewart and fickle William Forbes into Scotland. They headed north from Settrington, ordered to make contact with a host of nobles, including the earls of Atholl, Sutherland, Cassillis and Bothwell, and the lords Sempill and Seton. She had to know which men could be convinced to support her ambitious plan. The task of Stewart and Forbes was clear: 'to prove their good minds and affection towards the marriage of her son the Lord Darnley with the queen of Scots'.[15]

Her plot married an appeal to religious loyalty with political pragmatism. Although not all of these men were Catholic, they were all likely to be sympathetic. Bothwell was a reformer but, like the Lennox-Stewarts, a bitter foe of the Hamiltons. Even though Cassillis was the son of a Protestant and would eventually become one himself, his own beliefs were unclear in 1561. The rest were all Catholics and they heard the plan with interest.[16] Seton was apparently so committed to the idea of the Darnley match that he 'would spend his blood' in promoting it.[17]

Margaret was promoting Darnley in England and in Scotland as a Catholic husband for the Queen of Scots. But Mary Stewart was being courted by kings and princes across Europe, and Margaret saw that she would also need to make a case for her son to Catholics abroad. She had become exactly what the Elizabethan settlement had tried to prevent: a Catholic whose loyalties to her co-religionists prevailed over her loyalties to the English crown.

Unsurprisingly, she made her first overtures to Philip II, King of Spain and Mary Tudor's widower. During Mary's reign, Margaret had often been at court, in rooms near the queen's own. She named one of her children after Philip and she still saw him as an ally after Mary's death, even considering his Dutch territories as a refuge should she have to flee Protestant England.[18]

Margaret saw that she needed a means to get in touch with Philip and she turned to Francis Yaxley, a shadowy figure with ties to both English and European Catholics.[19] He had been a Clerk of the Signet under Mary Tudor and had stayed close to other members of her regime after Elizabeth's accession.[20] Yaxley admired Darnley, sending him a turquoise ring as a token of friendship, and Margaret acted as a patron for Yaxley, taking a young woman named Mabel Fortescue into her service on his recommendation.[21] He, in turn, was her link to the Spanish entourage at court.[22]

When Margaret spoke, Spain was willing to listen. Darnley gave Philip a way out of an impasse: the Guise were still petitioning him to marry his son Don Carlos to the Queen of Scots, and while he did not want to see Mary make another French alliance, he was not ready to offer his son instead. A Spanish match for the Queen of Scots would, at one stroke, undermine Philip's relations with Catherine de' Medici and with Elizabeth.[23] Both he and his ambassadors to Elizabeth's court came to see Darnley as the most acceptable of Mary's suitors.

Alvarez de Quadra, bishop turned ambassador, was alive to any hint that there might be a way to bring England back to Rome, and was well aware that Darnley had a claim to the English crown.[24] Much like his predecessor Renard, who had told Mary Tudor that her cousin Mary Stewart had the best right to the English throne, de Quadra thought the Scottish queen was the lawful heir. But he was also convinced that the Lennox-Stewarts, and especially the English-born Margaret, were popular and well-liked – in fact, it was worryingly possible that the competing claims of Mary and Darnley would divide English Catholics, to the detriment of the old religion.[25] He had believed this for some time; before Francis's death, he had suggested to Philip that if Elizabeth died childless, English Catholics might take up arms to make Darnley king.[26] Many would also be prepared to rebel and replace Elizabeth with Darnley at once, especially if Spain agreed to send troops.[27] For this reason, de Quadra wrote, most English Catholics supported matching Mary with Darnley rather than with a foreign suitor, as he 'would at all events be able to save the country from some turmoil by uniting his claim to that of the queen of Scots'.[28]

Darnley's standing as a potential British Catholic husband for Mary made his politics significant to the Spanish, who now saw the risks attendant on letting him be drawn into France's diplomatic orbit.[29] If he became King of Scots with French help, worried de Quadra, Scotland and perhaps England would ally with France, leaving Spain isolated.[30] De Quadra was determined that the Lennox-Stewarts remain linked to Spain. For him, Margaret and Darnley, with their Catholic supporters and their succession claim, were a vital piece of the Anglo-Spanish relationship.[31]

Then there was Mary herself, who left France and was back in Scotland by August 1561. She had been Queen of Scots for nearly twenty years but only now was she ruler in fact as well as title. In her absence and since her mother's death, the Protestant lords had had control of the government, and she had struck a compromise with them before coming home. She would worship in private as a Catholic, as she had done all her life, but otherwise, she would leave Scottish religion as she had found it – that is, Protestant. Elizabeth and Mary, though of different faiths, were both religious moderates, especially in comparison with their advisors. Like the lords, the queen wanted to maintain the amity with England – if Elizabeth remained unmarried, Mary had a strong claim to be her heir.[32]

In the midst of this complicated set of relationships, what mattered to Margaret was that Mary made it safely back to her own country. When she heard the news, she nearly collapsed with relief, thanking God that her niece had survived the voyage and telling the bystanders that God 'always had preserved that princess at all times, especially now'.[33]

Her allies in England, Scotland and Europe formed the core of Margaret's campaign, but the person she most needed to convince was Mary. According to Thomas Bishop, Margaret and Mary knew that they were being watched but kept up intensely dangerous and secret correspondence. Margaret invented her own codename for Mary and referred to her only as 'the hawk'. She burnt all of Mary's letters and told the queen that she should do the same with hers. Her goal was to make the same case in Scotland as she was making in England: that together, her Catholic niece and her Catholic son might reign in both kingdoms.

At the same time that Margaret was promoting Darnley, she and Lennox were also trying to rebuild their ties in Scotland and claim their inheritances. Lennox's cousin John, seigneur d'Aubigny, sent word that he was coming to Scotland, and the earl decided to send Darnley's new schoolmaster, Arthur Lallart, north to meet him. His mission was to inform d'Aubigny of Lennox's 'goodwill' and to ask him to deliver a message to Mary on behalf of the Lennox-Stewarts, asking her that no parliament confirm possession of the Lennox and Angus lands upon other claimants. If he could not find d'Aubigny or Thomas Stewart, Laird of Galston, Lallart was to speak to Mary herself.

Margaret helped plan the clandestine journey. They would be breaking the law, since Lallart did not have permission to go into Scotland. Together, she and Lennox decided that Lallart would go with a man named Wat Neep, Lennox's falconer. Neep, Lennox assured Lallart, knew Scotland well enough that the schoolmaster would not have to carry potentially incriminating letters or tokens – 'for my wife and I thinketh it not good'. Margaret's other servants, many of them Scottish, asked him to take letters to friends and family for them, but since he was not taking letters from Lennox, Lallart refused to take them from anybody connected to the earl and countess.

Once Lallart and Neep arrived in Edinburgh, they found that d'Aubigny had not come from France and that Thomas Stewart was away in England. Unsure what to do, the two men lingered in town, reluctant to leave with such a poor result. By chance, the falconer met the Earl of Sutherland, who was married to Lennox's sister, and the earl offered to introduce Lallart to Mary. He took the schoolmaster to Stirling, where they found the queen outside, surrounded by her ladies and on the point of leaving for Perth. Lallart bowed deeply and delivered his messages. Mary was frank: she was 'but newly and rawly' arrived and could not give him a full answer, 'but all that she might do for my Lord and my Lady her aunt for their right she would with time and place, desiring my Lady to be always her good aunt as indeed she knew her to be'. With that promise, she mounted her horse and galloped away, leaving Lallart to return home.[34]

Together with her fellowship of servants, friends and spies, Margaret had accomplished a great deal with impressive speed. Darnley was now talked of as a suitor to the Queen of Scots, he had support on both sides of the border, and so far, she had managed to escape any real interference from London. But late in the autumn of 1561 she received instructions from Elizabeth to come south and to bring her boys and Lennox with her. Officially, this concerned her overt friendliness to northern Catholics and failure to abide by the Elizabethan settlement, such that 'the Bishop [of York] dares not visit his diocese or punish any papist'. In truth, Elizabeth's counter-agents had been gathering intelligence on Margaret's spies.

Margaret was torn, terrified of being returned to the Tower or of seeing Darnley put out of the way, but half-convinced that she could bluff her way out of trouble. 'I am told,' said de Quadra, 'that she is resolved not to deny the allegation about the marriage of the queen of Scots as she says it is no crime, and as that Queen is her niece, the daughter of her brother, she thinks she has done no harm in advising her to do what she believes would be the best for her, namely, to marry her son.' If she did, 'all reason for strife would be avoided': Darnley was born in England and Mary would therefore be Elizabeth's heir, either in her own right or as the wife of her English-born husband.

De Quadra thought that the charges about religion were a ruse to make Margaret unpopular with Protestant Londoners, an effort to turn her into a symbol of treacherous papistry. This was a bitter blow to England's Catholics, he wrote, 'as they had placed all their trust in this woman and her son, and if they dared I am sure they would help her, and forces would be forthcoming in the country itself if they had any hopes of help from without'.[35]

14

The Time of Our Trouble

Master Secretary William Cecil had worked too hard to bring about the cross-border amity to let Margaret undermine it by attempting to seize the English throne. Armed with his own network of informants and news-gatherers, he noted the sudden energy of the Lennox-Stewart affinity with a calm that belied his sense of the stakes. To Cecil, their machinations were all of a piece. Margaret's religion, the contacts with France and Spain, the ties to sympathetic Catholics in England and Scotland were all threads of the same dangerous web. The Lennox-Stewarts were at work on their son's behalf, Mary Stewart was the object of all their schemes, and everything was in play: not only Elizabeth's crown, but the Protestant faith on the island of Britain.

As Margaret worked, so did Cecil. Despite their profound religious and political differences, the two of them were usually friendly with each other: Margaret admired Cecil's diligence and effectiveness as a royal servant, while he came to respect her love for her family and her work ethic. In the winter of 1561–2, however, he needed to know her plans in order to counter them. Some of Margaret's servants and confidants would have to be pressured into revealing what they had learned – and Cecil's men knew exactly how to apply that pressure – but for others, it was simply a matter of listening while they talked.

Inevitably, Lennox's old secretary Thomas Bishop was the first weak point. He and Margaret had been enemies from the start and it had been her treatment of him that set off the quarrel with Henry VIII just before the king's death. Bishop was more than happy to tell Cecil all about the gifts Margaret and her family had received from Mary Tudor – taking care to proclaim that in spite of the favours, Mary had always turned to Bishop for advice in Scottish affairs, rather than to 'her dear cousin of Lennox'. Worse, said Bishop, there was Margaret's 'unthankful, ungrateful, and cruel' behaviour towards Elizabeth: '[W]hat she hath otherwise said in secret, if all were known, she deserved not that great mercy that the pitiful nature of her majesty . . . have showed.'[1]

Another early target for Cecil was Francis Yaxley, who was arrested and ordered to explain his dealings with the Spanish ambassadors. The aggressive questioning left him in no doubt that he was in danger. Intimidated and terrified, he disobeyed his captors' command not to write any letters and got a message to Elizabeth's favourite, Robert Dudley. Yaxley sensed he was facing 'all extremity', fearing to be 'undone and cast away', and he begged Dudley 'for the bowels of Christ's passion, if ever you took pity and compassion of faithful subject and true servant of your own, to extend the same towards me'.[2]

In other cases, Cecil and his allies thought it best to move slowly, keeping an eye on the Lennox-Stewarts' messengers in the hope of learning more from them. William, Baron Grey, Warden of the Marches, let Thomas Stewart and William Forbes remain in Berwick for several weeks before seizing them for questioning.[3] When Cecil struck, however, he did it with force and precision. Lennox, in London on business, was arrested and confined in the Tower, leaving Margaret alone in Yorkshire with their sons. Her situation, so promising only weeks before, was suddenly grim. But though lonely and frightened, she was determined to keep Darnley out of Elizabeth's hands, even if it meant facing imprisonment herself.

By the spring of 1562, Margaret could not put off Elizabeth's summons any longer. Facing the inevitable, she came to London and was removed to Sheen, across the river from her old prison at Syon Abbey. Her children did not come with her, and Darnley's whereabouts for the next year remained a mystery. De Quadra reported that he and Charles Stewart were 'in safe hands' in York.[4] John Jewel, the vituperative Protestant pamphleteer who thought that Margaret was a fiercer Catholic even than Mary Tudor, believed that Darnley was in Scotland, and that sympathetic Catholics were plotting to marry him to the Queen of Scots. Still others reported rumours that he was in France.[5] Wherever he was, Margaret seems to have known: she petitioned constantly for Lennox's release but did not mention or plead for Darnley, suggesting that she knew he was not being held and had managed to go into hiding. Arranging an escape or hiding place for Darnley needed forewarning of Cecil's counter-spying and sympathetic assistance. Margaret's friends among the northern Catholic nobility would have been well placed to provide it.

Unbeknownst to Margaret, Cecil turned to Borghese Venturini, Ambassador de Quadra's long-serving and long-disgruntled Italian secretary. It took only a little bribery to get him to turn spy. In his first testimony, he reported de Quadra's belief that England's Catholics would rise up in favour of the Lennox-Stewarts: 'If the King of Spain wishes to support my Lady Margaret and her son . . . [they would have the support] of all the Catholics of the kingdom, and of the majority of the great nobles . . . [they would find] that it will be an easy thing to restore the Catholic religion in this kingdom'.

Venturini went even further in his next declaration, justifying his treachery by implying that he, rather than de Quadra, had

Spain's best interests in mind: 'In all his letters, [de Quadra] has always urged the King and his ministers to take up arms and wage war against the Queen in favour of the papists, and of the son of my lady Margaret . . . The ambassador thinks that we have here pots of money to make war, but we do not have the money, we do not want war with the English!'[6]

De Quadra soon realised the deceit of his secretary, prompting Venturini to quit his service; when the ambassador did his best to make amends and found his old secretary still hostile, he let him go – though Venturini, with supreme want of sensibility, was honestly affronted when de Quadra refused to pay him.[7] Elizabeth summoned de Quadra and accused him of 'always writing ill of her and her affairs', and he retaliated by pointing out that she had spied on him and questioned him about his diplomatic correspondence, 'against all precedent'. When she alleged that de Quadra wanted her overthrown and replaced with Margaret, he conceded that he had discussed Margaret's claim to the throne with the Duchess of Parma, though only as part of a plan for keeping the Lennox-Stewarts out of the French sphere of influence:

> [Elizabeth] at last said I could not deny that I had sent Dr Turner to Flanders to try to get her turned off the throne and substitute others (meaning Lady Margaret). I told her I had sent the doctor to arrange my private affairs and took the opportunity of his going . . . to tell him to give an account to the duchess of Parma of the state of the French negotiations and designs in this country which might be directed to securing the adherence of Lady Margaret to their side by taking her son and marrying him in France, by which means, even if the queen of Scotland . . . were to die, they would still have some claim to a footing in this country.[8]

Cecil observed tartly that 'the K[ing] of Spain is in great passion: his Servants hath secretly betrayed all his practices.'[9]

While Venturini was gathering information on de Quadra, Cecil's men took depositions from Thomas Bishop and William Forbes at the start of May 1562. Bishop now had a chance to unleash his venom: Margaret emerged from his statement as a domineering, greedy, deceitful character. She was power-hungry, aiming at Elizabeth's title and infecting her household with her own treasonous ambitions. According to Bishop, Margaret had 'usurped the name of second personage to the crown . . . and in default of the queen's majesty, she would give place to none'. It went almost without saying that she had no claim: she was not, he argued, English born, as her mother had not come to Harbottle '*in animo remanendi* [in the spirit of remaining]' but rather 'as a passenger and stranger', and soon after returned to Scotland with her daughter. And even if she were English-born, her parents' marriage 'was found null and of none effect from the beginning', so she was 'a mere bastard' – 'mere' was a double-edged adjective in the sixteenth century, meaning either 'nothing more than' or 'totally and unequivocally'.[10] Although a bastard herself, said Bishop, Margaret disparaged Elizabeth's right to the throne, saying that either Mary or Elizabeth had to be illegitimate, and 'as for Queen Mary, [Margaret] said all the world knew that she was lawful, and for herself, she desired nothing but her right'. Margaret wanted the throne herself, and her servants believed as she did, declaring that 'their mistress should rule ere long and they should have the ball at their foot'.

Just as dangerously, Margaret was a Catholic, upholding a false faith, kindling it in her eldest son, and using it to threaten the stability of the kingdom. All of the banned practices of the old religion lived on at Temple Newsam and Settrington: the Mass, the sacrament of confession, praying the Rosary. Darnley had been 'grafted in that devilish papistry' and even Lennox, Bishop's old patron, heard Mass with his wife and son, in a bedchamber decked with 'idols and images' – the devotional art of Catholic worship. Margaret had 'blinded', Bishop wrote, 'many of the gentleman in Yorkshire and some noblemen', and in order to win 'the hearts of papists . . . she hath contemptuously and openly declared her religion'. And where Catholicism could be found, so could all manner of spiritual deviance: 'By mediate persons she useth witches and soothsayers, and hath one within her house.'

All the crimes – the treasonous words, the heresy, the magic – came together in the service of one mortal political sin: Margaret's dealings with Mary Stewart and her plot to bring about the Catholic union of the crowns. Margaret tried to convince her niece Mary of 'what a godly thing it were to have both the realms in one, meaning the question of her son to the Scots queen, who then should be both king of England and Scotland, as her prophesiers at the death of her first son told her'.[11]

William Forbes, examined two days afterwards, either took the same line himself or was led to it by his questioners. His deposition closely echoed that of Bishop, albeit without the two decades' worth of accumulated bitterness underpinning the earlier testimony. In some instances, however, he went further than Bishop – unlike the former secretary, Forbes had been actively involved in Margaret's intelligence-gathering, and he had details that Bishop did not.[12] Forbes singled out the Earl of Westmorland as Margaret's chief ally among the Catholic nobles of the north, bound to her by religion and by love: he 'of all women beareth her his heart'. His professions of loyalty to Elizabeth were mere flattery; all the while, Westmorland and Margaret were reading Lallart's commentaries on the soothsayer Nostradamus and awaiting the day her son would be king. Not only could Lennox not control his wife – she was using her femininity to win the devotion of other men. Forbes also said that she attacked Robert Dudley and his family, a pointed reference to the Dudleys' role in the Jane Grey affair: 'I have heard her rail upon my Lord Robert and his blood, calling them traitors bred.' He repeated the tales of idols and witches, and drew that vague but sinister connection between Margaret, the fire at St Paul's and the dead men in St James's Park.[13]

Many of Bishop's and Forbes's stories are more or less true and confirmed by others examined at the time, especially the details of Margaret's ties to Spain. Some, like Bishop's views on Margaret's legitimacy, are opinions on matters of debate. Occasionally, they are the only sources for particular details that corroborate a broader picture, such as the intricacies of Catholic life at Settrington and Temple Newsam. But they also made crafty use of stereotypes.

Under the terms of the Elizabethan settlement, the parish church became a place in which to worship and show conformity, while the home stayed a haven for individual devotion. There was a distinction between public and private piety, though the idea that a Catholic could believe one thing in his heart and do another before his neighbours, met with swift condemnation from the Congregation of the Inquisition: 'Whosoever shall be ashamed of me and of my words, of him shall the Son of Man be ashamed.'[14] The statutes only applied to men, and it was common for Catholic noblewomen to maintain 'household Catholicism'. Protected from persecution by their sex, their rank and the settlement's line between public and private, they could worship as they liked inside their homes, and ensure that their families and their tenants had access to the sacraments.[15]

But, as Margaret discovered, there were limits to this freedom. Instead of a woman rightly concerned with her household's spiritual well-being, Bishop called her a domineering wife who made her husband act 'against his own nature'.[16] He and Forbes stressed the inversions in the house, where the woman ruled the man, and where the countess and her servants showed disrespect towards the queen and the Protestant nobility. Her taste for Catholicism was also a taste for witchcraft, and her royal blood, instead of offering social immunity, became a threat. Finally, the privacy of the Lennox-Stewart estates became a symbol of Catholic deceit, outward-looking rather than sheltered from the world. If there existed an acceptable Catholic noblewoman, Bishop and Forbes painted Margaret as her dark, inverted counterpart.

At the end of May 1562, Cecil drew up a list of questions to ask Margaret: what had she said about the supposed bastardy of Mary and Elizabeth Tudor? What had she heard about the men stricken 'with sudden death' on the day St Paul's steeple had burned down? What had made her say 'that touching the right to the crown, she would give place to none of the rest'? What message had she had from Lord Seton 'concerning his furtherance in setting forth of my Lord Darnley'? Beneath the questions were a series of prompts, reminders to himself: the names of her messengers, the charge of 'a fool in the house', and, ominously, 'Scottish Queen'.[17]

Members of the Privy Council came to Sheen to put Cecil's questions to Margaret and to charge her both with claiming to be heir to the crown and with plotting to marry her son to the Queen of Scots.[18] She defended herself and refused to give in to their intimidation – or, as Sir Henry Sidney recounted it, she was 'very obstinate in her answers to the Council'.[19] Her protestations did not convince them and it was decided to keep both Margaret and Lennox imprisoned.[20] With the Lennox-Stewarts cut off from their networks, Cecil could bring the full power of Tudor intelligence-gathering and intimidation techniques to bear on Margaret's servants.

Her servant Hugh Allan gamely tried to defend the Lennox-Stewarts, saying 'he spoke never a word of my Lady nor of no letters beyond the seas'. But when Yaxley named him as one of his messengers, Allan's examiners questioned him over and over again, unleashing a broadside of accusations. Their notes allow us to see just how relentless his interrogators were: 'Ye have been a continual messenger betwixt Yaxley and my Lady . . . he himself now at length sayeth ye know all. Ye knew he resorted to the Spanish ambassador, ye knew he had conference sometimes with other noblemen, sometimes with sundry clerks and secretaries . . . Ye carried like as this last touching the marriage, which ye would never have told unless ye had been pressed as you now be . . .'

Just as damningly, they told Allan, Arthur Lallart claimed that the two of them had 'been always secret friends in [the] house, and what the one knew, that knew [the] other . . . ye understood also that the laird of Galston was dispatched and the laird of Bar to the queen of Scots, especially Galston, and not only to entreat of my lord's living but also upon the marriage'. Piling crime upon crime, Allan had also questioned the legitimacy of the Protestant regime in Scotland: 'Ye said ye could not tell whether ye should call the lords there of [the] Congregation rebels or lords . . .'

Allan was not only a messenger, but an information-gatherer in his own right and well informed about Margaret's other spies, including the fact that 'one Brinkloo, my Lady's servant, lay here at London as a spy for her and had intelligence with the Spanish ambassador'. No 'natural Englishman', his examiners declared, could tolerate 'these lewd practices'. At last, though Allan denied delivering many of Yaxley's letters, he confessed that he had served as a go-between from Yaxley to Margaret. Not only that, he had discussed 'the respect and title of my lady and her son' with him, declaring that 'the same was likely upon the charge to take effect'.[21]

Thomas Bishop aided Cecil once again by taking letters to the Earl of Rutland, President of the Council of the North in Yorkshire, with instructions to interrogate both the servant Ralph Lacy and a priest known as 'Little Sir William', believed to have said Mass for the Lennox-Stewarts.[22] The priest was lucky: there was no proof against him and he was set free, but Lacy fared less well. Examined on 3 August 1562, he also denied as much as he could. Lacy admitted having delivered letters to Lennox's cousin d'Aubigny, but claimed he had only exchanged commonplaces with him, letting him know that Darnley had grown into 'a tall young gentleman'. He had not brought back letters from France, only instructions to commend d'Aubigny to the family. Although Lacy did his loyal best to avoid implicating the Lennox-Stewarts in any wrongdoing, he had returned from France to Settrington to find Margaret in Sheen and Lennox in the Tower, and was evidently so unnerved that he was 'not minded to serve them anymore but to take a farm and live thereof'.[23]

But Cecil's examiners would not take Lacy at his word, and one week later they questioned him again. 'We know ye have dissembled with us in certain things,' they said, adding 'ye will be confronted'. Stubbornly, he denied knowing of any messages sent to de Quadra; Lacy declared 'he hath neither heard in France nor in England of any marriage to have been brought about betwixt the Scottish queen and the Lord Darnley' and swore 'he hath not heard the Lady Lennox speak any evil of the queen's majesty nor otherwise than dutifully'.

There were, however, things that Lacy could not deny. To his knowledge, Margaret had not spoken of her claim to the throne and he could not see where any such claim would come from, but despite this, 'he heard it talked in that house that if King Henry VIII his will had not been, the Lady Lennox had had a title to the crown'. Moreover, Margaret had indeed written to the Countess of Feria in her own hand.[24] Lacy was imprisoned in York Castle.[25]

Yaxley was put through another round of questioning and labelled 'a right "Spaniziard", false and unnatural to his country . . . an espial here for my Lady Lennox these two years'. At length, 'with much ado', he confessed 'sundry writings sent from him to my Lady Lennox'.[26]

From her prison, Margaret began a long correspondence campaign, writing letter after letter to Cecil and having each one delivered by her servant Thomas Fowler. Cecil was responsible for her imprisonment but she could see that he was also her best hope of assistance: 'I cannot choose but trouble you with this my letter, for that I have no kin and not many friends to sue for me – if I had, I should have received some comfortable answer.'[27] In spite of this, she reminded him that she was still a member of the royal family: the queen aside, she said, she had 'no other kin in this realm but only by her highness's father's side'.[28]

Margaret knew of the attacks on her legitimacy and denied them, writing that she was surprised the queen was willing to listen to such slanders: 'I thought her majesty would rather have fortified and strengthened me . . . then to have hearing or sufferance to such a manifest wrong and injury against me, her poor kinswoman – but even as God hath made me so I am lawful daughter to the queen of Scots and the earl of Angus, which none alive is able to make me otherwise without doing wrong'.[29] She conceded the undeniable fact that Lallart had gone into Scotland without Elizabeth's permission, but wrote that 'for my part, except it were for the schoolmaster going into Scotland . . . I can remember no offence'.[30]

All the while they were away from Yorkshire, Margaret and Lennox were falling deeper into 'impoverishment which daily increaseth to our utter undoing'. Their household goods, livestock and lands were left in chaos, going 'to ruin and decay for lack of looking to', and she feared being left 'utterly impoverished now in my old age'.[31] Imprisonment was expensive in and of itself: she had to furnish her rooms at Sheen and pay her living costs, and was eventually reduced to borrowing.[32]

Worst of all, though her children were safe, Margaret knew what it was like to be imprisoned in the Tower, and she was deeply afraid for Lennox. 'Remember,' she asked Cecil, 'my intolerable griefs, which ariseth divers ways as well by my lord's imprisonment and mine, being thereby separated.'[33] Lennox fell ill in the Tower – with, Margaret said, 'a disease which solitariness is most against'. It is hard to say what this might have been, though the Lieutenant of the Tower complained to Cecil that Lennox was 'unquiet', suffering 'extreme passions' and disturbing the prison with his cries: '[T]ruly I am much weary of his continual exclamations.'[34] She begged that he be allowed more freedom or be given permission to come to Sheen: 'If it might please her majesty to suffer him to come to Sheen and to be kept here as I am, we should think ourselves much bound to her highness, for otherwise I know he cannot continue without danger of his life.'[35]

Unsurprisingly, given Bishop's testimony, Elizabeth saw Margaret as the leading half of the Lennox-Stewart partnership – and Lennox was not handling captivity well, alternately blustering that 'I did such service as I suppose my enemies, who now gather the fruit which I have travailed for, will never do the like', and then offering to give up all his lands in England in exchange for freedom.[36] But the implication that Margaret was Lennox's puppeteer was offensive to both of them, casting doubt on her femininity and Lennox's masculinity. Elizabeth demanded that Lennox's submission 'should come of himself and not by Margaret's teaching', and Margaret shot back: '[M]y lord needs not to learn at my hand how to use himself to the prince, wherein he was expert ere he came in England, and since his coming here has needed no such schoolmaster, though perchance some hath gone about to incense both her highness and Council to the contrary.'[37]

Although she was quick to spot any slight on Lennox's honour, Margaret wrote that captivity dulled her own wits, excusing her 'imbecility and weakness of brain' to Cecil.[38] To Margaret, Elizabeth's behaviour seemed capricious and unfair. It had first appeared to her, she wrote, that Lennox's 'liberty rested only upon his submission'. Now that he had made his submission to the queen, 'it pleaseth the queen's majesty not to accept it, I cannot tell what to think thereof, unless it be to prolong the time of our trouble'.[39]

Elizabeth fell ill with smallpox in the autumn of 1562, which gave Cecil a reprieve from Margaret's letters and Margaret a chance to reassert her loyalty. She held off writing until she had word that Elizabeth was recovered and then told Cecil she would 'pray to God daily to increase Her Majesty's health and strength and long to reign over us'.[40]

As the winter drew nearer, Margaret's petitions on Lennox's behalf grew more fervent, citing 'the long time of my lord's imprisonment and mine, and absence the one from the other, especially he being in the Tower, the winter come and that house both unwholesome and cold'.[41] She urged Cecil to remember the 'time of the year and ill air of the place where my lord is, he being sickly', asking for forgiveness, so that wherever Elizabeth chose to put them, 'we may be together'.[42] At last, in late November, Lennox got permission to leave the Tower and join her at Sheen.

Margaret was overjoyed, thanking Cecil for using his 'good means' to free her husband and reunite him with her.[43] It was not, however, an act of simple magnanimity. Elizabeth's brush with smallpox had terrified her advisors, and the succession was once more at the forefront of the political agenda. There was a surfeit of claimants to the throne, and although Margaret had been labelled a conniving, treacherous heretic, there were others who appeared even more dangerous.

15

Secret Charge

An agitated parliament met at Westminster in January 1563. Elizabeth's bout of smallpox had been a powerful reminder that there was no obvious heir to the throne. On the opening day the dean of St Paul's preached a sermon urging Elizabeth to marry and settle the succession.[1] Two weeks later both houses pleaded with the queen to come to a decision, warning of the 'evident and present danger and peril to all states and sorts of men of this realm' that would arise 'through want of understanding to whom they should hold their allegiance and duties, whereby much innocent blood is like to be shed'.[2] But Elizabeth was unmoved and unimpressed with the parliamentary meddling.[3]

Captive, impoverished and cut off from her network of friends and retainers, Margaret was now the least troubling of Elizabeth's relatives. The prospective marriage of Mary Stewart and Don Carlos of Spain, once rejected by Philip II as not worth the English and French displeasure it would provoke, was once again a possibility. In England, Jane Grey's eldest surviving sister, Katherine, had two years earlier married the Earl of Hertford in secret and without Elizabeth's leave. When the queen learned of the wedding and of Katherine's pregnancy, she sent both Katherine and Hertford to the Tower, were they had been ever since, their son declared the illegitimate child of an invalid marriage. When parliament met, Katherine was in double disgrace: she was eight months pregnant and her optimistic supporters were trying to get her named Elizabeth's heir. The Lennox-Stewarts, by comparison, seemed a minor problem.

But Margaret still believed that she could match her son to the Queen of Scots. Elizabeth's sudden show of magnanimity to the Lennox-Stewarts gave Margaret hope that she might get the support of both the English queen and Mary for her plans, but she was ready to act without Elizabeth. Before long, she was playing an even higher-stakes game than she had been before her imprisonment: she was still in close and secret contact with Spain and Scotland, but rather than plotting from Yorkshire, she was acting from within the paranoid world of Elizabeth's court.

She had to bide her time. Cecil sent one of Margaret's messengers back to Sheen with a curt reply warning her not to ask for too much, and she hurried to conciliate him: 'I am sorry that you impute me to be so unthankful as to blame you for the slow proceedings of my suit, considering that always I have rested and hath had my full confidence in all my suits only on you, not attempting any other but by your advice. And to say the truth, I have from time to time understood you to have taken such pains in soliciting my causes that I have rather just occasion to give you thanks and to requite your gentleness if it may lie in my power.'[4] For Margaret, it was easier to be patient now that she had Lennox back and that it seemed they would eventually get their freedom.

Her hopes were vindicated. In February, word came that Margaret and Lennox could return to London. Their jailor, Sir Richard Sackville, was a cousin of Elizabeth's on the Boleyn side. He moved them from the rural environs of Sheen to his house in crowded Fleet Street, a short walk west of the still-damaged spire of St Paul's Cathedral.[5] To be free, however, was not enough for Margaret. She wanted forgiveness and preferment, and for those, she and Lennox needed to see Elizabeth in person. As she wrote to Cecil, 'notwithstanding that those of her highness' Council did declare to my lord and me that her majesty had forgiven and forgotten all her displeasure towards us and was pleased to set us at liberty, yet we cannot account ourselves to have received the same so long as we be restrained from doing our duties to her majesty's presence'.[6] If Cecil could arrange this, 'I shall account myself more bound to you than in all the rest, for that it shall be most to my comfort of any worldly thing, as knoweth God.'[7]

Elizabeth left Margaret to fret. She had freed Margaret and Lennox to serve as a tactical counterweight to Mary and the Greys, not because she thought they were innocent. If she could split English Catholics over the succession, getting some to favour Mary and others the Lennox-Stewarts, all the while also proving that she could not be manoeuvred into naming Katherine Grey as heir, she could leave the succession unsettled until such time as she chose to settle it – if she chose to at all.[8]

Cecil also stalled, in spite of Margaret's relentless letter-writing. He wanted a stability that only a sure succession could provide, and he was gathering evidence on Margaret's legitimacy. He had already examined a Scot named Alexander Pringle, who had told him that Margaret's parents had never been married: the upshot was that Margaret 'was openly taken and reputed a bastard in Scotland'.[9] He also interviewed William Barlow, Bishop of Chichester, and Margaret's old friend William Howard, the men who had gone to Scotland in 1535 to give the Order of the Garter to James V. Although their accounts differed in details, both agreed that Margaret was a bastard and that Henry VIII had been told as much.[10] Cecil himself kept a book of pedigrees, noting the bare facts: Margaret had been born in England, her parents had divorced and both of them had remarried.[11]

A man by the name of John Hales was circulating a tract in favour of Katherine Grey, stoutly denying Mary's claim on the grounds of foreign birth: 'If you will put strangers and right Englishmen in one case, what availeth the liberty of England?' Margaret did not emerge unscathed, and Hales's writings so closely echo Bishop's deposition that it seems certain he was familiar with it. Sometimes he elaborated on the images. Margaret was not English, as Angus had come to England as 'a guest, or as a bird that leaveth for a time her native country while the foul weather lasteth, or as a wild beast, that is chased with hounds out of his haunt, and flyeth till he perceive they persecute him no longer'. The child of a Scotsman born in England could not be called English: 'No man can serve two masters at one time (sayeth the right law-maker, and also common reason).' And even if all this logic went unheeded and Margaret could be considered English, she was still a bastard.[12]

If the Lennox-Stewarts overstepped their bounds again, Cecil had evidence that he could use against their claim, so it was finally safe to let them come back to court. Elizabeth at last relented and summoned the Lennox-Stewarts to her. Margaret made condign obeisance to the queen, protesting her innocence and loyalty, and swearing that she would never let Darnley marry without Elizabeth's consent.[13]

Darnley came out of hiding and was reunited with his parents, and he, Lennox and Margaret spent the summer in Elizabeth's company.[14] For Margaret, who had not seen her son for a year, it was a heady few months. Elizabeth was taken with her young cousin and before long he was the subject of court gossip, mentioned as a suitor to the Queen of Scots or even as Elizabeth's successor in his own right. De Quadra wrote of him constantly. Although the ambassador had poor contacts in Scotland, he suspected that there were Scots who would prefer Darnley for their king if Mary wed the Austrian Archduke Charles than the wealthy Spanish Don Carlos: '. . . many of her people will incline rather to Lady Margaret's son than to the Archduke, because if they cannot come into the hands of your Majesty they would rather have an Englishman than a poor foreigner'.[15]

It was around this time that Margaret and Lennox, despite their straitened finances, commissioned a double portrait of their sons. The boys were both dressed in sumptuous black, Charles in the long skirts of a small boy, Darnley in doublet and hose, emphasising his athletic legs. Margaret was already a keen collector of timepieces, and she fastened one around Darnley's neck for the occasion. There was a family resemblance between her sons – they shared the same reddish-brown hair – but while Charles looked tired and baggy-eyed, Darnley was a striking young nobleman: beardless but showily handsome, his hand resting protectively on his younger brother's shoulder, a sword at his waist.

Furthermore, Elizabeth was finally showing some willingness to help the Lennox-Stewarts recover their estates in Scotland. William Maitland of Lethington had arrived at court and Margaret and Lennox asked Elizabeth to intervene on their behalf either with him or with Mary herself. One week later, Elizabeth wrote to Mary on behalf of 'our dear cousin the lady Margaret and her husband the Earl of Lennox', calling to mind 'the nearness of her blood to us both' and asking that she give some consideration to their suits.[16] They retreated to Yorkshire in the autumn, but before long were back at court.[17]

Was Elizabeth being sincere? On the one hand, the Lennox-Stewarts had already proven that they could create difficulties in England and it would have been a relief to get them out of the country. On the other, they were likely to be even more troublesome in Scotland, where they would be free to pursue their own ambitions for their son and to make themselves into a terrible threat to the Protestant Anglo-Scottish amity. They would be Catholic magnates in their own right and as parents of a Catholic suitor to the Queen of Scots – for such a triumph, their over-extended English estates would be only a small sacrifice. The likeliest explanation is that Elizabeth did not think Mary would restore them to their titles and estates. After all, Lennox was a traitor and letting Margaret into Scotland would reawaken the old question of the earldom of Angus. For Elizabeth, there was no apparent downside to writing the letter: it would please Lennox and Margaret without changing the status quo.[18]

But Elizabeth herself then altered the situation by proposing that Mary should take Robert Dudley as her husband. From Elizabeth's perspective, this made good sense. Dudley was devoted to her as well as being a convinced Protestant, and if Mary were married to him, she could not choose a Frenchman or a Spaniard. Unfortunately for Elizabeth, it would have been a very bad bargain for Mary. She was being asked to make a marriage that would neither strengthen her claim to the English throne nor bring her a European alliance. It was also beneath her dignity as a Guise and as a queen: marrying a Scottish earl would have been one matter, but taking a minor English nobleman with no title of his own and making him into the King of Scots was quite another.

Thomas Randolph, the diplomat charged with making the case for the Dudley marriage in Scotland, used the language of amity to describe the good that the match would bring the Scots: 'I have perpetual peace to offer them, a firm amity to assure them of.'[19] But it was not going to be easy, not least because none of the three participants actually wanted it to happen: Mary wanted a more impressive match, Dudley did not want to move to Scotland, and although Elizabeth believed the plot could work, she inwardly wanted Dudley to stay in England and she had to force herself to make the offer. Meanwhile, Mary continued to negotiate a Spanish match, though the death of Ambassador de Quadra slowed the pace of talks.[20]

Two issues refused to go away: the question of Lennox's return to Scotland and the related matter of Darnley's marital prospects. In April 1564, Mary gave her consent to Lennox's homecoming, and many in Scotland expected that Margaret and the children would arrive with him. John Knox, digesting the news, wrote that 'God's providence is inscrutable to man', before confessing that 'to be plain . . . that journey and progress I like not'.[21] The return of the Lennox-Stewarts did not bode well for Scotland's godly Reformation.

For Margaret, it was an uncertain summer. She lived at court, was often in the queen's company, and in July 1564 served with her as joint godmothers to Cecil's daughter Elizabeth.[22] Darnley, now a young man, was also becoming a regular presence, and Margaret was exceptionally proud of him. She even allowed him to inscribe a poem in the Devonshire Manuscript, the first new entry in two decades. In a slim italic hand – a hand neither of his parents seem to have been able to write – he entered twelve lines of rhyming verse on the popular theme of the wooing lover:

My hope is you for to obtain
Let not my hope be lost in vain.
Forget not my pains manifold,
Nor my meaning to you untold.
And eke [also] with deeds I did you crave,
With sweet words you for to have.

To my hap and hope condescend,
Let not Cupido in vain his bow to bend.
Nor us two lovers, faithful, true,
Like a bow made of bowing yew.
But now receive by your industry and art,
Your humble servant Harry Stewart.[23]

Elizabeth made Darnley part of her carefully orchestrated welcome for the new Spanish ambassador, Guzman de Silva, who arrived at Richmond Palace on 27 June 1564. She sent Darnley to escort the new ambassador to her presence chamber – where she impressed him with her fluency in Italian and Latin – and to guide him back to his barge after his first meeting with her. De Silva heard it rumoured that Elizabeth was after all going to propose Darnley as an alternative marriage prospect for Mary.[24] On the other hand, though Lennox had leave from Mary to go back to Scotland, Elizabeth and Cecil were reluctant to send him. It was only in September that he was finally allowed to depart.[25] After their spells of lonely imprisonment, Margaret wept at yet another separation from Lennox.[26] But she was otherwise in hopeful spirits, assuring the new Spanish ambassador that Mary would never marry Robert Dudley: 'She says he is undeceived and has told her so himself.'[27]

Darnley was also with Elizabeth in September 1564 when Sir James Melville arrived at court. A young Scotsman in his late twenties, Melville had served Mary Stewart in Scotland, France and on the Continent, and now he 'had a secret charge' from her: it was his task to meet Margaret and get leave for Darnley to go into Scotland, so that he could see the country for himself and then accompany his father back to England. Melville did not reveal this to Elizabeth, though she told him that Darnley was one of the two suitors she was considering offering to Mary. Perceptively, Elizabeth could see that Melville took more interest in Darnley than in Dudley, now a noble in his own right as Earl of Leicester. Darnley was bearing the sword of honour before her 'as nearest prince of the blood' and the queen, pointing towards him, observed to Melville '[Y]e like better of yonder lang [tall] lad.' Melville demurred: 'No woman of spirit would make choice of such a man, that was liker a woman than a man; for he was very lusty, beardless, and lady-faced.' He was doing his best to keep Elizabeth off the scent, for he 'had no will that she should think that I liked of him, or had any eye or dealing that way'.

Meanwhile, Margaret arranged to meet in secret with Melville. They impressed each other: he later wrote that Margaret 'was a very wise and discreet matron, and had many favourers in England for the time'. She, in turn, decided to trust Melville and enlisted him to be her messenger. Margaret offered him messages and advice to give to Mary, as well as a series of gifts: a diamond ring for the queen; an emerald for Lennox; a diamond for the queen's half-brother James Stewart, by now the Earl of Moray; a ruby ring for Melville's brother Robert. Drawing on her own collection of watches, she sent William Maitland of Lethington an 'orlege or montre' set with diamonds and rubies. To Melville, her aims were obvious: '[S]he was still in good hope, that her son my Lord Darnley should come better speed than the earl of Leicester.'[28] Later that month, Mary told Elizabeth she was planning to restore Lennox and Margaret.[29]

Now the question became whether or not Darnley should also be allowed to go to Scotland. Margaret was determined that he go, which put her at odds with both Elizabeth and her counsellors. Unusually, the queen and her advisors were of one mind on Scottish policy: they doubted the wisdom of letting Darnley go, though Leicester – who might otherwise have been sent north of the border himself – was more sympathetic to the idea.[30] Then Elizabeth began to vacillate, one day congratulating Margaret on Lennox's restoration and offering to give Darnley licence, the next declaring that Lennox was not being frank with her and revoking the grant. Margaret, by now well versed in Elizabeth's sudden changes of mind, was able to talk her into re-giving permission, but the queen retracted it once again.

Margaret had to hold her nerve as the queen's ministers grew ever more perplexed about her motives. 'This is the way with everything – absolutely no certainty,' vented an exasperated Ambassador de Silva in a despatch to Philip. Margaret told him that Elizabeth and her ministers behaved towards her 'as if they were frantic', and de Silva agreed that they 'are so suspicious, so excited, and so anxious . . . [that] certainly she is not far wrong'.[31]

In Scotland, Darnley's return had been expected since the summer, and anxiety was in the air. On 7 November 1564 the English diplomat Thomas Randolph wrote to Elizabeth that Margaret and Darnley were both awaited. Randolph was of two minds about Darnley's proposed 'release' into Scotland. He felt the same way he had about Lennox's return – 'or rather worse'. Darnley, married to the queen of Scots, could upset the religious balance in Scotland. But if Margaret were able to get hold of the earldom of Angus, she might damage her own claim and her sons' to the English throne: 'If she claim here the earldom of Angus, there will be a gap open to disprove a greater title that she pretendeth unto, nearer your Majesty's self than that is which she seeketh for here . . . I trust she shall be all the days of her life, or any of hers, far enough from wearing of a crown.'[32]

Randolph may have imagined that holding a Scottish title would make it difficult for Margaret to claim English birth, but she did not need to have been born in Scotland to be recognised as the lawful Countess of Angus. In light of later events, however, he had a point: if Margaret had asserted a successful claim to her father's earldom, thereby alienating all her Douglas relatives, it would have been almost impossible to win them over to her plans for Darnley.

The winter of 1564 was one of the bitterest that Scotland could remember, and the members of parliament assembled in snow-covered Edinburgh did not dawdle over their work. Lennox was welcomed home and restored to his rights after two decades in English service. Within a week he was boasting that his son would marry the Scottish queen. Thomas

Randolph downplayed the threat. Before Lennox's arrival, Darnley had been an unknown quantity and a topic of constant gossip, but now he was little discussed. Randolph told Cecil that Mary had no love for the Lennox-Stewarts: the marriage, 'by that which hath been spoken of her own mouth, both of [Darnley] and his mother . . . shall never take effect if otherwise she may have her desire'.[33] He did not know of the exchange of gifts or of the secret communication between the countess and the queen.

All the same, Margaret frightened him. He feared her temper, her ambition, and above all her Catholicism: 'The father is now here well known, the mother more feared a great deal than beloved of any that knoweth her.' He invoked the spectre of Mary Tudor:

> I am not so forgetful of my duty . . . that to think that my Lord Darnley should marry this Queen and his mother to bear that stroke with her that she bore with Queen Mary, which she is like to do, as you can conjecture the causes why, would alienate as many minds from the Queen's Majesty my sovereign by sending home as great a plague unto this country, as that which to her majesty's great honour and perpetual love of the faithful and godly she drove out of the same when the French were forced to retire themselves that daily sat in their necks [of their harbours] with ready knives to cut their throats.[34]

Margaret was free, at court, and Countess of Lennox in fact as well as in title for the first time in her marriage, but to Randolph, she was still the woman who had been rightfully imprisoned in Sheen: scheming, ruthless and Catholic, determined to restore the old religion, unite the crowns and reinvent herself as the power behind the British throne.

16

Running at the Ring

One February morning in 1565, Margaret oversaw the final preparations for a long journey. Trunks were already packed with travel provisions, clothes for the hard Scottish winter, tokens and gifts to smooth Darnley's first entrance into his father's home country. The year had begun well. For the first time in years Margaret and the queen exchanged gifts on 1 January, Elizabeth presenting her with a set of gilt bowls together with a salt-and-pepper box.[1] Then, Margaret had at last got the long hoped-for permission: Darnley was free to go to Scotland. After months of refused requests, promises of good faith and furtive messages to Scottish, French and Spanish ambassadors, the moment had come for him to depart. As Margaret looked at him, it is easy to imagine what she felt: grief at the coming absence of her cherished son; tremendous pride in his looks and manners, his accomplishments, his prospects; and perhaps, mingled with the excitement, fear. They both knew what was at stake: the hand of the Queen of Scots.

But there were other things that Margaret did not know, or that she refused to see. Her charming son, raised in her devoutly Catholic household, was a craven young man of no real religious convictions. His classical education and elegant handwriting belied his abysmal political instincts and utter want of common sense. And as he vanished to the racket of horses' hooves, he was leaving her and her advice behind for ever.

Ostensibly, he was going to help his father in the restoration of his estates and to learn something about the country – Darnley was the heir to at least one Scottish earldom but had never been to Scotland. Randolph's letter of the previous November suggests that the earldom of Angus may also have been a factor, and that Margaret had given Darnley the task of meeting with their Douglas relations. There is no doubt that he had good reason to go to Scotland, but Darnley was attractive, Catholic and Tudor-blooded, and there were long-standing rumours that he was a suitor to the Queen of Scots. Elizabeth had long been reluctant to let him go, so why did she suddenly change her mind?

In the absence of letters to Thomas Randolph explaining the decision, the reasoning behind Darnley's 'release' remains a mystery. The choice may have been Elizabeth's: it is possible she agreed with Randolph's observation that the Lennox-Stewarts would be better off ensconced as Scottish nobles than as claimants to the English throne. Other observers gave her credit for a longer-term strategy: that she hoped Mary would wed Darnley, rather than Dudley or a foreign prince – although Elizabeth was always reluctant to indicate a favoured successor, and matching Darnley and the Queen of Scots would certainly have made them and their children her obvious heirs. It could have been a feint from Dudley, who had no desire to move to Scotland.[2] In the envoy Melville's view, it was Cecil's doing rather than Elizabeth's.

Cecil did not want either Darnley or Dudley to marry the Queen of Scots; his goal was to keep Mary single for as long as he could, buying himself time to settle the English succession decisively on some other heir. He believed that Darnley would not marry without Elizabeth's consent, since his family had lands in England that would be forfeit and since his mother was still at court, likely to pay the price of any disobedience.[3] With Elizabeth and Mary still in talks and Mary not rushing to make a foreign marriage, the gamble seemed less risky than it was. If this really was Cecil's strategy, there were factors he failed to take into account: the fact of Mary's independence as a queen in her own right, the strength of Elizabeth's reluctance to name a successor, and the intensity of Margaret's ambition for her son.

Before long, Darnley was in Scotland and on his best behaviour. He stayed three days in Edinburgh, waiting to hear from his father whether he should join Lennox or go to Mary, who was then at the cliff-top castle of Sir John Wemyss in Fife. Randolph met Darnley twice and found him distasteful: 'There are here a great number that do wish him well. Others doubt what he will prove, and deeplier consider what is fit for the fate of their country, than (as they call him) a fair jolly young man.' Still, he conceded that 'his courteous dealing with all men deserveth great praise and is well spoken of' – and he lent Darnley a pair of good horses so that he could continue his journey. Lennox told him to go to the queen, and on 17 February 1565 he met Mary.[4]

We do not know what Darnley made of Mary, but she was certainly impressed with him. Although younger than she was, her cousin was athletic and tall – and Mary stood nearly six feet. Darnley, she declared, 'was the lustiest and best-proportioned lang [tall] man that she had seen', and he had been 'well-instructed from his youth in all honest and comely exercises'.[5] The princely upbringing paid dividends: Darnley could turn a galliard, play the lute, join the queen in hunting and hawking.[6]

He took care to offend as few people as possible. Just as Margaret had been careful to court Protestants as well as Catholics, she and Lennox seem to have instructed Darnley to make himself agreeable to Scottish reformers. He attended John Knox's sermons and became acquainted with Mary's Protestant half-brother James Stewart, Earl of Moray.[7] Moray, once destined for a Church career, had become an inveterate politician: chilly, pious and devoted to the Reformation. Neither Moray nor anybody else in Scotland seems to have believed Darnley to be a Catholic ideologue, which was an accomplishment given his family's reputation in England.

But that did not mean everybody was glad to have him in Scotland. Randolph still saw him as a mother's boy under Margaret's thumb, reporting with a sneer that 'My Lord Darnley, though I would not have it known to my Lady's grace his mother, hath taken a little cold.'[8] At first, Randolph was inclined to downplay the risk of Mary choosing Darnley, but others were more anxious. The Earl of Argyll, a devout reformer and a cousin of the Duke of Châtelherault, told Randolph how unhappy he was about the Lennox-Stewarts' return. Darkly, he declared 'that the affections of women are uncertain'.[9] Many reformers did not like the idea of a Catholic marrying the queen, no matter how many Protestant services he attended.

Margaret was still at the English court, guarding her favour with Elizabeth and careful not to reveal her hopes for Darnley too openly. On Shrove Tuesday she dined with the queen and the French ambassador at a banquet given by Dudley, watching the action of the afternoon tournament, listening to the evening masque on the relative merits of chastity and marriage.[10] In those first critical days she and Darnley were still in contact, careful not to say too much since they were exchanging letters via Randolph.[11] She soon had word, however, of how warmly Darnley had been welcomed.

This was exactly what Margaret had hoped to hear. She wrote in haste to de Silva, near to crowing at Darnley's reception. Moreover, the French were now courting her, offering their support for the match, although Margaret told de Silva she suspected this was merely an attempt to learn what she had planned and might even be Elizabeth's doing – further binding the Spanish ambassador to her cause by casting suspicion on the French.

She affirmed her trust in Spain, saying 'that she and her children have no other refuge but [Philip], to whom she and they will always remain faithful'. Margaret also asked for Spanish support for the Darnley match, or for the Lennox-Stewarts themselves in the event that Elizabeth died childless. De Silva advised her to keep in contact with the French, promising that he would do the like 'as proof of the great affection [Philip] bears her for many reasons and especially for her high Christian character'.[12]

Margaret then had a stroke of luck that she could not have hoped for. Elizabeth changed the terms of the deal with the Scottish queen, writing her a letter on 5 March announcing that she would settle the succession only once she – Elizabeth – was married or formally decided not to marry. Randolph received the letter nine days later and realised with horror that Elizabeth meant to break her promise to name Mary her heir if she married Dudley. He took a day to decide what to do next. Reluctantly, he delivered the letter to Mary on 16 March, and despite his earnest efforts to convince her nothing had changed, Mary answered:

> [S]o long time to keep me in doubt, and now to answer me with nothing, I find great fault, and fear it shall turn to her discredit more than my loss. I will content myself with my smaller portion and maintain that as God will give me grace; when better cometh it shall be thankfully received of Him, I assure you, and of non other. I would that I might have been most bound to my sister, your mistress; seeing that cannot be, I will not fail in any good offices towards her, but to lippen [rely] or trust much from hence further in her for that matter I will not.

She strode out of the room, leaving Randolph sputtering and Moray 'stark mad' with fear that the Anglo-Scottish amity was teetering and set to tumble. The next day, Mary stood on the sands of Leith and watched Darnley 'running at the ring'. A wooden post had been set up and a small hoop suspended from it. Darnley mounted his horse, picked up a short lance and charged down the beach, aiming to put his weapon through the ring. It took significant skill, but executed well there was no more dashing feat of athleticism – and the queen did not look away.[13]

Mary was falling in love with Darnley and he was becoming a source of ever-greater worry to Randolph, who said 'in wisdom he doth not much differ from his father', but the honour Mary showed him 'maketh him think no little thing of himself', and there were many around him ready to say 'that there is no less goodwill born unto him by many of this nation than that they think him a fit partner for such a Queen'.[14] Randolph brooded, telling his fellow diplomat Sir Nicholas Throckmorton that it had been a mistake to let Darnley come: 'This Darling of yours is so dandled amongst us that I fear we shall show some part of our folly.'[15]

By mid-April, Randolph was convinced that disaster was near. He met with Châtelherault, who gloomily told him that the Hamiltons were soon to be 'quite overthrown . . . [H]e trusted much in the Queen's favour towards him; now he seeth his present undoing, and all his adversaries' fetches [plots] tending to that end. The godly cry out and think themselves undone. No hope now of any sure establishment of Christ's true religion but that all shall turn to confusion.'[16]

At this critical moment, Darnley became sick. He was afflicted with stabbing pains in his stomach and head, and de Silva reported that it was smallpox.[17] It was, in fact, probably recently acquired syphilis, picked up shortly before or somewhere along the journey north.[18] But even venereal disease seemed to work in Darnley's favour. Mary visited him constantly, moving the Earl of Bedford to write that 'it appeareth by her tenderness over him that she feared not whether the sickness were infectious'. Margaret, he was certain, 'will like well that her son is so much made of there'.[19] When Margaret did hear that he had recovered and that Mary was being so solicitous with her ministrations, she was sure that her plan was going well.[20]

The days of entente, however, were over. As Margaret was preparing to leave her apartments, she received orders from Elizabeth to keep to her chamber. Margaret had had secret communication with a foreign ruler and should 'consider herself a prisoner'. Knowing Elizabeth's changeable mind, Margaret tried to bluff. She protested that she had only just received the news from Scotland and had been coming to show the letters to the queen. In response, Elizabeth told her she should think herself lucky: she would still be allowed to receive guests, a privilege not afforded to most prisoners. If Margaret had not realised it before, it now became clear: not only was Elizabeth not going to support the match, she was going to punish Margaret harshly if Darnley dared to marry the Queen of Scots.

But if Elizabeth thought she had put her cousin out of play, she was wrong: Margaret had spent more than three years working for this marriage and she refused to be defeated now. She smuggled a message out to de Silva, saying all was going Darnley's way and asking him to tell Maitland that Spain was in favour of the match.[21] And there was still one final gambit that she could make in Scotland.

The Douglases opposed Darnley's suit. The family had tended towards Protestantism since Angus's day and they were allied with the Hamiltons, both politically and by family ties – Margaret's cousin Morton and Châtelherault had married sisters, which also meant that the same strain of mental illness ran in both their families. Randolph wrote that there was 'no small fear' among the Douglases about what might ensue if Mary wed

Darnley, though he tried to convince 'them in good hope the best I can that there is no danger that way'.[22]

Randolph had not counted on the old affair of the Angus earldom. Margaret believed wholeheartedly that she was her father's heir, and if Darnley were to become King of Scots she might someday be able to reclaim her title. At that moment, however, she had no way of getting hold of Angus's earldom. She decided that if ceding her largely impracticable claim meant she could divide the Douglases from the Hamiltons and bring them over to her side, it was a sacrifice worth making. By the start of May 1565 secret negotiations had begun.[23] On 12 May the parties gathered to settle the affair. Her rival claimant was young Archibald Douglas, the ten-year-old grandson of Margaret's uncle George. Margaret was named her father's heir, but she agreed to acknowledge her cousin as Earl of Angus in return for his support – and that of Morton – for the Darnley marriage:

> And on the other part, the said Archibald, Earl of Angus, with express consent and assent of the said James, Earl of Morton, his tutor . . . shall, with the assistance of his haill friends [all his friends] and all that will do for him within the realm of Scotland . . . solicit, advance, and set forwards the said Henry, Lord Darnley . . . to the marriage to be contracted and solemnised betwixt her highness [Mary] and the said Lord Darnley . . .

Away in London, Margaret did not sign the agreement on 12 May. That task fell to Mary, Lennox, Darnley, Angus and Morton. However, the final line of the text notes that 'the said Lady Margaret has subscribed the same', and her name is on the reverse: '[T]o the earl of Lennox my husband.'[24] This is the exterior of the document that would have served as a cover or envelope. It is not clear when Margaret signed. Either Lennox or Darnley might have carried the parchment with him into Scotland, giving some credence to Randolph's speculation about the earldom of Angus the previous November. Alternatively, Margaret could have had it smuggled out of England in the spring of 1565. Whichever happened, it was a canny political bargain: years after the fact, the Elizabethan Member of Parliament Peter Wentworth would write '[i]t was a well-lost earldom which brought home a kingdom'.[25]

On 4 June the English Privy Council met and confronted the dangers of a match between Mary and Darnley. It was the first step on an obvious path to the overthrow of Elizabeth, the union of the crowns of Britain and the restoration of the Church of Rome:

> The first of this sort of perils was that by this marriage with the Lord Darnley there was a plain intention to further the pretended title of the queen of Scots not only to succeed the Queen's Majesty . . . but to occupy the Queen's estate . . . the second was, that hereby the Romish religion should be erected and increased daily in this realm.[26]

Marriage with Darnley meant that the spectres of pan-Britannic Stewart monarchy and Catholicism were 'knit together', since his Catholic supporters would help him claim his wife's rights in England.[27] There was panic in the English court, as the terrible folly of Darnley's release became clear.

The blame fell on Margaret. The Privy Councillors were convinced she was behind the scheme and recommended that she be imprisoned in 'some place where she may be kept from giving or receiving of intelligence'.[28] Until then, she had been allowed to see visitors, but this was no longer to be tolerated. The safest place for her was the Tower: she would be isolated from court and kept under heavy guard. Many of Elizabeth's nobles, finding this unduly harsh, recommended a lighter sentence, but the queen was resolute. In early June, Elizabeth had made up her mind to send Margaret to the Tower, and it was only a question of when she would be forced to go.[29]

In the last week of June, Cecil and William Howard came to Margaret's chamber with a message from Elizabeth: she was going to the Tower, and she had only until the tide rose to prepare herself. Perhaps for the first time, Margaret realised just how treacherous Elizabeth thought she was, and how severely the queen was ready to punish her. She had steeled herself for confinement within the palace, but the prospect of returning to her old prison was terrifying. Desperate, she implored the two men to tell the queen 'that she did not know the cause of such an injury being done her', and asked for the mercy of one more day. They agreed to intercede, but warned her that they were unlikely to persuade Elizabeth and that she should not wait to begin packing.

The household moved into hurried action, folding clothes and linens into trunks and deciding which attendants would go with her. Although it was nearly summer, they readied for the cold: for Margaret, a black velvet gown and taffeta nightgown, both trimmed with rabbit fur, along with a French hood and six pairs of velvet shoes; for every servant, two pairs of blankets; for the prison chamber, equipment to build fires and write letters.[30] For Margaret herself, those must have been anguished hours, dreading the return to the Tower, worrying what would happen to her sons, holding on to the forlorn hope that Cecil and Howard could win her the extra day. How difficult was it to remember that all this was in the service of making Darnley into a king?

The implacable tide rose. Early the next morning, Sir Francis Knollys, Vice Chamberlain of the Queen's Household, came to her room with six guards. Three women stood to meet them: Margaret and her two attendants, probably Elizabeth

Hussey and Elizabeth Chamberlain. They walked through the corridors and out into the summer air before boarding one of Elizabeth's barges and embarking for the Tower, journeying down the river for the whole city to see.

When Mary's envoy arrived at court the next day, he asked to see Margaret and to give her letters from Mary and from Lennox. Elizabeth turned him down, saying that Mary could not expect that one 'imprisoned for so grave a crime' would be permitted to see visitors. She might let Margaret read the letters, but only after she had read them herself: Margaret had only been released from her captivity at Sheen 'on her solemn oath that she would not allow her son to marry without [Elizabeth's] consent, and she had deceived her'. As for Lennox, who had written to her as well as to Margaret, she sent the letter back, 'saying she would not accept letters from a traitor, as she should very soon proclaim him to be, and his son as well'.[31]

Ambassador de Silva, frustrated at his inability to help, wrote to Philip that he was not finding it easy to maintain a diplomatic silence: 'The affair has been so public and her claims on us are so strong that I should have taken some step in her favour but that I do not want to arouse the suspicion of these people, and I have therefore not said a word.'[32]

Philip himself was pleased. He wrote to de Silva, telling him that he would approve the match:

> the bridegroom and his parents being good Catholics and our affectionate servitors; and, considering the Queen's good claims to the crown of England, to which Darnley also pretends, we have arrived at the conclusion that the marriage is one that is favourable to our interests and should be forwarded and supported to the full extent of our power . . . failing the Queen [Elizabeth] there is no doubt that people would

all flock to the queen of Scotland and Lord Darnley, and this must be the object to which all energy must be directed. You will make Lady Margaret understand this, and that not only shall I be glad for her son to be king of Scotland and will help him thereto, but also to be king of England if this marriage is carried through.[33]

17

A Son Lost

This time, Margaret's prison was a house on Tower Green, less than twenty years old and one of the newest parts of the palace. It faced the chapel of St Peter ad Vincula, its door a minute's walk from the spot where five women well known to Margaret – Anne Boleyn, Jane Boleyn, Katherine Howard, Margaret Pole and Jane Grey – had met their deaths. She had five attendants, three women and two men, and amongst them they shared a small set of rooms. These attendants were the only company Margaret could rely on: all other contact would depend on their skill as messengers, her friends' ability to get news to her, and the generosity of Elizabeth.[1]

For nearly a month Margaret petitioned the Lieutenant of the Tower to let her write to her friends. At last, after 'much ado and persuasion', he allowed her to send a letter to Cecil and to the Lord Chamberlain, Lord William Howard. Margaret – still signing herself Countess of Lennox and Angus – was godmother to Cecil's daughter Elizabeth and to Howard's daughter Douglas, and she appealed to them as parents: 'You both are fathers: consider therefore, for God's cause, what I suffer being as not hearing from my lord my husband and son there, not yet from my child being in Yorkshire.'[2]

Margaret was being punished for her own actions but she was also a hostage, and Elizabeth tried to use her imprisonment to get Darnley and Lennox to return home. The queen ordered John

Thomworth, setting out for Scotland, that if he met Lennox and Darnley he should 'remember to them the hard case of the Lady Margaret now in the Tower whose well doing must depend upon their behaviour there'.[3] Darnley's younger brother Charles, only ten, found himself in the custody of the formidably Protestant Thomas Young, Archbishop of York.[4] Margaret's beautiful Temple Newsam was appropriated by the crown, its contents inventoried and itemised, every gift and tapestry counted. The commissioners did not fail to spot that the hangings around Lennox's bed were presumptuously embroidered with the arms of England, or that Elizabeth was conspicuously absent from the family portraits in the Great Hall.[5] Settrington was seized as well, the inventory-makers observing how worn and aged its furnishings were: 'Old tapestries . . . A little old pair of regals [an early organ] . . . A chair of old green velvet.'[6] The French ambassador Paul de Foix reported that Margaret was suffering: 'her goods are seized . . . the poor treatment that they give her extends even to her food and drink'.[7]

Nonetheless, Margaret did not despair. She and her friends devised methods of exchanging news, relying on her servants and the occasional chance to meet in person. De Silva had 'secret and suitable means' figured out within two weeks of her imprisonment, and de Foix became similarly organised, finding 'the means to visit her quite often and to send her news'.[8] For her part, Margaret had an old gentlewoman who delivered her letters every two weeks, sometimes directly, sometimes passing them on to friends so that they could come by a more circuitous route.[9] She had not lost her old intelligence-gathering skills.

At first, the letters brought good news. Mary had already made Darnley Earl of Ross in May. On 22 July 1565 she named him Duke of Albany, a title usually given to a member of the Scottish royal family. It was proclaimed that the two of them would rule together, and that Darnley would not be merely a consort, but King of Scots. By the time Elizabeth gave her instructions to Thomworth, it was already too late. On 29 July, Lennox and Atholl brought Mary to the altar of the chapel at Holyrood, where she and Darnley were married by Catholic rites. After years of imprisonment, politicking and constant hope, Margaret's plan had succeeded.

Now that the match was concluded, requests came from Spain, France and Scotland that Margaret be set free.[10] Mary herself wrote in August, noting that Margaret was both her mother-in-law and near relative, 'so tender of blood to her', and asking that Elizabeth release her from the Tower.[11] But petitions on this side proved as futile as Elizabeth's hostage gambit had been on the other.

Even in summer, the riverside damp of the Tower left it humid in the daytime and skin-chilling at night. Worse, as soon as Margaret adjusted to one set of restrictions, she had to adapt to another. On 23 July de Silva was in the midst of reporting that Margaret had been given more freedom when he had to contradict himself: '[Her] imprisonment, which I had just written had been moderated, is now again been made hourly more severe. The changes here are constant.'[12] By autumn, Margaret was ill, and de Silva, always one of her most ardent advocates, was spurred to act, asking Elizabeth for mercy. The queen coldly informed him that Margaret had been warned of the consequences of lying to her and could not complain of ill treatment:

> Lady Margaret deceitfully asked leave for her son to go to Scotland to take possession of his father's estates. She had given her this license, telling her at the same time to take care she did not deceive her and let her son do anything else, or she [Margaret] would find herself the person deceived . . . She was therefore justly indignant with the Queen [Mary], and especially with Lady Margaret, as they had both deceived her.[13]

Margaret had to accept that this time Elizabeth would not change her mind.

It might have been bearable, had the situation from Scotland not quickly turned bleak. All along, Margaret and Lennox had known that the match needed Protestant support if it were to succeed. Mary herself was in the difficult position of trying to maintain her own religion and protect her co-religionists without alienating the Protestant polity. At first, Darnley seemed to understand this. He and Lennox drew Protestants into their affinity, and Darnley walked out of his own wedding rather than hear the Mass.[14] But these nods to the state religion did not seem to win him new supporters. When Mary had him proclaimed King of Scots in Edinburgh and the herald cried out 'God save the king', the shout met with almost total silence: the only man who replied 'God save His Grace!' was Lennox.[15]

Although Margaret and Lennox had patiently won tolerance if not outright support for the match from many of Scotland's nobles, they had not convinced either the queen's half-brother, Moray, or the Earl of Argyll, both keen supporters of the Anglo-Scottish amity. Naturally, they had not won over Châtelherault or any of the Hamiltons. The marriage had scarcely taken place before Moray, Argyll and Châtelherault raised up armies and rebelled, claiming that Mary's match with Darnley portended the overthrow of the Kirk and a return to state Catholicism. Mary was masterful. She had already recalled the Earl of Bothwell, a Protestant who had nonetheless stayed loyal to Mary of Guise and was an unbending enemy of Moray. Now, Mary pursued the rebels on horseback, armed with a pistol and followed by Darnley and the massed ranks of her own forces. By mid-October she had driven Moray into England.[16]

It was a triumph, and soon after, Mary learned that she was pregnant. But Darnley, now thinking himself absolved of the need to conciliate Protestants, promptly set about the task for which his princely Catholic upbringing had prepared him: presenting himself to France and Spain as the powerful, devout and Catholic King of Scots. On his orders, Margaret's old Hispanophile ally Francis Yaxley journeyed to Philip II's court. He was tasked with arranging an alliance between Spain and Scotland, discussing the possibility of a joint invasion of Catholic Ireland, and urging Philip to intercede on Margaret's behalf. This did not work out well for anybody – there was no invasion, Margaret remained in the Tower, and the long-serving Yaxley drowned on the way back to Scotland. More fruitfully, Darnley petitioned Charles IX for the Order of St Michael, the great French order of chivalry that his grandfather Angus had won after the victory at Ancrum Moor.[17]

Later, Margaret would later tell de Silva, with some exaggeration, that it was impossible for her to 'trust heretics'. Darnley also professed a liking for 'the papists in England' above the 'Protestants of Scotland'.[18] He had been brought up a Catholic and taught to see his royal blood as vitally connected to his religion. But there was also a more mundane explanation for his newfound religiosity: Mary faced the task of maintaining her own religion without alienating Scottish Protestants, and by allying more openly with his fellow Catholics, Darnley could build his own network of supporters independent from those of his wife.[19]

He was not, however, an astute politician, and it was not only Protestants who came to despise him. Once married, Darnley no longer felt he had to be charming or even respectful towards Mary. The two of them had a blazing fight when she decided in December 1565 to pardon the rebellious Hamiltons. Mary had had her husband called king, and coins had been minted with both their names appearing, but Darnley had never been crowned King of Scots. Now, the earlier hints that he would get the crown matrimonial vanished.

Immured in the Tower, Margaret was only able to get a fractured picture of events. Shortly before Christmas 1565, Lennox did send her a letter, downplaying the worst of the tensions. Addressing her as 'My sweet Mage', he told her he missed 'the commodity and comfort of intelligence by letters that we were wont to have passing between us during our absence'. Darnley was well, Mary was pregnant, and there was good reason to be glad: 'Yet of my part, I must confess that I want, and find, a lack of my chiefest comfort, which is you . . .' He assured her that he was doing all he could to encourage them to intervene with Elizabeth on her behalf and prayed that God 'send us with our children a merry meeting'.[20] Lennox could not keep everything from her, particularly not the news that while Châtelherault was still in exile the Hamiltons were restored to favour. When Margaret heard this, she told de Silva she was both troubled and surprised: Mary had told her 'that she would not return the Duke's rank as he was so great a heretic'.[21]

There was a brief entente between Mary and Darnley in the first weeks of 1566. Mary encouraged the nobility to attend Darnley's investiture with the Order of St Michael, letting him use the ceremony as a pseudo-coronation in front of Scotland's Catholic lords. She also continued to petition Elizabeth for Margaret's release, inadvertently confirming her new mother-in-law's role in the marriage negotiations by asking rhetorically 'whether she deserves punishment for merely wishing well to her child'.[22]

But the thaw between Mary and Darnley did not last, and the terrible mistaken assumption at the heart of Margaret's plan was becoming clear. From the moment of Francis II's death, Margaret had thrown all her energies into wedding Darnley to Mary. Amidst all her strategising, intelligence-gathering and diplomatic manoeuvring, she had taken it for granted that Darnley would know how to behave himself.

This was a calamitous error. Since his wedding, Darnley had showed himself to be not only unfaithful – rumour had it that he and David Rizzio, Mary's winning and musical Italian secretary, were lovers – but also arrogant, abusive and power-hungry.[23]

It is impossible to know why Darnley was such an appalling husband and any explanation is necessarily conjecture. Although his youthful accomplishments are well documented, there are almost no traces of his character before his journey into Scotland, and it is worth remembering that he probably became infected with syphilis around the time of his release – a disease that can cause dramatic personality changes. Lennox never behaved towards Margaret as Darnley did towards Mary, so it was not that Darnley grew up seeing such behaviour as the marital norm. But early modern thinking held that men were superior to their wives, and perhaps Darnley remembered the mocking accusations that his mother dominated his father and feared being the subject of such slurs himself. His parents had taken every chance to remind him of his royal blood – he heard it from friends and servants, saw it in the family portraits on the Great Chamber walls, knew it was the reason Elizabeth kept him so close at court – and they had spent five years angling to have him made King of Scots or named Elizabeth's heir. Now, Mary was refusing to give him the crown matrimonial, which he saw as simply his entitlement as her husband. Finally, he was just twenty and had been brought up in an atmosphere that combined love and luxury with enormous familial expectation; without Margaret and his tutors, there was nobody to keep him under control.

Darnley was jealous when it came to Mary and thought himself wronged by her refusal to make him king. It did not take long for all other considerations – including his Catholicism – to fall by the wayside as he tried to make himself Scotland's real ruler.

Although he had no interest in the day-to-day work of running a kingdom, Darnley was prepared to do anything that would secure him real power. In the weeks after his investiture with the Order of St Michael, an unlikely alliance of nobles agreed to a plan that would isolate the queen. The instigator was Margaret's cousin, James Douglas, Earl of Morton – he had sworn to be her ally and support the Darnley match, and he was once more offering aid to her son, but it was a poisonous sort of help. Darnley would get the crown matrimonial, Moray and his supporters would return home, and the Reformation settlement would be reaffirmed. They also agreed on a scapegoat: Mary's secretary, Rizzio, would be cast in the role of wicked papist counsellor who had misled the queen and set up divisions between her and her husband, and suffer death as a consequence.[24] Darnley compounded the treachery of inviting back the rebels with shocking hypocrisy and ruthlessness: he was no Protestant, and he and Rizzio had been friends – if not lovers.

On 9 March 1566 the conspirators burst into Mary's apartments and murdered Rizzio in front of her, dragging him out of the tiny supper room to stab him to death, threatening her with a loaded pistol when she tried to intervene. Virtually all of Margaret's nearest relatives had been involved in the plot: her husband, her eldest son and her first cousin. But they seem to have kept her in the dark and there is some doubt about when she heard the news. At first, de Silva reported that she only learned of the plot when informed of it by Elizabeth, at some point after the murder; three weeks later, however, he wrote that 'the day prior to the night of the murder, Cecil informed Lady Margaret of it as an event that had occurred'. The murder and the company her son was keeping left Margaret profoundly unsettled.[25]

Following one stunning miscalculation with another, Darnley now lost his nerve, betrayed his co-conspirators and crawled back to Mary, who swept to a comprehensive revenge. Just as her father, James V, had taken vengeance on the old Earl of Angus, Mary moved against the Douglases. She named them traitors, drove them into England and seized Tantallon. It had taken Margaret's earldom to win her Douglas cousins over to the Darnley match, but now her son left them to their fate, saying that he had had nothing to do with them and their plot against Rizzio. They swore revenge, and sent Mary proof that Darnley had agreed to the murder.[26] She had taken Darnley back, but she now knew exactly what he was, and the reconciliation was a mere show.

Watching Darnley waste the opportunity that his mother had struggled for years to win him, many contemporary observers wondered whether events would have unfolded differently if Margaret had escaped to Scotland with him. In his *History* of Mary's reign her secretary, Claude Nau, wrote that Darnley often failed to honour his father: more than once, Mary was obliged to remind him to behave more respectfully towards Lennox.[27] De Silva made the same point to Philip in May 1566, implying that Margaret, not Lennox, was known to have sway over Darnley: 'These people [England's Privy Council] have not done badly for their ends in detaining her, because if she had been in Scotland they are sure her son would not have been led astray, nor would these disputes have taken place, as she is prudent and brave, and the son respects her more than he does his father.'[28]

But Margaret's own relationship with Mary was under tremendous strain. They had still never met and it was by now becoming clear to each of them that the other had used her for her own political ends. In the spring of 1566, Margaret sent Mary letters that either 'greatly offended' her or caused her 'great sorrow', or possibly both.[29] The letters are lost, so there is no record of what Margaret said to upset her niece – though as Darnley's mother and a Douglas, there was little she could have said that would have endeared her to Mary at that moment.

Mary was due to give birth within weeks of getting the letters, and she drew up a will in case she did not survive, setting aside a pair of black-enamelled diamond rings for Lennox and Margaret as well as another diamond for Margaret alone. Out of context, it seems a lavish gift, but by the standards of the will it was not – there were jewels for many others. Moreover, Mary set out a plan for a regency in the event of her death, and it did not include Lennox: she had no tenderness for or trust in any of the family.[30]

Mary gave birth to a son. Far from reconciling with Darnley, she no longer had need of him: she had an heir. They were both desperately unhappy in the marriage and Darnley, whose misery was far less justified than Mary's, was talking of leaving Scotland for safe Catholic shores.[31] Once Mary had recovered her health, the boy was christened in a sumptuous Catholic ceremony in the chapel of Stirling Castle, conducted by Châtelherault's half-brother, the Archbishop of St Andrews. The child's first name was Charles, in honour of his godfather, Charles IX, but he was always known by his second name, James, like his royal Stewart forebears. Elizabeth herself acted as godmother, sending an extraordinarily expensive font made from 333 ounces of pure gold.[32] Although several Protestant lords refused to attend the ceremony, the celebratory banquets that followed saw foreign dignitaries and Scottish nobles of all confessional stripes joining together to welcome the new prince. It was a show of unity nearly on a par with Mary's own coronation twenty-three years earlier, with two unmissable exceptions: neither Lennox nor Darnley was there.[33]

Margaret had a better sense of appearances than Darnley and she arranged to have a 'fair and rich' bearing cloth sent to Scotland for use in James's baptism.[34] When she learned that Darnley had not attended, she found it hard to understand. It was a dreadful show of division for Darnley not to be present at the font, especially when his son was being christened a Catholic. But even from the Tower, Margaret was the practical operative, determined to save the situation if she could. Knowing that Darnley and Mary were again at odds, she wrote to de Silva, venting her frustration and anxiety and asking him to do all he could to reconcile her son and daughter-in-law. Yet determined as she was, Margaret was slowly being ground down under the bodily and monetary pressures of her imprisonment, and worse was still to come.[35]

On 19 February 1567 the door opened and two women entered Margaret's room. They were new visitors: Margaret, Lady Howard, and Mildred, Lady Cecil, mothers to her two goddaughters Douglas and Elizabeth. For a moment, perhaps, Margaret hoped for a reprieve and that the queen had sent these two women to bring her news of freedom. But thirty years before, when Margaret had needed to tell somebody of her secret betrothal to Thomas Howard, she had found a confidante in Lady Howard. Now, it fell to the same Lady Howard to give Margaret devastating news from Scotland.

The syphilitic Darnley had been gravely ill. He had been removed to Kirk O'Field, a house on the margins of Edinburgh that Lennox would later say Darnley found 'vile', 'too little and unseemly for him to lie in', and generally 'much against his liking'. There, he underwent a regimen of bathing and purging meant to help the gruesome sores.[36] By 9 February he was showing some improvement, and Mary came to visit him that evening before returning to Holyrood, where a wedding reception for two of her favourite servants was in its final hours. Shortly after the revellers went to bed, a violent explosion cracked the quiet of the Edinburgh night: Kirk O'Field was annihilated in a blast of gunpowder. But this, it seemed, was not what finished off Darnley. He and his servant William Taylor were found nearby, apparently unharmed by the blast but unmistakably dead: they had been strangled.

The circumstances of Darnley's death remain mysterious. It seems clear that he and Taylor had left the house before the explosion: perhaps the assassins' plan was to kill Darnley and then use the explosion to destroy the body, but he heard them and fled. An Italian diplomatic account quoted witnesses who testified that Darnley's last words were a plea for mercy, addressed to *fratelli miei* – his kinsmen, suggesting it was the Douglases who put their hands around Darnley's throat.

As she tried to understand the unendurable news, Margaret gave way to grief that looked and felt like madness. The Dean of Westminster and Robert Huick, physician to the Tudors since the last years of Henry's reign, were summoned, and stayed with her in the Tower through the night, trying and failing to relieve her 'passions of mind'. She had gone two years without seeing her son, living and dying – alone – by word of his triumphs and his failures, and now she would never see him again.

Cecil confided to the English ambassador in France, Sir Henry Norris, that he hoped Elizabeth would 'show some favourable compassion for the said lady, whom any human nature must needs pity'.[37] In the presence of such pain, it seemed petty to recall their religious differences and even Margaret's double-dealing with Scottish and European Catholics. Elizabeth moved swiftly and Margaret left her prison two days later. Once again, she was under the tutelary custody of Elizabeth's Boleyn cousins at Sackville House in Fleet Street, home to the young courtier-poet Thomas Sackville and his wife, and less than two miles from the Tower.[38]

Thirty years before, Margaret had left Syon Abbey convinced that she could not survive her grief at Thomas Howard's death. Darnley's demise was far worse: it left her sick, haggard, unable to control her emotions. But this time, death gave her purpose.

She was convinced that Mary was responsible for Darnley's end. She was determined to be revenged on the Queen of Scots and to see that her only grandchild – the Catholic-christened boy who was heir to the thrones of England, Scotland and Ireland – would grow up to fulfil the destiny she had meant for his murdered father.

Part Three

WHAT WE RESOLVE

18

Memorial

In the last days of February 1567 a ten-year-old boy with serious grey eyes journeyed from Westminster to the neighbourhood of St Paul's. He had spent the past eighteen months being shuttled between the homes of various ecclesiastical dignitaries and now, with the queen's permission, he was bound for Sackville House. When he reached his destination and saw his mother, Margaret held him and wept: she had had eight children, and young Charles Stewart was the only one still alive.

She was not left alone to grieve with her son. Robert Melville, older brother of Sir James Melville and Mary's ambassador in London, heard reports that Margaret was slandering the Queen of Scots. De Silva tried to calm him, reminding him that 'grief like this distracts the most prudent people, much more one so sorely beset'. Melville, however, was determined to see for himself, and went to speak to Margaret in person. Cagey, she told him that she was ready to believe Mary innocent of Darnley's death, but that she knew her niece had treated her son badly, and she flatly refused to write to Mary without permission from Elizabeth.

Margaret was cold to Melville, but she was showing tremendous self-control. Privately, she had no doubt about Mary's guilt – and, de Silva observed, she was not alone.[1] To the courts of Europe, Darnley living had been an upstart and a disgrace; Darnley dead was the innocent victim of a horrifying regicide.

The Earl of Bothwell instantly became the chief suspect, with the Queen of Scots talked of as his accomplice. Elizabeth, unconvinced of Mary's guilt and revolted by the slanders against a fellow monarch, wrote to Mary saying she was more grieved for her than for Darnley and urging her to take care for her own reputation 'rather than look through your fingers'.[2] Cecil summed up the matter in a letter to Sir Henry Norris, the English ambassador to France: 'The common fame in Scotland continueth upon the Earl Bothwell, to be the principal Murtherer of the King, and the Queen's name is not well spoken of.'[3]

Margaret was convinced that general opinion was right; Lennox, though his supporters were calling for vengeance against Mary, was more willing to make overtures to the queen, provided she showed no mercy to Darnley's murderers.[4] He asked Mary to call a parliament and try 'the bloody and cruel enactors of this deed'.[5] She promised that she would, but Lennox had no patience for delays. He was writing to Cecil just over two weeks after his first letter to Mary, asking that Elizabeth avenge Darnley, 'so near of her Majesty's blood, born and brought up as her subject within her realm' and reminding Cecil of 'the good will and acquaintance that was between you and him'.[6] A short time before, all of Margaret and Lennox's hopes had centred on their connections to the Queen of Scots; now, their faith in Mary destroyed, they pivoted from her and reasserted the ties that bound them to Elizabeth.

Mary held on to the support of many of her nobles, but there was no aid from England or Europe, and she turned to the Earl of Bothwell. Protocol dictated that she should have been in solitary mourning for Darnley, but instead she was out in public, often with the earl. Popular opinion condemned them both, Bothwell as a murderer, Mary as at best an unloving wife and at worst an accomplice in her husband's death. Balladeers compared the queen to every reprehensible woman they could find in myth and scripture. She was Delilah, who double-crossed her lover Samson, or Clytemnestra, who butchered her husband Agamemnon, or even Scylla, the tentacled sea monster who seized and devoured unsuspecting men.[7]

A long ballad addressed to Mary by an anonymous English Catholic lamented that 'The Protestants now of every Region/ Have found delight with shameless voice to cry/Behold and mark the fruit of papistry.' The author reproached her ingratitude in the face of Margaret's sacrifices:

Did he [Darnley] not for thy fickle favour lose
The friendship of his loving native Queen?
Did she not through his fault (alas) depose
His parents from their livings quite and clean?
Did not his mother in the Tower sustain
A woeful bale [misfortune] without hope of rescuing?[8]

Although Darnley and the Douglases had betrayed each other over and over again, another ballad, printed in Edinburgh, urged Margaret's family to remember her and seek vengeance:

Now, every Douglas of an heartsome [daring] mind,
Think on dame Margaret sometime in the Tower,
And of young Charles, prudent of ingyne [temperament]:
I pray God let them see a joyful hour.[9]

But Mary did not change her course, even though many of the broadsides against her were written up and posted on the Tolbooth for all Edinburgh to read.[10]

Weeks went by and Margaret was on the verge of despair, increasingly desperate for revenge, but powerless to take it, able to envision only the bleakest scenarios. Lennox, she was sure, would be murdered, while James would be seized by

Protestants and brought up a heretic. She had preserved her dignity in front of Melville but confessed to de Silva that she could no longer keep control of her emotions, though she knew it would be better if she could. Everybody around her felt her temper. When the Lord Treasurer told her that he was unable to help her recover her lands, she was short with him, thinking him unkind and unwilling to aid her. In spite of this he told Cecil he wanted Elizabeth to 'let [Margaret] have her lands again in her own receipt and so she would be best pleased, whereof I shall be very glad . . . because her need is great'.[11] Lennox wrote to her, but Margaret did not write back, leading him to send an anxious letter asking after her: '[S]ince her liberty she has sent no servant of her own to let me understand the present state she is in so that I fear much she is not well in health . . .'[12]

Margaret had gone silent with grief and impotent rage just when Lennox most wanted to hear from her. He had charged Bothwell with Darnley's murder and a trial was fixed for April, but he had so few friends in Edinburgh that he was unable to enter the city and testify. Bothwell, unsurprisingly, was acquitted – grim news that neither de Silva nor anybody else wanted to give to Margaret.[13] Shortly afterwards, parliament met and condemned the broadsides, and ratified a series of grants of land from Mary to various nobles – including Bothwell and the Douglases.[14] Any doubts Lennox had about Mary's complicity vanished.[15]

Mary, however, was not the person driving events. Bothwell recognised that he would never again have such an opportunity to seize power in Scotland. On 19 April 1567 he and his allies swore a bond, committing themselves to a plan: they would do their best to get Mary married to Bothwell, whom they proclaimed innocent. But when Bothwell proposed, the queen turned him down. On 24 April he abducted Mary and took her to Dunbar Castle. Mary was deeply affronted, but some unsympathetic observers – John Knox for one – claimed that this was nothing but a show, and that she had planned all along to go with the earl.

With the political situation so uncertain, many of the most important nobles made strategic retreats. The queen's half-brother, the Earl of Moray, had already left the realm. Lennox, having tested the political waters and found them too hot, was making for England by way of France. Châtelherault remained out of the country. Those who stayed were bitterly divided. Many swore that they were going to set Mary free, but Bothwell then divorced his wife, with the assistance of the Catholic Archbishop of St Andrews, John Hamilton. This left Bothwell at liberty to wed the queen by Protestant rites on 15 May.[16] The bemused French ambassador noted that the royals of England and Scotland made 'a strange habit' – inherited from their medieval forebears – of sudden divorces.[17] Now, many of Mary's longest-standing allies abandoned her.[18]

As Mary's resolve faltered and her positioned weakened, Margaret gained in strength. She arranged for a ship to sail to Brittany to bring Lennox home.[19] By June, he was back in England, pledging his devotion to Elizabeth and swearing 'to offer my service unto your highness, even from the bottom of my heart', trusting that she would remember 'the most cruel murder of him that was your majesty's poor kinsman till upright justice may be had for the same'.[20] Margaret and Lennox had not seen each for nearly three long, difficult years.[21] It was hardly the 'merry meeting' Lennox had once promised her.[22] They had no money, their beloved son was dead, and Scotland was in turmoil. But Margaret, somewhat recovered from the first shock of grief and heartened by Lennox's return, was now ready to re-enter the political fray.

She left Sackville House and went to court. Elizabeth was planning to spend the summer at Richmond Palace and Margaret secured an audience with the queen on the day of her departure. Seeing them together, it would have been hard to remember that they were of the same generation, first cousins and both grandchildren of Henry VII: Margaret, in heavy mourning, was nearly twenty years older than the summer-dressed queen, and she looked it. But when Margaret asked her cousin for help to avenge her son, Elizabeth promised she would do her best. Robert Dudley, Earl of Leicester – once Darnley's rival for Mary's hand – came and commiserated with her, as did Cecil, who promised that they would do their best to rescue James from Scotland and bring him to her. This was encouraging. So was the news that the Earl of Mar, a good friend of Lennox who had custody of James, was refusing to allow Bothwell anywhere near the infant prince.[23]

Shortly afterwards, Margaret and Lennox set off for Richmond themselves. Margaret met with the queen first, and Elizabeth was warm and charming, telling her to bring Charles with her soon. The day after, Lennox spoke with Elizabeth for two hours, giving his own account of events in Scotland and asking for help against Mary. She told him that the past was forgiven but that she 'could not take any part against the person of the Queen'.[24] This was to be an enduring fault line between Margaret and Elizabeth. Margaret wanted revenge against a queen, even if meant allying with rebels, whereas Elizabeth, sympathetic though she was to the lords, was just as reluctant to side with rebels against an anointed monarch now as she had been during the Reformation that overthrew Mary's mother.

Elizabeth did not have to choose. On 15 June, Mary's forces met the lords' men at Carberry Hill and the Queen of Scots, seeing that she had no hope of victory, surrendered. Bothwell was allowed to go into exile, fleeing Scotland altogether in favour of Denmark. He was eventually arrested – having had the bad luck to be recognised by a jilted Norwegian lover – and shut up in

Dragsholm Castle, where he suffered a slow descent into insanity. Mary was taken back to Edinburgh, disgraced, humiliated, and a prisoner. She was pregnant with twins, but she miscarried in July.[25]

Margaret received word of Carberry Hill when her illegitimate half-brother George Douglas arrived in England. He came straight to her and Lennox and asked them to help get Elizabeth's support for the Scottish lords. There was nothing Margaret was more willing to do, and she made immediately for Richmond to speak with the queen. All through the night, she remained at the palace, trying to persuade Elizabeth to join forces with Mary's enemies.[26]

The lords now demanded that Mary abdicate in favour of her one-year-old son James. Carried out under terrible duress, this was less abdication than overthrow. The new king was crowned on 29 July 1567 at Stirling Castle, in a Protestant service with a sermon by John Knox. Mary's long-ago coronation had occasioned a bold show of unity – even Lennox and Châtelherault had put aside their rivalry for the day. Her son's brought palpable division. Only a handful of nobles attended and England kept its envoy, Nicholas Throckmorton, away; the ambassador and all his men put on mourning clothes.[27] But Margaret suddenly found herself the grandmother of a king.

She now faced a new dilemma. Mary's half-brother, the Earl of Moray, was heading back to Scotland to assume the regency for his nephew. Unexpectedly, given that they had never found themselves on the same political side before, he stopped to speak with Margaret, offering condolences and whatever help he could give her. Not certain what to make of the visit, Margaret spoke to her old confidant, the Spanish ambassador de Silva. She promised him she could not 'trust heretics'.[28] In fact, since Darnley's death, she had been doing precisely that: her hopes rested on the goodwill of Elizabeth and the political ingenuity of Cecil, even as she feared the consequences of having James raised by Protestants. Could she reconcile her rejection of Mary with her own Catholicism?

At first, she believed she could. Mary had lost her crown and her freedom, but even now, Margaret did not think herself thoroughly revenged. She commissioned the Dutch artist Livinus de Vogelaare to create a painting that would encapsulate her family's pain and ensure that Mary's young son grew up believing his father was a hero and his mother a murderer. The result was *The Memorial of Lord Darnley*.[29]

The painting shows James and the Lennox-Stewarts in a chapel at prayer, kneeling beside an effigy of Lord Darnley and facing an altar with a statue of Christ triumphant. The young king is nearest the altar, set slightly apart from his father's family with his own kneeler, still a child but already crowned and wearing his kingly regalia. He prays: 'I ask that you rise up, Lord, and avenge the innocent blood of my father the king, and defend me with your right hand.'

Behind him are the Lennox-Stewarts, all in sombre black with white at the collar and cuffs, all having taken off their gloves to pray. Charles, furthest from the altar, sickly pale and bulging-eyed, prays: 'I pray that you, Lord, avenge the innocent blood of my brother the king and that you make me an instrument of your vengeance.' Lennox is nearest the altar and Margaret in the centre, their faces weary and grim, and they speak together: 'Hear our cry, Lord, and avenge the innocent blood of the king our beloved son, and give his son the king long life . . .' Inset, just below the altar, is an image of Mary's defeat at Carberry.

It is a carefully constructed composition. Lennox and Margaret dedicated the painting to James, so that if they died 'before the majority of their descendant, the King of Scots, he [would] have a memorial from them, in order that he shut not out of his memory the recent atrocious murder of the king his father, until God should avenge it through him'.[30] The painting stresses James's British heritage by evoking his father's English and Scottish rights. The Scottish royal arms appear on a banner above his effigy and on a crest upon the base of the sarcophagus, and two crowned unicorns sit by his head, while his English arms also appear as a banner and crest, and his feet rest upon two lions.

The painting is also explicitly Catholic. A letter written in December 1567 from John Baptista Castagna, nuncio in Spain, to Cardinal Alessandrino, shows that to the minds of European Catholics the Lennox-Stewarts remained in the Catholic fold, and the *Memorial* supports his claim.[31] James and the Lennox-Stewarts are praying for revenge, rather than for the soul of the dead Darnley, and the presence of Latin prayers in worship does not guarantee that the sitters were Catholic. Nonetheless, the use of Latin suggests that the prayer books next to the kneeling Lennox-Stewarts were not copies of the Book of Common Prayer, and that the family had not adopted the vernacular rites of the Church of England. On the altar is a three-dimensional, haloed Christ, who stands next to a wooden cross, suggesting that the Lennox-Stewarts kept at least one devotional statue in their chapel, using both the language and the devotional objects of the old faith.

Margaret could not really afford the painting: getting her lands and revenues back was proving a drawn-out process, and she and Lennox were still labouring under 'great impoverishment'.[32] She was also ill through the autumn of 1567 and worse by the New Year, suffering from what she called 'my old colic'.[33] But she did not ask Livinus to idealise her or any of her family when it was time to sit for their portraits. Although the images are not sparing, they are determined. For all that the Lennox-Stewarts look haggard, worn and miserable, their faces are set: confident in the rightness of their cause and merciless in their condemnation of Mary. The *Memorial* is directed to James, stressing his British-Catholic heritage, but it also claims him for the Lennox-Stewarts – though set apart by his royalty, he belongs to their family, son of his martyred father and not his treacherous mother.

Mary's abdication created a new divide in Scottish affairs, splitting the political class between supporters of the infant king and those of the overthrown queen. Although reformers dominated the king's party and Catholics the queen's party, neither religion nor blood was a safe guide to allegiance. There were Catholics on the king's side, Protestants on the queen's. In England, Mary divided Elizabeth from her counsellors, in defeat as in power. Cecil was delighted to see her gone but Elizabeth believed she was still the rightful ruler.[34]

Mary refused to stay idle. She tried and failed to escape in March 1568, but on the evening of 2 May she disguised herself as her attendant Mary Seton and fled Lochleven. Once free, she headed for Hamilton, where she met supporters and raised an army, ready to overthrow her half-brother and take back her throne. But the Regent Moray emerged triumphant and she was forced to flee again. Three days later she crossed the border into England. Although understandable, her actions were unwise: they left the queen's party in Scotland with no figurehead and they placed Elizabeth in an impossible position.[35]

Margaret was in no such difficulty. She and Mary, once allies of convenience, had become passionate foes. Each strove to undermine the other with Elizabeth. Mary, knowing how Margaret had been called a traitor for promoting the Darnley marriage, invoked old memories: 'It is not only from this hour that she [Margaret] had had a bad opinion of queens: because she is so much an enemy to me . . . when it shall please you, I will tell her teachings before you.'[36] But Margaret was in good standing with the regime: Cecil was asking her to help him gather intelligence.

She interrogated a Scotsman in Lennox's service and reported back to Cecil that Mary had been in contact with Bothwell since leaving Lochleven. Margaret was frustrated that she could not give him more information: 'This is all that I can learn. I would to God I knew the truth to satisfy you, but my hope is in God that all those which were guilty therein shall be known.'[37] Mary's blows upon Margaret merely glanced off.

Over the autumn of 1568, Mary's commissioners met with those of Moray and Elizabeth, first at York and then at Westminster. It gradually became clear that this was to be a trial of Mary for Darnley's murder. The Lennox-Stewarts, in anticipation of the Westminster event, had drawn up their own evidence. Lennox told stories of horrible fights between Mary and Darnley: she mocked him for his red-faced fury, Darnley answered that if he was 'high coloured' it was because of 'her extreme words', and Mary snapped back if he 'had bled as much blood as the earl Bothwell bled, it would make him look fair in the face'.[38] But there was to be far more dramatic testimony.

Moray told Cecil he had evidence that would destroy the queen's reputation – letters, written by Mary to Bothwell, proving her guilty of adultery and murder. Kept in a small silver box and recovered from Bothwell, the so-called Casket Letters have provoked debate ever since: whether or not they are genuine and what they claim to be. The critical thing was that Cecil either believed their contents or wanted to believe them, as they seemed to prove, with Mary's own words, her adultery and her complicity in Darnley's death: 'You have heard the rest. We are tied to with two false races [Mary and Bothwell were both married]. The good year untie us from them. God forgive me, and God knit us together forever for the most faithful couple that ever he did knit together. This is my faith; I will die in it . . . Cursed be this pocky fellow [Darnley] that troubleth me this much . . .'[39]

Elizabeth was torn and at her instigation the tribunal neither convicted Mary nor absolved her. She went back to prison without having had the chance to address the judges or to meet Elizabeth herself. As for the Lennox-Stewarts, the Casket Letters only confirmed what they already believed: that the Queen of Scots had killed their son.

19

Constant Hope

In the midst of Mary's trial, Margaret and Lennox went to Elizabeth. Together, they begged her to remove the young King James from his chaotic country and bring him into England. Elizabeth was characteristically non-committal, but early in 1569 she issued a proclamation at Hampton Court. Printed shortly afterwards, the text denied a series of wild rumours about events in Scotland and especially any plans to remove James from his kingdom. Elizabeth conceded that she had been asked to bring James into England, not least 'by the Earl of Lennox and the lady his wife (being, as it is known, parents to the late murdered father of the Prince)' – but the king would stay in his own kingdom.[1]

George Talbot, Earl of Shrewsbury, assumed custody of the deposed Queen Mary. Almost immediately, she became the focus of plots and rebellions. The fourth Duke of Norfolk, a freshly widowed Thomas Howard with royal aspirations and flexible religious views, concocted a plan to marry the Queen of Scots himself and seize the throne. When Elizabeth learned of this scheme, she had Norfolk imprisoned. The unintended consequence of this move was to spark rebellion in northern England. Margaret's old admirer, Henry Neville, Earl of Westmorland, had died in 1564 at the age of forty, leaving the title to his son Charles – Norfolk's brother-in-law. The new earl had supported the Norfolk marriage scheme, as had Thomas Percy,

Earl of Northumberland. In November 1569, Westmorland and Northumberland led an ill-starred uprising in favour of the old religion.

The revolt ended in amateurish disarray, but more than ever before Protestants saw Catholicism as the religion of treachery. Throughout the 1560s, Catholics who kept out of high politics – unlike Margaret – were largely free from active persecution and left to grapple with their own consciences in peace. The Northern Rebellion, however, cast a pall of suspicion over all English Catholics. Their position became even more intractable in February 1570, a mere two months after the failure of the rebellion. Pope Pius V, having held off formal censure of Elizabeth for more than a decade, chose this moment to issue the papal bull *Regnans in Excelsis*. It excommunicated the queen as a heretic and persecutor of the true Church, proclaimed her a usurper with no claim to the throne of England, and declared that all who had sworn oaths to her should consider those oaths forgotten. It was now the duty of every Catholic to resist Elizabeth's religious settlement.

Margaret managed something that few Catholics did. Provoked by the rebellion and the papal bull, the regime began persecuting in earnest: any Catholic could be untrustworthy. A new English self-image was starting to take shape, one of a Protestant nation under threat from the Catholic powers of Europe. It is therefore remarkable that there does not seem to have been any doubt about Margaret's loyalty to Elizabeth. She and Lennox were still known to be Catholics, both at court and in the country: in 1570 the story of her punishing her reforming tenant John Hume got into print, appearing in the second edition of *Acts and Monuments*, John Foxe's magisterial history of English Protestantism.[2] Yet neither Margaret nor Lennox was seen as a political threat. Perhaps this was because Margaret, as the newly minted Spanish ambassador Guerau de Spes wrote in

January 1570, '[deserved] every good thing' but had no major political following.[3] Margaret and Lennox no longer lived in Yorkshire and many of their old northern Catholic friends and retainers were dead. Moreover, they were so closely identified with their murdered son that their Catholicism seemed less important than their well-known hatred for the Queen of Scots.

The closest that Margaret came to being connected with the rebellion was the testimony of her old foe Thomas Bishop. He and Margaret seemed destined to be forever on the opposite side of any political question: just as Margaret was growing more distant from English Catholicism, Bishop was reinventing himself as an unlikely Catholic sympathiser and rebel in the northern rising. But even Bishop, who now found himself on the sharp side of questions about northern Catholics, the Queen of Scots and the Spanish ambassador, only referred to Margaret to mention that he had 'sav[ed] my lady Lennox's gentlemen and a servant of the Queen's', and that she had been friendly with the Percys and the Nevilles in the early 1560s. These friendships, such a concern ten years earlier, no longer seemed dangerous.[4]

In Scotland, the Regent Moray had some success in subduing the queen's party, reconciling those he could and putting others out of the way. Chief among these removals was the Duke of Châtelherault, who had returned home in 1569 and was still James's heir presumptive as head of the house of Hamilton: devoutly pro-Mary, he was imprisoned.[5] But Moray's victory did not last long. On 23 January 1570 the Regent was shot in the stomach – the bullet went through his body, mortally wounding Moray and striking an unfortunate nearby horse.[6] He was the victim of a Hamilton plot. Not only was the murderer, James Hamilton of Bothwellhaugh, a relative of Châtelherault, but he escaped on horses lent to him by John Hamilton, Archbishop of St Andrews and Châtelherault's half-brother.[7] Elizabeth was dismayed and even Margaret, who had never wholly trusted Moray with her grandson, called it 'discomfortable news'.[8]

Once again, Margaret and Lennox asked Elizabeth to bring James – her 'fatherless and desolate poor orphan and kinsman' – into England. They sent her a petition in which their own nationality became confused – James was 'the King our sovereign', though they were also Elizabeth's 'most humble and faithful subjects'. But their conviction was clear: Scotland was too dangerous a place for the King of Scots.[9]

Even as she petitioned Elizabeth, Margaret saw another possibility. If James could not come to England, Lennox could go to Scotland, and if she could not convince Elizabeth, she might be able to persuade Cecil. On 2 February 1570 she wrote a letter on Lennox's behalf that on the surface disclaimed any pretensions to the regency but in its subtext suggested that Lennox not only wanted the task but would be James's 'chiefest pillar and strength'.

She spun a vivid story for Cecil. Lennox, long subject to melancholia – he had struggled with it in the Tower – was suffering under the news from Scotland. Margaret was grieved, she said, to see her husband – 'who and I have been together this twenty-six years' – falling again into depression: '[If] he continue anytime in the same, I fear he cannot long endure, his inward grief is such.' Lennox muttered over and over again that 'unless God of his great mercy and pity put to his helping hand, he seeth plainly the destruction of that little innocent king near at hand'. Margaret could not do anything to turn his mind away from Scotland, and listened to him say that he would rather God 'take him out of this miserable life' than let him live to hear of his grandson's death.

Lennox was convinced that there were two reasons Elizabeth would keep him in England. First was the fear that he wanted the regency for himself. Margaret protested that he had never wanted the job: Lennox was in his mid-fifties, making him some fifteen years older than Moray. His only aim was to be 'an assistant to such noble men' as Elizabeth and the Scots would choose to govern the realm, serving only as guardian 'of the said king's person', keeping him out of danger, whether in Scotland, England or Europe.

The other reason against his going, Margaret wrote, was worry about 'religious cause'. Answering this concern, she wrote that '[a]s for religion it should never have fared the worse for him, but rather the better'. This was what Elizabeth might have called an 'answer answerless', but the implication was that Lennox was not going to undermine the Protestant amity, whatever his own beliefs – or Margaret's. But, she concluded, Lennox was nowhere near strong enough to go – and in any case, she had recently been compelled to sell some of her jewellery in order to meet their ordinary expenses, so she could not 'see how his purse can be able to take that chargeable journey in hand'. Margaret was not being subtle. She knew that her arguments against Lennox's going were far less compelling than those in favour of it.[10]

Margaret was not alone in making the case for a Lennox regency. A Scots ballad printed in Edinburgh encouraged the lords to summon him back to Scotland: 'Now fie for shame, fetch Lennox home.'[11] The queen's first cousin Henry, Lord Hunsdon, wrote that 'sundry of the best' would welcome Lennox as head of the king's party, 'being a Stewart and by marriage a Douglas'. He warned of the consequences of letting the Hamiltons seize power – 'if the Hamiltons should bear the sway, the French shall not be long absent' – and of the malevolence of France: 'Assure yourself that if ye do not take heed of that Scottish queen she will put you in peril ere it be long, for there are many practices abroad.'[12] Cecil, knowing that Margaret and Lennox were now implacably anti-Mary, liked the plan.[13]

Not everyone was so convinced. While there were loud calls in Scotland for Lennox to return, there were those – even within the king's party – who felt that he should stay in England.[14] Elizabeth was among the doubtful. Scotland remained divided, and with Moray's death, the Hamilton-dominated pro-Mary faction was re-energised. Elizabeth wanted Mary restored – the idea that rebels could force a monarch from her throne was abhorrent to her – but she also wanted to maintain England's friendship with the king's party. The last thing that she wished to contribute to this political situation was the fractious presence of Lennox. Being the king's grandfather did not make the earl an avuncular, politically neutral figure. Lennox was a lifelong rival of the Hamiltons and a bitter enemy to Mary when what Scotland needed, Elizabeth thought, was a conciliator. The choice of Regent was up to the Scots, but Elizabeth could delay.[15]

For two months she did: in late March, Guerau de Spes reported to Philip that '[t]he negotiations here about the earl of Lennox have been quite forgotten'.[16] But later in the spring, though she had not yet endorsed his regency, Elizabeth let Lennox go.

Once again, Margaret watched Lennox depart for Scotland. When he had last left for Scotland in the hopeful autumn before Darnley's release, Margaret had wept at the separation, but this time she was dry-eyed. They both believed that the fate of the king's party and of the king himself rested on Lennox's going, and the political stakes were too high to give weight to other considerations – not the expense, neither the danger nor the loneliness. She swore that she would be his best ally at court and Lennox, in turn, resolved to stay in constant contact with her; with those promises given and received, he rode northwards. Whatever loss and fear Margaret felt, she did not show.[17]

The mission started badly. Soon after Lennox reached Berwick, he came down with a raging fever, suffering fits so violent that the attending doctor nearly despaired. Lennox wrote to Margaret, though he concealed the worst: 'I do send a letter herewith to my wife,' he told Cecil, 'to let her understand of my sickness, but not the extremity thereof, for if she did I think it would trouble her.'[18] For nearly a month he remained at Berwick, undergoing relapses of his 'sore ague', waiting for news from Scotland, and petitioning Cecil for money.[19] But by the second week of May, he told Margaret that he was better and Cecil that he was ready to go to Scotland and 'to pull the feathers off the other party's wings'.[20]

Before leaving Berwick, Lennox wrote a long letter to Elizabeth, entrusting 'your poor kinswoman my wife and only son' to the queen's protection and asserting their loyalty: 'Although she and I hath given but small cause to any to bear us evil will yet I do know we are not without some false friends, and what cause they have so to be I know not unless it be in doing your majesty service, which we do not repent us of nor never will.'[21] Returning to Scotland, he harried prominent Marians out of Glasgow and revived his old alliance of convenience with Margaret's Douglas relatives.[22] Come the summer, the king's party were determined to have him as Regent, and Elizabeth assented to what had become inevitable.[23]

Just after Lennox's arrival, Cecil let Margaret know that her husband had made it safely to Scotland and that the queen's party was in disarray. Lennox had specially instructed him to tell her about James: 'I have seen the king her *oye*, greatly to my comfort.'[24] Margaret had not spoken Scots for years, but the short, Gaelic-derived word could only mean one thing: *oye* was Scots for 'grandchild'.

It was probably at this time or shortly afterwards that Margaret commissioned the locket known as the Lennox or Darnley Jewel. This piece of jewellery, now in the Royal Collection, has inspired many theories concerning both its date of creation and its intended audience. It has been variously interpreted as the 'marvelous rich and fair jewel' that Margaret sent to Mary in 1564 when she was trying to finalise the Darnley match; a memorial to Lennox commissioned some time after his demise; and a gift to James made shortly before Margaret's own death.[25] However, internal clues raise another possibility, namely that the locket was made for James either during or as a prelude to Lennox's regency.[26]

The heart-shaped locket tells a story in gold and precious stones, aided by seven cryptic Scots mottoes. That story's theme, apparent at first glance, is dynastic right. In the centre of the locket is an egg-shaped sapphire, surmounted by a crown. When the crown is opened, the monogram MSL, for Margaret and Matthew Stewart Lennox, and the motto 'What we Resolve' are found beneath it. Under the blue gem is a *memento mori*, a skull bearing the inscription 'Death Shall Dissolve'. The white enamel border surrounding the locket bears the motto 'Who hopes still constantly with patience shall obtain victory in their claim'. The claim is evidently the crown, mounted above the egg and supported by the figures of Victory and Truth, who stand above Hope and Faith. James was already King of Scots, so the claim in question was almost certainly the English crown: Margaret envisioned her grandson as Elizabeth's successor.

The reverse embroiders the theme of dynastic triumph through perseverance. It depicts a sun, beneath which are found a crowned salamander in flames, a phoenix in flames, a pelican feeding its young with its own blood, and the body of a young man, from whose recumbent form a yellow flower grows. The image tells the story of the Darnley match from the grief-stricken vantage of the Lennox-Stewarts: a young man dies, sacrificing himself, like the pelican, for his son. That son becomes a symbol of the future, and unites the claims of the Tudors and the Lennox-Stewarts, via the blood of the house of Douglas. Hence the dynastic emblems: on the obverse, the Lennox fleur-de-lis, and on the reverse, Elizabeth's phoenix with the Douglas salamander and heart.[27]

As an art form, lockets are secretive; there is a face visible to the world, and an interior known only to the wearer. The panel revealed when the locket is opened is the most densely iconographic section of the jewel. Its images refer to Mary's complicity in Darnley's death and to the union of the Lennox-Stewart and Tudor claims to the English throne. The image of a queen imprisoned on her throne is associated with Cassiopeia, the beautiful mother whose vanity nearly brought about her child's death – an apt avatar for Mary. The duel and the woman being taken captive may refer to Darnley's murder and Mary's abduction by Bothwell. The Scots mottoes on this panel also serve as anagrams, adding another layer of secrecy to this already secret panel: they can be arranged to spell 'Margaret is Leil', or true; 'Mat[thew] S[tewart] L[ennox] ye Real [Royal] Reg[ent]', and 'My PS [princess] Eliza rules me'. The lack of reference to Mary, the stress on the Lennox-Stewarts' loyalty to Elizabeth, and the mention of Lennox's regency, reinforce the idea that the locket was made after Moray's death in 1570 and prior to Lennox's own in 1571.[28] The use of Scots is unique in Margaret's surviving writings, and apart from the odd word, Lennox did not use it in writing to her. This suggests that the locket was meant for a speaker other than Lennox, one with a claim to a greater throne – James.

Although Margaret was committed to the idea of James as king of a dynastically united Britain and was willing to work with Protestants to bring about her dreams, she did not abandon her own religious convictions. Heart-shaped jewels were popular in the mid-sixteenth century, as were pendants based on family symbols, so it was doubly unremarkable for a Douglas to commission a heart-shaped jewel – the family emblem was the heart of Robert the Bruce. But heart-shaped jewels with images of the saints were also popular with Catholics, who used them as devotional aids. Concealed beneath the crown and above the intertwined letters MSL are two hearts bound with a golden knot and pierced by two arrows, evoking the sorrows of the Virgin Mary. Margaret turned artistic convention towards her own political and religious ends.[29]

For more than twenty-five years Lennox had been trying to gain control of the government of Scotland by bolstering his ties to the royal family and diminishing the influence of the Hamiltons. When he finally managed to secure power, it was as Regent to a king who was his own grandson, with support from Scots and English alike – it was, in short, a good political hand. He and Margaret both knew that, played well, it augured still more – and the Lennox Jewel promised that constant hope would be rewarded with an even greater crown.

20

The Lady Regent

Shortly before Lennox was named Regent, Margaret was summoned to Elizabeth's presence and handed a letter. It was addressed to her, and under the queen's eyes Margaret unfolded and read the message. The letter came from Mary, Queen of Scots, and she had entrusted its delivery to her emissary, the Bishop of Ross. Mary wrote that Margaret 'had not only as it were condemned me wrongfully but so hated as by your words and deeds hath testified to all the world a manifest misliking in you against your own blood'. In spite of their kinship, Margaret heeded 'wrong and false reports' from men treacherous to herself as well as to Mary, 'enemies . . . alas too much trusted of me by your advice', who had convinced Margaret 'against my innocence (and I must say against all kindness)'. For these reasons, Mary had put off writing to her, hoping 'with God's grace and time to have my innocence known to you'.

Time, at least, had done nothing to convince Margaret of her niece's innocence. But Mary explained that she now had to write to Margaret on a matter that concerned them both: bringing James, 'your little son and my only child', into England. Mary was open to the idea, but wanted Margaret's advice, 'as in all other things touching him'. She intended to 'love you as my aunt, and respect you as my mother-in-law', not 'showing therein any unkindness to you, how unkindly that ever you have dealt with me'. She gave her commendations to Charles, but did not mention Lennox, and concluded by praying God would 'cause you to know my part better [than] now you do'.[1] It was an olive branch, albeit one offered with less grace than it might have been.

Margaret wanted nothing to do with Mary. Having read the letter, she was still unmoved, resolved to work for Lennox and maintain her good relations with both Elizabeth and Cecil. But in Scotland, Lennox's welcome soon gave way to mistrust and broken faith, and he, having come into the country with the hope of finally holding and enjoying government, grew paranoid and obsessive. Although Margaret did her utmost for Lennox and, with the mind of one who had once been in charge of a formidable news-gathering network, proved adept at keeping misinformation from him, she could not save her husband from the consequences of his own failures.

She had London lodgings in Somerset Place on the Strand. It was a stately palace built on land that Protector Somerset had acquired in the wake of Henry's Reformation, when the medieval riverfront 'inns' or houses that had once belonged to bishops and abbots were suddenly on the market. Somerset had spent freely, pulling down the old inns and building a new residence with a be-columned classical facade.[2] From here, Margaret once again started collecting intelligence. There was palpable tension during the first weeks of Lennox's regency: the English were trying to broker a peace between the queen's party and the king's, an idea Lennox was resisting. Elizabeth also wanted Mary back in Scotland, where she was rightfully queen and where she would not be such a dangerous focal point for the plotting of disaffected English Catholics. At the end of August 1570, the Scottish queen's supporters agreed to a truce, and Margaret heard rumours that commissioners were set to go to Mary herself to treat with her for her liberty.[3]

The news sent Margaret into a fury, and she hurried to write to Cecil. Mary's freedom was a horrifying prospect: not only was Mary guilty of 'the grievous murder which by her means only upon my dear son her husband was executed', but she would also make it impossible for Lennox to 'so well serve the queen's majesty's turn as now'. As she tried to warn Cecil against letting Mary return to Scotland, her writing grew agitated, the pen pressing hard into the paper, words started and then crossed out in frustration: '[Her Majesty] I trust will hold me excused considering whereupon I ground my desire for stay of her who otherwise I doubt shall stir up such ill as hereafter all too late may be repented.'[4] After writing to Cecil, she wrote immediately to Lennox.[5]

When it came to the Queen of Scots, Margaret and Lennox were in complete agreement. He wrote as much to her in October, making the arguments that would hold the most sway with Cecil: 'But for all my own simple opinions, there is no surety for her highness to enter in any treaty with the Queen, tending always to her preferment or liberty.' He pointedly recalled that moment in Mary's past that had always seemed most sinister to Elizabeth's secretary, the moment when Mary, then still in France, had 'usurped [Elizabeth's] style, title, and arms'.[6]

Margaret saw that she now had a new role to play in British politics. She became Lennox's chief intermediary with Elizabeth and with Cecil. 'My good Meg,' Lennox wrote, 'you must sustain a part of my burden to use the place of a solicitor and agent, as well in delivering of my letters to her Majesty and to my lords . . . I cannot well commit the handling of those matters, being of such weight, to any other than your self.' He had faith in her likeability and political sense: 'Neither am I assured if other messengers should be so well liked of, nor if the personages with whom you have to deal, would be so plain and frank with others as they will be with you.'[7]

At first, Margaret played her part from Somerset Place, sending the letters off to Cecil with a plea that he take them seriously and give Lennox a speedy reply: 'My hope is only in God and your wisdom to foresee the perils and dangers that may happen if that realm may understand the parliamenting with the queen of Scots as by these notes you may perceive. I shall desire you . . . that my lord may have answer by his said servant with such convenient speed as ye may for that my lord will think the time long.'[8]

Shortly afterwards, however, Margaret joined the court at Windsor to make her case in person. After 'much ado' over finding her a set of rooms, she met with the queen to talk Scottish politics. Elizabeth was not pleased about the harsh line taken against members of Mary's party, but she did not blame Lennox – the fault rested with Margaret's cousin James Douglas, Earl of Morton, her old opponent over the earldom of Angus. When the conversation turned to the Queen of Scots, Margaret told Elizabeth that Mary had had far gentler treatment than she had any right to expect: 'Her Majesty was good lady to her, and better, I thought, than any other prince would have been if they were in her case.' In a rare display of family feeling, Elizabeth asked her how she was bearing up under Lennox's absence. The queen could recall other times when the Lennox-Stewarts had been separated and Margaret had 'wept and wished my lord at home'. Margaret replied that the seriousness of Lennox's role allowed no time for tears, for 'since that time [Lennox] had a great burden laid upon him, which made me not to do so now'. Elizabeth agreed that only James was a strong enough reason to keep Margaret and Lennox apart: 'If it were not for that little one she thought he could not like her being there.'

Margaret reported all this to Cecil, with whom she was still finding common cause. The correspondence was a political responsibility and a personal outlet: 'Thus I unburden my mind to you as to him whom I know hath most care of the good estate of the realm and the preservation of the queen's majesty and a friend to me and mine.'[9]

But there were already difficulties. Lennox was taking a hard line in Scotland and winning himself unnecessary enemies. He had imprisoned the elderly mother of Mary's close friend and lady-in-waiting Mary Seton, for the crime of writing to her daughter. Elizabeth had to write to the Earl of Sussex, Lord President of the North, to get him to talk Lennox into a less aggressive approach.[10] Worse, one of Margaret and Lennox's servants, a man by the name of John Moon, was found to be an agent of the Queen of Scots. Under repeated torture, Moon confessed to having been in contact with the Bishop of Ross through the mediation of the perpetually antagonistic Thomas Bishop, and that he – Moon – had been keeping some of Margaret's reports from Lennox.[11]

Still, Margaret and Elizabeth were on better terms than they had ever been. At the New Year's celebrations of 1571, Margaret gave Elizabeth a much more personal gift than the usual purse of gold: 'a round kirtle with a pair of bodies loose of gold and silver tinsel striped bordered with two yards of black velvet embroidered with pipes and spangles of venice silver'. It was the sort of present she might once have given to Mary Tudor. Elizabeth, in return, gave her more plate than on any other occasion: an elaborate basin as well as a ewer and a covered goblet. Shortly thereafter, she gave her a grant of £800.[12] The two were often together, Margaret seen to be 'most busy of all' on Lennox's behalf.[13]

In Scotland, Lennox was growing ever more ruthless. In April he seized the Marian stronghold of Dumbarton: some solace, perhaps, for his nearly three decades in exile, as he had been born in the castle and had struggled fruitlessly to win it for Henry VIII back in the 1540s. He then took gruesome revenge on the Hamiltons. Châtelherault's illegitimate half-brother John Hamilton, Archbishop of St Andrews, was a committed Marian of long standing: he had baptised her son, given her shelter after her escape from Lochleven, and stayed loyal even after her flight into England. More damningly, he had helped his kinsman James Hamilton of Bothwellhaugh to assassinate the Regent, Moray. Lennox captured him on 2 April 1571 and put him on trial, finding him guilty of involvement in the deaths of both Moray and Darnley, though it is unclear whether or not Hamilton had any hand in Darnley's death. Four days after his capture, he was hanged in the public marketplace at Stirling.

The Marians, however, were not broken. They still held Edinburgh Castle, and when Lennox assembled a parliament in the city in May, members were forced to crawl on their hands and knees into the Canongate while their enemies shot at them, earning the episode the nickname 'the creeping parliament'.[14]

Margaret was becoming increasingly impatient to see Lennox and James, whom she had yet to meet. By June, her husband had been in Scotland for more than a year and there was talk of 'my lady Regent' leaving England and taking up residence in Holyrood, first converted into proper royal lodgings for her mother's use.[15] But she then received a letter from her cousin William, Lord Ruthven. He assured her that her grandson was doing well, growing every day 'in person and judgement'. Nonetheless, he told her gently that Scotland was simply too dangerous for her and for her surviving son Charles: '[I] wish to God that there was such quietness here that your grace might with pleasure arrive in this realm to the comfort of the king my sovereign and my lord your grace's husband.'[16] So Margaret, growing apprehensive, remained in England.

Over the summer, Lennox's relationships in Scotland deteriorated, especially his alliance with Margaret's cousin Morton. His letters mingled tremendous optimism with flashes of frustration and despair. Lennox was curt even with Margaret: on the one occasion that his messenger failed to bring back letters directly answering his own, even though he had warned Margaret of his imminent departure, Lennox wrote 'I thought great marvel that I received no letter from you . . . except two letters dated of old . . . I think long to hear from you'.[17] In August he declared 'it was and is most untrue that the nobility had left me' and the next month he wrote of his confidence in the success of the king's party.[18] At the same time – knowing that Margaret would convey his letter to Elizabeth – he complained that the one charge his adversaries could lay against him was his loyalty to England: 'I have been termed of the adversaries, by writ and otherwise, a sworn Englishman.'[19] In fact, consciously or unconsciously, hints of Scots were creeping back into his writing – not many Englishmen would have written 'meikill mair short' when 'much shorter' would have served.[20] Lennox's real difficulty was not that he was pro-English, but that he was obsessively anti-Marian.

His regency, he wrote, had served both his home and his adopted countries. After Moray's death, 'it is well known that there was no such thing as governing [Scotland], but a confused desolation, every man standing on his own guard and taking private revenge on such as they had offended against . . . Fire and bloodshed during that time were not only in the bowels of the realm, but also her majesty's own realm and subjects suffered the same plague.' He had come to Scotland 'for the affection I bear to the preservation of this innocent king and to the preserving of this peace and amity betwixt the realms'.[21]

Nonetheless, Margaret took Lennox's assurance that Morton was still in alliance straight to Cecil, who had already heard an opposing opinion from William Drury, marshal of Berwick and one of England's most trusted and experienced lieutenants in Scotland. Drury apologised for having contradicted the Lennox-Stewarts, telling Cecil he hoped he would not think that 'in a matter of such weight he would hastily or unadvisedly have advertised upon every hearsay or writing'.[22] Margaret was determined that Lennox's portrait of events should be the one most trusted by the regime.

At the same time, Margaret sent out her servants to gather intelligence so that she could get it to Lennox before he could have it from any other source. When John Case, provost marshal of Berwick, gave him a report that contradicted one of Margaret's, Lennox told him that he had already heard the opposite, adding morosely that 'it is no matter: it is better to be happy than wise'.[23] Confident in her contacts at court, he trusted her information best.

But though Margaret was doing her utmost to pass intelligence to both Lennox and Cecil, there were efforts under way in Scotland and England to cut her out of the loop. Case told Drury that 'my Lady Lennox getteth most of your advertisements and writes them unto him, which maketh him so much to mislike with you', leading Drury to ask Cecil to keep information from her, 'otherwise I shall not receive such knowledge as I have done'.[24] Meanwhile, Lennox's letters were becoming self-deluding.

At the beginning of September 1571, Lennox wrote confidently to Margaret that 'it appears to look favourable on his highness [James] and all his cause, nothing in effect resting if the town and castle of Edinburgh well were made obedient, for the which nothing in me shall be omitted and left undone'.[25] But as parliament assembled at Stirling, disaster awaited.

The streets of Stirling were narrow, steep and silent as a group of queen's men rode in at daybreak. They moved freely through the town, each one knowing just where his intended captive would be lodging. David Spence of Wormiston came to Lennox's house, pushed past his terrified servants and seized the Regent from his chamber. Some of the king's men, though scarcely more awake than Lennox, put up more resistance. Before long, the streets were filled with brawling men and the crack of musket fire. Lennox nearly managed to free himself and escape on horseback, but amid the confusion came a cry: 'Shoot the Regent!' A single bullet went through both Lennox and his would-be captor, leaving the earl with a mortal stomach wound.[26]

In spite of the trauma, Lennox was able to stay mounted and ride towards the summit of the dizzying hill, determined to reach the fortress of Stirling Castle. His companions, perhaps guessing how badly he was hurt, tried to encourage him. Lennox replied 'If the babe be well, all is well.' When they came to the courtyard, men helped him off his horse and into the stony chill of the Great Hall, where servants rushed to prepare a bed and stoke the vast fireplaces. It soon became clear that Lennox was dying. He summoned the nobles to his bedside and said once again that he had never sought to become Regent:

> but your choice that brought me to the charge I have this while sustained, which I undertook the more willingly, that I was persuaded of your assistance in the defence of the infant King, whose protection by nature and duty I could not refuse. And now being able to do no more, I must commend him to the Almighty God, and to your care . . . And I must likewise commend unto your favour my servants, who never have received benefit at my hands, and desire you to remember my love to my wife Meg . . . whom I beseech God to comfort.[27]

Lennox lingered on for hours after being shot. He had had no perceptible religious views since coming into Scotland – and all his chief allies had been Protestants – but there was a hint of the old faith on his deathbed. He prayed continually and asked the nobles 'to assist him with their prayers', though it is uncertain whether he simply wanted the support of their voices as he prayed or if he was asking them to intercede for his Purgatory-bound soul.[28]

In death, Lennox served the useful purpose of uniting the king's assorted adherents, as they swore a bond to avenge the late Regent's murder. Captain George Bell and Captain James Cawdor admitted their roles in Lennox's assassination. Within ten days they had both been put to death and Cawdor, who had pulled the trigger, died 'after the manner of France, arms and legs broken and set upon a wheel'.[29]

Elizabeth and Cecil were away from court when they had word from Scotland. The queen had been on her summer progress and she and most of the Privy Council were at Lees, a country mansion in Essex belonging to Lord Rich.[30] Cecil absorbed the news and instructed the men who brought it to keep silent until they could confirm it and tell Margaret. 'I would have no knowledge come to the Lady Lennox,' he wrote, 'but she shall hear it from the Queen's Majesty.'[31]

When it was found to be true, there was disagreement over Lennox's legacy. William Drury, hearing rumours of Lennox's death, wrote 'if it be true, the Queen's Majesty hath received a great loss: the like of affection she will never find of a Scottish-born person.'[32] Morton, whose loyalty had so obsessed Lennox in his final weeks, was coolly objective: the queen's party had suffered casualties whereas the king's party had lost only a handful of men and no nobles – 'saving only my lord Regent's grace'. As for the new Regent, John Erskine, Earl of Mar, he had 'better opinion and knowledge of this country and the affairs thereof nor had my lord Regent's grace which is lately departed'.[33] Antonio de Guaras, a Spaniard living in London, had written in July 1570 that Lennox and Margaret were Catholics who had not forgiven Elizabeth for their past imprisonments: Spain, he believed, could not hope for a better governor in Scotland.[34] Lennox, however, did little to justify these Catholic hopes, and by the time of his death the Spanish ambassador Guerau de Spes had no sympathy: 'the only one who paid the penalty of his bad government was Lennox'.[35]

But Margaret did not care that Lennox had been a poor Regent or that he had disappointed Catholics in Europe and Scotland. When Elizabeth broke the news to her, there was only one possible reaction. She and Lennox, as she had once told Cecil, had 'been together' for nearly thirty years, through the loss of seven children as well as long spells of imprisonment, poverty and political frustration, bound to each other not just by the force of their British ambitions for their family but through an instant attraction that had deepened and softened into love.[36] As Cecil had foreseen, Margaret was inconsolable.

The new Regent wrote to her with words of comfort and she forced herself to reply. Although Margaret had made herself into an Englishwoman, Scotland had been her childhood home, her husband's country, her son's kingdom, the means by which she hoped to see her family ascend the throne of a united Britain. Now, she could not bring herself to write its name: 'Perverse fortune hath been such in that realm towards me that there I have lost my chiefest comforts, having cause sufficient thereby that the remembrance of the country should be grievous unto me.' The grief was still so raw that her husband was not 'my lord', 'the late regent' or even 'Lennox': he was simply '[he] . . . that is gone'.[37]

Lennox was buried in the chapel of Stirling Castle, and Margaret paid for a substantial tomb, with Latin verses written by the historian George Buchanan and a pair of doggerel English poems. The brief epitaph for 'a prince and potentate . . . godly, just, and fortunate' concluded with the assurance that although 'thus respects the death no wight,/When God permits the time,/Yet shall the vengeance on them light that wrought that cursed crime'. The second 'heroical verse' took a longer view, celebrating Lennox's match with Margaret and naming them both descendants of Brutus, the mythical first King of Britain: 'Thus did king Brutus blood conjoin, for both by grace divine/Are come of Northwales princes *hault*, which were of Trojans' line.'[38] Their Anglo-Scottish marriage had always been more than a romance: Lennox was dead, but the promise of their union survived him.

21

A Lone Woman

Overcome with shock and grief, Margaret could hardly move. It was as if she were in a trance, and it took some time before she could turn her mind to anything other than mourning. She stayed in the village of Hackney, just outside London, overwhelmed by the loss of Lennox, her terror for James and a passionate desire for revenge. But her friends sent messages urging her back to action, playing on her concern for her surviving family members. Although she was 'now a lone woman', as she put it to Cecil, she had 'awakened my self'.[1] A month after Lennox's death, she was dictating letters to the new Regent in Scotland.

Lennox's death left her with dozens of small matters and practicalities to handle, from making sure that his friends and servants were repaid any money they were owed to recovering a pair of falcons that she wanted to give to a friend in England. But it was the protection of the young king that commanded her attention: she wanted him kept safe and she wanted revenge for Lennox's 'cruel end'. Whatever she could do in England, she would: 'What I may do in the advancement of his actions I shall not leave anything of my power unapplied thereto.'[2] Her focus now was the safety and happiness of her family.

Margaret also had cause to worry about her surviving son, Charles Stewart. The puffy-faced boy painted in *The Memorial of Lord Darnley* was now sixteen years old and had grown up with a father absent in Scotland and a mother often locked away in prison. It was with some guilt that she compared Charles to Darnley. Unlike her eldest son, who had been educated and raised 'only at home with his father and me', Charles had reached late adolescence 'somewhat unfurnished of qualities needful'. Keen to remedy the gap, Margaret made a proposal to Cecil, who had recently been raised to the peerage as Baron Burghley. In order that Charles might 'serve his prince and country hereafter', she suggested that Cecil take him into his own household, where he could 'be brought up and instructed . . . so long time as shall be needful'. Such a serve, she wrote, 'shall not only bind me but him and his friends to pray for your Lordship'.[3]

It was both an ordinary and an extraordinary request. The idea of sending Charles away was not intrinsically strange: Darnley had not been very much older when he had gone to Scotland to romance Mary, and Cecil had shown himself willing to take young noblemen into his household, especially when their fathers' deaths brought them into their titles at an early age.[4] For a man expecting a career in royal service, Cecil House on the Strand was the perfect political finishing school, close to the Inns of Court and the London palaces, a hub for London's Elizabethan elite. But Margaret cannot have had any illusions about the kind of schooling her son would get in Cecil's house. Devout Protestant worship set the rhythms of the inhabitants' lives; there would be no chance of Charles being brought up 'in that devilish papistry' that Margaret had impressed upon his older brother.[5]

In response, Cecil and Margaret seem to have worked out a similarly Protestant alternative. Rather than moving to the Strand, Charles took up lodgings at Gray's Inn, that seedbed of reform where Cecil had started his own legal career.[6] He also acquired an unlikely tutor, probably with Cecil's help. The post went to the Swiss Protestant Peter Malliet, 'led by both the prayers and the promises of the great of this kingdom'.[7] Margaret had raised her eldest son to be a Catholic king, but her youngest was being groomed for service in a Protestant state.

Her English loyalty and her willingness to downplay her own religious beliefs brought more material help. On Lennox's death, his earldom had reverted to the Scottish crown, since King James was his nearest heir. Cecil proposed that Charles should get his late father's title, and James's council, acting on his behalf, agreed.[8] Charles had never set foot in Scotland and wrote a letter thanking the lords for their magnanimity 'towards me, unknown to you, or to the most number of you'.[9] The grant was confirmed by the parliament of January 1573, although there was some grumbling that Charles ought to come and live in Scotland 'as became a good Scottish man'.[10] His new title did not bring any special wealth – the land had all been mortgaged – but it was a show of good faith, and Elizabeth thanked the new Regent, the Earl of Mar, for his 'goodwill and favour towards our said cousins both the mother and son'.[11]

The key to Margaret's alliance with Cecil and Elizabeth lay in her enduring enmity for Mary, Queen of Scots. Sensing this, Mary ceased her efforts to reconcile with Margaret and once again tried to divide her from Elizabeth. The Scottish queen declared that the entire Darnley marriage scheme had been Margaret's idea, promoted relentlessly from long before Darnley's 'release' from England. But Margaret refused to let Mary distract her. She devoted her time to helping the Regent, delivering messages from him and from James to Elizabeth, never failing to give the queen her own anti-Mary counsel on Scottish affairs. Mar, however, suddenly died in October 1572 and was succeeded by James Douglas, Earl of Morton.

It was not easy for Margaret to trust her ambitious cousin. Morton was her old rival over the earldom of Angus and an instigator of the plot against Mary's Italian secretary David Rizzio.

He had had a role in Darnley's death as well, though Lennox never seems to have grasped this and was obsessed in the last weeks of his life with keeping Morton on his side. But whatever else he was, Morton was James's Regent, so Margaret struck up a correspondence with him.[12]

One of the great tasks Morton faced was the recapturing of Edinburgh Castle, still in the possession of the queen's party. Mary's supporters were gradually growing weaker: in early 1573 the Earl of Huntly and the Hamiltons submitted to the king's party and were pardoned. Margaret was far from pleased with this magnanimity towards her deceased husband's foes, but there was something she could do.

The English diplomat Henry Killigrew wrote to Cecil that Margaret could have her revenge by convincing Elizabeth to fund the taking of Edinburgh Castle. It would help to conclude the war swiftly and end the danger to James: 'If Lady Lennox be not satisfied it would be asked whether war would make the matter better or worse, and whether it be not more necessary to preserve him that is alive than to continue the danger of his life in seeking a revenge for the dead; yet if she were to persuade the Queen to send the Regent means to win the Castle, she could not be better revenged, nor do the Queen and this young babe greater service.'[13] Elizabeth did at last agree to send aid – though the influence of Margaret's urging is uncertain – and the king's party recovered the castle in the spring of 1573. Morton turned to Margaret in the aftermath of his triumph, counting on her to thank Cecil and Leicester for the 'great goodwill' they had showed the king's party.[14] Later, he sent 'most heartily thanks for the great care and good will you show to the furtherance of the king your dearest nephew's affairs there [in England], wishing of God that you may long continue in good health and so be able to stand him in stead as you have always heretofore'.[15]

Margaret's grandson appeared safe, and she could content herself that she had worked on his behalf.

It may have been for James's sake that Margaret now decided to leave London and return to Yorkshire. The French ambassador, Bertrand de la Mothe Fénelon, suspected that her proposed visit was merely an excuse to travel northwards. Her real destination, he was convinced, was Scotland: 'From [her house] she will cross into Scotland to see the young prince, her grandson, which I judge can be for no other end than to try to get him into her hands, in order to bring him [into England].'[16] The Spanish ambassador reported it as a fact, declaring that Margaret 'was already on the road to receive [James] if they [the Scots] would consent to give him up'.[17] Elizabeth, however, expressed doubts about Margaret's going, which raises the possibility that Margaret may not have had an official diplomatic mission and may simply have wanted to be closer to James.[18] With a team of oxen granted by the Privy Council, Margaret's servants packed her household goods into carts and prepared for the trip from Hackney to Temple Newsam.[19]

Shortly before she set out, Margaret met with Elizabeth and tried to allay the queen's anxieties about her proposed journey north. Along her route lay Chatsworth House, where the Earl and Countess of Shrewsbury were hosting – and guarding – the Scottish queen. Enquiring as to whether Margaret might go to Chatsworth if invited, Elizabeth asked that she avoid the house, lest she give the appearance of being in sympathy with the Queen of Scots. The suggestion was laughable, even offensive, and Margaret, with a force and directness that surprised Elizabeth, demanded 'if she could think so, for I was made of flesh and blood and could never forget the murder of my child'. The queen, struck by Margaret's gravity, replied 'nay, by her father she could no, not think so, that ever I could forget it – for if I would, I were a devil'.[20] With Elizabeth reassured, Margaret and Charles set out together for Yorkshire.

It was at this point that Margaret let herself be drawn away from her original plan. As she and Charles travelled onwards, Margaret received a message from the Countess of Shrewsbury asking her to stop at Rufford Abbey, a long-suppressed Cistercian monastery acquired by the earls of Shrewsbury after the dissolution. Good manners dictated that she accept the invitation, especially as the abbey was not more than a mile out of her way and would take her towards 'a much fairer' route than the one she had planned. Margaret agreed and met the countess herself as she approached the abbey.[21]

The Countess of Shrewsbury, better known as Bess of Hardwick, had been born Elizabeth Hardwick, daughter of an obscure Derbyshire gentleman. Sharp, experienced and practical, she had risen by a series of fortunate marriages to become one of the wealthiest noblewomen in England. In November 1567 she had married George Talbot, Earl of Shrewsbury, who became chief captor to Mary, Queen of Scots, in 1569. In spite of their marked social and religious differences – Bess was a confirmed Protestant – Mary and Bess got along reasonably well. When Bess was at Chatsworth, they could often be found sewing or embroidering together.[22]

Mary was not at Rufford Abbey, but Bess was not alone: accompanying her was Elizabeth Cavendish, her daughter by her second husband. Meeting the wealthy and well-spoken young woman, nineteen-year-old Charles was smitten with 'sudden affection'.[23] Elizabeth, for her part, had been recently 'disappointed' by a former suitor, and Bess encouraged her to consider Charles instead.[24] Before long, Charles was pleading with Margaret to let him marry Elizabeth.[25]

Charles's sudden passion took Margaret by surprise. He was old enough to marry and she had started to give some thought

This portrait of William Cecil, 1st Baron Burghley, is attributed to the Flemish artist Marcus Gheeraerts the Younger. It shows the statesman riding a mule. Despite their deep religious and political differences, Margaret and Cecil had a cordial and sometimes even friendly relationship.

This double portrait of first cousins Mary, Queen of Scots and Henry, Lord Darnley was painted c.1565, near the beginning of their disastrous marriage. It later belonged to Bess of Hardwick, who had close connections to both sitters: she was one of Mary's guardians during the Queen's captivity in England and mother-in-law to Darnley's younger brother, Charles.

This miniature of James Hepburn, 4th Earl of Bothwell, shows him in his early thirties. It was painted to mark his wedding to Lady Jean Gordon in February 1566. Fifteen months later, the marriage was annulled and Bothwell married the Queen of Scots.

The Memorial of Lord Darnley, a large painting by Livinus de Vogelaare, was dedicated to James VI. It depicts the young king together with Lennox, Margaret and Charles, all in mourning and all offering up Latin prayers for vengeance. The inset in the lower left corner shows Mary's defeat at Carberry Hill.

The heart-shaped locket known as the Lennox or Darnley Jewel. Made of gold, glass and gems, it was commissioned by Margaret – whose initials, along with those of Lennox, appear beneath the crown.

This miniature by the portraitist Nicholas Hilliard shows Margaret in 1575, not long before her death.

Rijksmuseum, Amsterdam

Portrait of the young Arbella Stewart, daughter of Charles Stewart and Elizabeth Cavendish. She was Margaret's only granddaughter and principal heir.

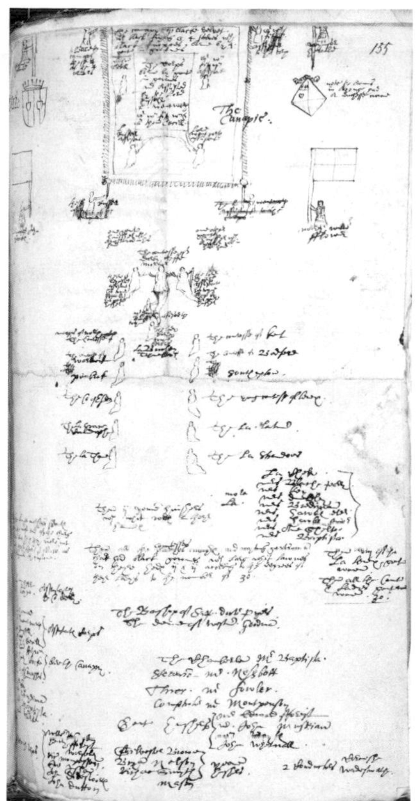

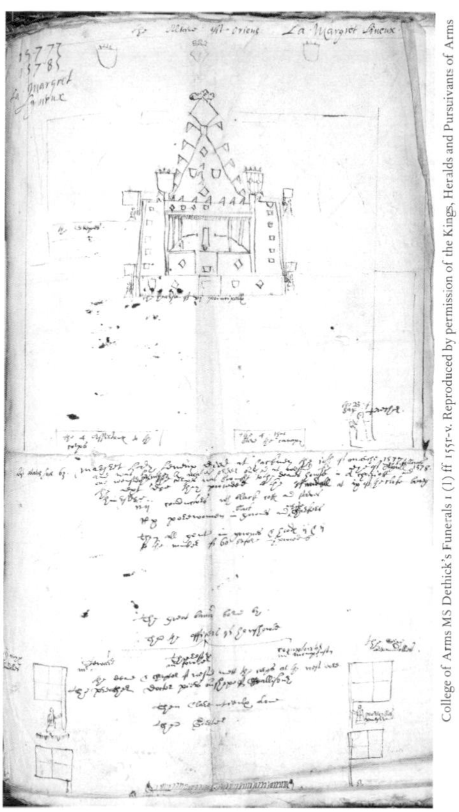

This manuscript contains details of Margaret's funeral procession at Westminster Abbey as well as a drawing of her hearse. The mourners included leading nobles, her household staff, and, as she set out in her will, a hundred poor women gowned in black.

As she requested, Margaret was buried in Westminster Abbey along with her youngest son, Charles. She shares the south aisle of the Lady Chapel with her niece Mary, Queen of Scots and great-grandmother Margaret Beaufort.

'Progeny', in seventeenth-century English, could mean both offspring and ancestors. This 1619 line engraving depicts James VI and I as the flower of a royal family tree with its roots in the marriage of Henry VII and Elizabeth of York. Margaret Douglas is second from the right in the central row.

to a match for him – one 'other than this', as she later wrote to the Earl of Leicester. Elizabeth Cavendish, although she was stepdaughter to the Earl of Shrewsbury, was not of noble birth herself, and she was the daughter of a firm Protestant. But Margaret, in spite of her private beliefs, had been distancing herself from her fellow English Catholics for nearly ten years. Bess of Hardwick was rich in her own right, something the Lennox-Stewarts, for all their royal blood, were not. And it is possible that having been in love twice herself, once with Thomas Howard and again with Lennox, and having pushed Darnley into a loveless marriage that caused his death, Margaret could not stand to disappoint her youngest son. So when Charles came to her for help, and she saw that her 'only son and comfort . . . had entangled himself so that he could have none other', she agreed to the match.[26]

Margaret does not seem to have been as ambitious for Charles as she had been for Darnley, but she had made a terrible political misstep. Although Charles lacked his elder brother's flash and had spent little time at court, he was Margaret's son and therefore a potential claimant to the English throne. Although wedding Elizabeth Cavendish did nothing to bolster that claim, descendants of Henry VII could not marry without the queen's permission. Queen Elizabeth was furious, and the fact that Bess was one of Mary's closest companions lent the situation the air of treason.

As soon as Margaret realised the scale of her mistake, she enlisted help to fix it. She begged Bess's husband, the Earl of Shrewsbury, to write to the Privy Council and protest her innocence of all wrongdoing. Shrewsbury agreed: Margaret, he said, was 'a subject in all respects worthy the Queen's Majesty's favour' and he asked that Cecil and the Council 'save her from blemish, if no offence can be found in her towards her Majesty'. The real concern was not the marriage, 'nor the hatred some bear to my Lady Lennox, my wife, or to me, that makes this great ado, and occupies heads with so many devices; it is a greater matter . . .' He was not being particularly subtle: the fear was that this marriage would somehow help the Queen of Scots. But Shrewsbury declared he would not have stood for the marriage if it could be of any help to Mary or any danger to Elizabeth: 'I would not have her Majesty think . . . that I could or would bear with it . . . for [Margaret's] sake, or for my wife, or any other cause else.'[27]

Shrewsbury's intervention was not enough: the queen ordered Margaret back to London. Margaret made her way haltingly, and her mules – with a keen sense of timing – wore themselves out as she neared the town of Huntingdon. Glad of the delay, she turned to both Cecil and Leicester for help.[28] Leicester had an unusual bond with her in 1574 in that his mistress, Douglas Howard, was her goddaughter. Margaret had already sent him a detailed explanation of events, which he had brought to the queen. Thanking him, she reiterated her innocence and said she had kept well away from anywhere the Queen of Scots might have been:

> I did not mistrust her Majesty would have been offended with me for seeing the countess of Shrewsbury so that I had neither gone to Chatsworth, which the place her Majesty did mislike of nor yet near Sheffield by thirty miles in the least. And . . . as touching the marriage, other dealing . . . was there none but the sudden affection of my son . . . I beseech your lordship to be a means unto her majesty . . . to have compassion on my widowish estate.[29]

But this explanation convinced nobody.

Queen Elizabeth was engaged in marriage negotiations with the French royal family, which were going poorly. Sir Francis

Walsingham suspected that this sudden Stewart-Cavendish match was an attempt to thwart the talks and destabilise the succession.[30] Walsingham, a stern-faced, Cambridge-educated Protestant who had been a diplomat in France and recently replaced Cecil as Elizabeth's Principal Secretary, was just as impressive an intelligence-gatherer as his predecessor. He also shared Cecil's conviction that the Queen of Scots was the single greatest threat to Elizabeth's throne. He believed that Catholic plotters, European spies and the Queen of Scots had all had a hand in this marriage, and Margaret's household was the link between them.

Once again, Margaret's servants found themselves facing interrogation. Her secretary Thomas Fowler was kept in 'close and strange custody' for nearly a week between questioning sessions and warned of the 'great peril' he would face if he did not talk: 'Some such kind of persuasion cunningly used may perhaps breed such fear and deep conceit in him as may cause him to utter such truth as otherwise may hardly be drawn out of him.' Walsingham instructed the notoriously anti-Catholic Earl of Huntingdon to question Fowler not just about the marriage but about Margaret's politics. The queen and he had received intelligence that Margaret had met in secret with the Bishop of Ross and the Laird of Kilsyth, who claimed or 'pretend[ed] to be enemy to the Queen of Scots'; in fact, both men were devout Catholics and loyal servants of Mary Stewart. According to this intelligence, Margaret had also sent a Portuguese man to Sheffield with letters concerning the marriage of Charles and Elizabeth – the implication being that such a match would please the Queen of Scots.[31]

Walsingham's spies were busy gathering evidence. They found that the Spanish ambassador Antonio de Guaras was trying to learn whether or not Margaret would be committed to the Tower, so they stuck to him and reported whatever they found suspicious: he was endeavouring to rent a boat – 'for the transportation of some wheresoever upon the sudden any need be'. It also came out that one of Charles's servants was 'by former Profession a Popish massing priest', who was immediately suspected of being a spy: '[W]hat all miscreants such disguised men of his calling oftentimes have been and are in these days most like to be your lordship knoweth or may easily conjecture.'

Margaret had to steel herself for questioning as well. When she had been examined about Darnley's suit to Mary, she had been judged stubborn and defiant. But she had been more than a decade younger, matriarch of a devoted family, and determined to carry off an audacious dynastic marriage. This time she was isolated and did not have any such ambition to give her courage – and it was a far more dangerous thing to be a Catholic in 1574 than it had been in 1562. When questioned, she was frightened, which Walsingham took to mean that she was not revealing all she knew about the marriage. To his mind, she seemed 'fearful . . . as though some part of her dealings not yet discovered might reach unto herself'. Just as Cecil had understood the Darnley marriage in 1565, Walsingham understood the Cavendish marriage as the product of Margaret's machinations with British and European Catholics.[32]

Mary herself seems to have had no idea that the marriage was planned, writing that Walsingham's suspicions of her ambassadors' meeting with Fowler were 'so badly-founded, that I expect they will not succeed in anything'.[33] The French ambassador believed that the English had utterly misread the situation. They thought Mary was behind the match and that she wanted to bring Margaret and the Protestant Catherine, Duchess of Suffolk, into league with Bess. 'On the contrary, she fears, more than anything else in the world . . . the meeting of these three women – of whom two have always been her strong enemies . . .'[34] The match could end up being to

Mary's disadvantage, and though the French ambassador was relieved that the marriage had forestalled any plans Margaret might have had to go to Scotland, he feared that she, 'having made friends with the countess of Shrewsbury, may make her [Bess] an enemy of the Queen of Scotland'.[35]

Others close to the situation doubted that Mary had had any involvement. The Regent Morton disclaimed all knowledge and affected prim displeasure, telling Walsingham that it was all a question of money and that his cousins' conduct was shameful to James VI, the earls of Lennox, and his own house of Douglas: 'I cannot but be sorry that my aunt, my lady his mother, and he should have proceeded as they have done', especially as they had not consulted him, in spite 'of the honour [Charles] has to be so near cousin to the King, and of the proximity of blood between him and myself, as also for the respect of his house, and the earldom of Lennox here in this country . . .'[36]

Elizabeth eventually forgave Bess of Hardwick, but for Margaret, eight years of entente with the queen had come to an abrupt end. Once again, Margaret found herself in the Tower. By this third spell of imprisonment, she was nearly sixty and her hair had become completely white. In the drawn-out, unvarying Tower days, she took to embroidery, fashioning her own hair into a delicate piece of needlework known as *point tressé*.[37] Cut off from her only surviving child and with her still-unseen grandson far away in Scotland, Margaret turned all her attention to crafting a small, white square of lace.

22

Watches and Dials

This time, Margaret only had to endure a brief spell in the Tower. She was soon back with Charles and his wife Elizabeth, now parents to a little girl named Arbella. Margaret – whose four daughters had all been stillborn or died as infants – adored her granddaughter, the only one of her grandchildren that she would ever meet. They were living in the King's House, a Hackney manor where Margaret's old friend and cousin, Mary Tudor, had made peace with Henry VIII after acknowledging him head of the Church of England. It was a two-storey brick house, some 100 years old, with nearly 200 acres of land. In its earlier history, it had had a vibrantly frescoed chapel, though by the time Margaret worshipped in the room it had probably been given a Protestant coat of white.[1] As this small, three-generation family took shape in Hackney, Margaret heard news that forced her to reconsider the past eight years of her life.

Reports reached England that Mary Stewart's third husband, the Earl of Bothwell, was dying and that he had made a deathbed confession. In fact, he was lingering on in Denmark, still chained to his pillar in Dragsholm Castle and long since sunk into madness. But this forged account of his repentance was spectacular enough to warrant an English audience. Darnley's death, Margaret heard, had been entirely the doing of Bothwell and his allies. Notable among these men were Mary's half-brother Moray, John Hamilton, Archbishop of St Andrews, and Margaret's own cousin Morton. She also read that Bothwell was an inveterate womaniser who had won Mary by witchcraft. The Queen of Scots had had no role in or knowledge of Darnley's death: like her murdered husband, she was a victim of Bothwell's treachery.[2]

All her life Margaret had been implacable when the stakes were high: in her love for Thomas Howard, her ambition for Darnley, her conviction in Mary's guilt. But after eight years of hatred and denial, she was at last able to admit to herself that Mary might have been innocent of Darnley's murder. Much of the forged confession confirmed what she already believed or found all too easy to believe. Her own husband Lennox had put John Hamilton to death for his part in murdering Moray and been convinced that the archbishop had had a hand in Darnley's end. Margaret's dealings with Morton had never been better than uneasy. He was a reformer, had blocked her claim to her father's earldom, and he was one of the men who had dragged her son into the plot against David Rizzio – and whatever his protestations of familial feeling, he had not acted to help her to any of her revenues in Scotland. If Bothwell, acknowledged as the driving force behind the murder, vowed that Mary was innocent, Margaret found herself believing it.

She had sworn never to go near the Queen of Scots and had faithfully reported all contact with her to Elizabeth, but now, quietly and secretively, she sent a messenger to Mary. He carried a letter written in her own hand, and probably a token as well: the piece of shimmering *point tressé* lace that she had stitched in the Tower.[3] Mary, surprised but delighted, kept Margaret's letter and her gift, and replied with a message of her own, some of it written in a letter and the rest entrusted to the messenger. It was a whole-hearted reconciliation. There were gifts for young

Arbella, who was both her niece by marriage and her first cousin once removed by blood, and for Margaret herself. Above all, there was the question of King James VI.

Margaret immediately dispatched a messenger – whom she called 'our trusty' – to Elizabeth's court. He was instructed 'to understand the state present and for prevention of evil to come'. While there, he met with men who Margaret believed could be trusted, 'such as both may and will have regard for our jewel's [James's] preservation and will use a bridle to the wicked when need requires'. Now, she wrote back to Mary, telling her how much the letter, message and gifts had comforted her. They were bound together by their mutual love and fear for James:

> especially perceiving what zealous natural care your majesty hath of our sweet and peerless jewel in Scotland, not little to my content. I have been no less fearful than careful as your majesty of him, that the wicked governor should not have power to do ill to his person, whom God preserve from his enemies . . .

Arbella was another tie between them, and another focus of hope. Margaret thanked the queen for her 'good remembrance and bounty to our little daughter here, who someday may serve your highness'. When it came to Mary, Margaret had always assumed a certain auntly authority, respecting her queenship but also telling her what she thought best. This old character came back quickly, but there was a new measure of tenderness and affection too: 'I beseech your majesty fear not, but trust in God that all there shall be well, the treachery of your traitor is known better than before. I shall always play my part to your majesty's content, willing God so as may tend to both our comforts.'

As Margaret finished writing, her daughter-in-law Elizabeth added a postscript. Whatever the tensions between her mother,

Bess of Hardwick, and Mary, Elizabeth pledged herself to the Scottish queen's service. She told Mary she could 'but wish and pray God for your majesty long and happy estate till time I may do your majesty better service, which I think long to do, and shall always be as ready thereto as any servant your majesty hath', swearing that she loved and honoured the queen 'unfeignedly'.[4]

Around the time of her reconciliation with Mary, Margaret sat for a miniature portrait by Nicholas Hilliard, the most accomplished artist of Elizabeth's court. She tucked her white hair under a plain white cap and dressed in a high-collared black gown, trimmed with fur, sleeves slashed to reveal black-and-white embroidery, a small white ruff at her chin. Her eyes and lips were pale and the bones of her skull showed through her delicate skin, its pallor heightened by the contrast with the bright lapis background. Unlike Livinus de Vogelaare, who portrayed her haggard with grief and rage in the *Memorial of Lord Darnley*, Hilliard caught her beauty: at sixty, her skin is still unlined, her expression guarded, even piercing, observing the viewers who observe her. Characteristically, she looks like a woman with a secret.

A little over a year later, Mary wrote a will. She commended her son to the protection of the King of France and to her Guise relatives, leaving him 'both my estate in Scotland, and my right in England', on condition that he became a Catholic and abandoned his alliance with Elizabeth. If he died before converting, she left her Scottish rights to the next in line. The old question of whether the Lennox-Stewarts or the Hamiltons could claim to be 'second persons of the realm' endured, but this time Mary wanted religion rather than legitimacy to determine the matter. The next heir was either 'the earl of Lennox, or [Châtelherault's younger son] Claude Hamilton, whichever shows himself the most faithful to me, and the most steadfast in religion, in the judgement of the aforesaid dukes of Lorraine and Guise'.[5] For the first time, Margaret had put her younger son in a position where he might find himself fulfilling the kingly, Catholic destiny she had wanted so badly for Darnley.

But before Charles could achieve such heights – before Mary had even written her will – he fell sick. He died at the age of twenty-one. It was a horrible misfortune: he was the last of Margaret's children. In less than a decade she had lost her husband and both her sons, and the joyful interlude marked by the birth of Arbella and the reconciliation with Mary was over. Bowed down with grief, Margaret buried Charles in the parish church near her house in Hackney.

Charles's death threw her into a struggle that would last until the end of her life. At first, it seemed that she would not have the strength for it. On 24 April 1576 she wrote to William, Lord Ruthven, a Scottish nephew on the Douglas side. It was, she said, 'the first that I have written to any since my son's death, for I have small care of worldly matters'. Nonetheless, at the urging of her friends, she wanted 'to know how the state standeth of the earldom of Lennox because my son hath left a daughter behind him'.[6]

At her husband's death, the Lennox earldom had passed to James, who had given it to his uncle Charles with the approval of a Scottish parliament. Understandably, Margaret believed that Arbella now had the right to be called Countess of Lennox and to draw the revenues of the earldom. A portrait of the little girl, painted in the year after her father's death, shows a serious, red-haired child, wearing a cream dress embroidered with flowers and holding a doll. The inscription labels her 'Arbella, countess of Lennox'. But Margaret now found herself in a humiliating and infuriating posture: for Arbella's sake, she had to apply to Morton for help, asking him to give her the wardship of the Lennox lands as well as her own dower lands. The Regent refused to give them up or even to acknowledge Arbella as heir to the earldom. It was the start of another fight.[7]

Margaret was also defending her lands in England from contesting claims. She had never been easy about money, excepting the brief interlude of Mary Tudor's reign. There were some circumstances she could not control – she did not have access to her Scottish revenues – but she also found it hard to adapt to financial straitening. As early as her first imprisonment, when she had taken on Thomas Howard's servants without being able to pay them, she found it simpler to make decisions first and work out the financial consequences later. Her son's marriage to Elizabeth Cavendish had not brought any of the wealth that cynical observers thought she was expecting. In fact, Margaret was in debt to Bess of Hardwick for £500 per annum. Now, a pair of men laid claim to a small wood at the centre of her land in Whorlton Park in Yorkshire, with plans to cut it down. She was incensed, and writing to Cecil, seemed to relish the prospect of a fight. She would happily prove her title to the land to any of Elizabeth's Privy Council, but if she were found not to be the owner, she would somehow find the money to buy it herself: 'I would be loth,' she wrote, 'to have a stranger to fell the wood within my park.'[8]

Although she thought that her son's death would break her, it left Margaret as the head of her family, and she was as busy as she had ever been. Hackney was still rural but popular with wealthy Londoners. In spite of Margaret's strained resources, she now rediscovered her old fondness for writers, and gave the London poet and author Richard Robinson help in editing the *History of Gesta Romanorum*, a series of elaborate allegories drawing on Roman history to provide moral instruction to the reader, usually involving emperors as stand-ins for God. He dedicated it to Margaret with prayers for her 'long and prosperous good estate . . . in this life: And finally for your established felicity immutable in the life everlasting'.[9] After her death, a handful of people remembered her as a literary patron: one French author, dedicating his *History of France* to the ladies of Elizabeth's Privy Chamber, encouraged them to read it in the manner of 'many high and lofty ladies, who often times to be met with wearisomness, exercised themselves in study and reading of worthy writers', offering a long list of examples headed by 'Marguerite, countess of Lennox'.[10]

These admirers stressed Margaret's taste and patience rather than her politics, which may have been her doing. William Camden was an Oxford-educated humanist who would go on to become one of his generation's best-known historians. From 1575 onwards he was second master at Westminster School and close to Cecil's circle at court, which is probably where he encountered the elderly Margaret. He claimed to have heard her say she 'was thrice cast into prison . . . not for matter of treason, but for love matters': first for Thomas Howard, next for Darnley, and finally for Charles.[11]

But Camden was being disingenuous: she was as political as she had ever been. Although she took on the struggle for Arbella's rights, for her own dower lands in Scotland and for her own estates and pastimes in England, her greatest hopes were still for James. She had long wanted to see him grow up as he had been christened – a Catholic – but she had concealed her hopes, letting her fury with Mary and her fear for James's safety convince her that he would be safest if brought up in Protestant England. Now that she was wholly convinced of Morton's treachery, compromise lost its attraction. She and Mary both feared that James would be removed from Scotland and brought up at Elizabeth's Protestant court. In secret, they came to a common goal: to have James taken to France. In November 1577, Mary wrote that Margaret 'does not desire this transport less than myself'. They wanted him 'safely brought into France', where he would be raised by Mary's French relatives in their shared Catholic faith.[12]

With this promise to give her hope, Margaret had one more dynastic proclamation to make, knowing that it would long outlast her. She was sixty-two and wanted to be buried in Westminster Abbey, where her cousin Mary and her Tudor forebears had been entombed. She commissioned the monument and arranged its building before she died.[13] Old sorrows were carved in stone: eight alabaster figures knelt in mourning by the effigy, statues of her children. She had outlived them all, and her second son 'was murthered at the age of twenty-one years'. She downplayed her part in politics, casting herself as a pious royal matron, more important because of her familial ties than because of anything she did – though she wanted to be remembered as a Tudor, for the detailed inscriptions in both English and Latin set out her place in the Tudor family tree. The Douglases did not come into it: as she had told the late Regent the Earl of Mar, 'remembrance of [Scotland] should be grievous unto me'.[14] But there was one provocative and telling detail: she declared her relationship 'to her niece and daughter-in-law Mary, queen of Scots'.

In the winter of 1577–8 she became sick, and she wrote her will on 26 February. It was common for children who died in infancy to be buried in their parents' tombs, less so for adults, but Margaret asked that Charles be moved from his resting place in Hackney so that his body could be 'laid with mine, both in one vault or tomb'.[15] The bulk of the estate was to go to Arbella, including all her jewels. For King James, 'as a remembrance of me his grandmother', there was a black velvet bed embroidered with flowers. There was a ring with four diamonds for Cecil as well as a golden pomander and a portrait of Henry VIII for Leicester. There were charitable bequests: money to be given out on the day of her funeral, and gowns for a hundred poor women. Her servants were all remembered, particularly her executor Thomas Fowler, who got the very practical gift of her entire stock of sheep and the more personal one of 'all my clocks, watches, dials, with their furnitures'. Collecting was a means of showing power and taste, knowledge and intellectual curiosity, and she had been gathering timepieces for at least fourteen years. Now they became a fitting gift for one of her oldest servants.[16]

One of the witnesses to the will was Lawrence Nesbit, Lennox's long-serving retainer, who had once been thrown in the Tower for failing to show sufficient deference to the queen.[17] But there was nothing subversive about the will, no indication of strong Catholic or Protestant allegiance: Elizabeth was 'our sovereign lady . . . defender of the faith'; Margaret left her 'soul unto almighty God, my saviour and redeemer' – and there was no bequest for Mary Stewart.[18]

Margaret died at Hackney in March 1578. Sometime after her death a pamphlet entitled *Leicester's Commonwealth* accused the Earl of Leicester of being a practised poisoner. Among his putative victims was Margaret. The author, apparently repeating testimony he had had from Margaret's servants, wrote that Leicester visited her in Hackney and that the two of them talked together for some time with no hint of ill-will. When he left, however, Margaret suddenly became sick with a violent flux, suffering massive bleeding. Both she and the entire household were convinced that Leicester had poisoned her. The author observed darkly that 'this art of poisoning is perfecter with my lord than praying, and he seemeth to take more pleasure therein'.[19] There was, however, no talk of this at the time.

There is a certain irony in the fact that her closest correspondents by the time of her death were Mary, Queen of Scots, on the one hand and Elizabeth's nearest advisors on the other. For all that Margaret had been called a deceitful and untrustworthy woman during her lifetime, her earlier spying had usually been discovered: in her last years, however, she learned how to keep her secrets.

When Mary learned of Margaret's death, she wrote to James Boyd, Archbishop of Glasgow, in a reflective mood: 'This good woman was, by the grace of God, very well reconciled to me for the past five or six years that we had intelligence together, and acknowledged to me, with letters written in her own hand – which I keep – the wrong she had done me in her unjust pursuits . . . as she let me know . . . [she had been] badly informed, but principally by the express commandment of the said queen of England and the persuasion of her council, which had always forbidden our meeting, until having learned of my innocence, she wanted to stop pursuing me, so far as totally refusing to avow that which they did against me in her name.'[20] In fact, it had probably been closer to three years, but the relationship mattered: Mary always kept the lace that Margaret had given her.

Margaret died in such debt that Elizabeth paid for her funeral.[21] Her body was laid in a lead coffin and she was interred in the chapel built by her grandfather to honour the Virgin Mary and house the bones of his royal descendants. She rests under the fan-vaulted ceiling of the Lady Chapel's south aisle, to the west of her great-grandmother Margaret Beaufort – another woman who had never been queen but who had overcome the stigma of bastardy and seen both her son and grandson become kings.[22]

It was a splendid occasion. Her hundred poor women, dressed in their newly furnished gowns, followed the clergy. Then came an array of mourners: her chaplains and servants, including Lawrence Nesbitt and Thomas Fowler, executors and household officers, heralds at arms. Eight gentlemen carried her body, leading a still grander set of dignitaries: Margaret Clifford, Countess of Derby and a great-granddaughter of Henry VII, served as chief mourner, with a baroness to carry her train and Cecil and Leicester in attendance. Five pairs of noblewomen followed, with Margaret's daughter-in-law Elizabeth and Lettice Knollys, Countess of Essex, in the central position. In contrast to Margaret's tomb, which proclaimed her membership of the Tudor family, she was memorialised as a Douglas. Heralds carried the banners setting out her descent from the first Earl of Angus, who had married the daughter of Robert III of Scotland, tracing her heritage through six generations and culminating with her own arms – the fleur-de-lis of the earls of Lennox on the left, the heart of the Douglases on the right. Behind them came a crowd of yeomen clad in black.

It was undoubtedly a Protestant burial service. The preacher was John Piers, Bishop of Salisbury and the queen's own almoner.[23] Whatever the bishop said in the sermon went unrecorded, but it was depoliticised, if the work of the fiery Protestant pamphleteer John Phillips is any indication. He wrote her a one-page epitaph in rhyming verse. On some points he was quite accurate. His description of her marriage – 'faith knit love's knot' – was true enough, as was his account of the deaths of her sons: of Charles, he wrote that '[his] want in her a double dole [grief] did place', and of Darnley, '[his] death did nip this countess to the gall / yet did she joy, his seed was safe from thrall'. He caught her generosity and managed a good pun on her name, *Margaret* meaning 'pearl':

> You suitors poor have lost a Margaret dear
> A precious pearl, the pillar of your trust:
> Who willing was your due demands to hear
> And to the prince to further causes just.

On the other hand, John Phillips was a devout Protestant, and he did his best to portray the Catholic Margaret as his own co-religionist. This took a deal of polite fiction, especially when he wrote that 'From God nor prince, her thought could never change'. For one who had lived 'in dread for to transgress the law', she had spent many years in prison, and she would not have recognised herself in Phillips's Protestant account of her piety: Margaret died a Catholic, unconvinced that faith alone would 'purge her sin and make her just'.[24]

Above the vault, the tomb of colourful painted alabaster took shape: the effigy, crowned with a countess's coronet; the kneeling statues of her eight children; the proclamation that she was *aedita princibus princibusque parens* – descended from princes, parent to princes. By October 1578 the monument had been completed and installed, its politely apolitical portrait fixed in stone.

Epilogue
KING HENRY'S CHAPEL

Being a Tudor and being a woman meant that Margaret's relations with her kin informed every choice she made. Some opportunities appeared at random – her brother's quarrel with her father brought Margaret to her uncle's kingdom, and her eldest son only became suitor to a queen because the King of France died young. Others, however, were her own creation. It was not for nothing that Elizabeth's Privy Council had recommended shutting her in prison in the panicked days before Darnley finally wed the Queen of Scots: Margaret had evolved from a girl who was thrown in prison for falling in love without her uncle's permission to an independent political actor who was on the point of confounding every plan that Elizabeth and Cecil had for Mary Stewart.

Margaret was her own person: she fell in love at the direction of her own heart; quarrelled rashly but fearlessly with nobles and monarchs; stayed a staunch Catholic in a country that was slowly embracing its new identity as a Protestant kingdom. Often forced to be reactive, she became a skilled reactor: she established a place for herself in a new country at a new court; moved faster than anybody else in the aftermath of Francis II's sudden death; admitted, when she read the forged Bothwell confession, that she had been wrong about Mary and hastened to reconcile with her. Thomas Randolph called her 'more feared than beloved', and any student of Machiavelli would have replied that 'Fortune is the arbiter of one half of our actions, but . . . she still leaves the control of the other half, or almost that, to us.'[1]

Above all else, she had a vision of her family and of what they were meant to do – to claim the crowns of England and Scotland, and to restore the old faith. Even at the very end, when she stood widowed and childless, neither mother, wife, nor England's queen, she was working to see that James grew up in her Church and not in the Scottish Kirk.

Most of Margaret's foes came to ugly ends. Morton lost the regency in the same month that Margaret died, and though he recovered power shortly afterwards, he was never secure again. On New Year's Eve 1581 he was accused of involvement in Darnley's murder. Found guilty, he was beheaded by the 'maiden', a Scottish guillotine. Châtelherault had died in his bed in 1575, after over a decade spent watching, heartsick, as his heir struggled with severe mental illness.

However, neither of Margaret's two daughters-in-law had long or happy lives. Elizabeth, dowager Countess of Lennox, struggled to secure Charles's earldom for Arbella, and had no more luck than Margaret had had in her long campaign to be acknowledged Countess of Angus.[2] Four months after Margaret's death, James VI gave the earldom to her brother-in-law – Lennox's younger brother Robert, Bishop of Caithness.[3] Elizabeth died in 1582, commending Arbella to Queen Elizabeth's care.[4] Bess of Hardwick, so devastated by her daughter's death that she '[could] not think of aught but tears', wrote to Cecil that 'your lordship hath heard . . . how it hath pleased God to visit me, but in what sort soever his pleasure is to lay his heavy hand on us, we must take it thankfully'.[5]

Mary, Queen of Scots and dowager Queen of France, spent the last nineteen years of her life in English captivity. By the 1580s she was trying new means of getting her throne back: she did her best to convince both James and Elizabeth to let her share the crown of Scotland with her son, but this came to nothing. As her hopes of ruling jointly failed, she became involved in a plot to destroy Elizabeth, and the English queen could not ignore it. Mary was put on trial and sentenced to death in December 1586. Despite protests from James and her own great reluctance to condemn a fellow monarch, Elizabeth finally gave the order for Mary's death. The Queen of Scots died at Fotheringhay Castle on 8 February 1587, dressed in the clothes of a Catholic martyr, suffering multiple strokes of the axe from an incompetent headsman. She was buried in Peterborough Cathedral. Mary had been a constant of British politics since the reign of Henry VIII, at first as a pawn in the dynastic schemes of the Tudors, the Guise, the Valois and the Scottish nobility, then as an often unpredictable ruler in her own right. For all that, she died at the age of only forty-four.

Margaret's two grandchildren had their own tragedies. Sir Walter Mildmay, a serious, reform-minded counsellor who had served Henry VIII and all his children, wrote that the young Arbella would grow up 'like her grandmother, my old Lady Lennox'.[6] This proved extraordinarily prescient. Arbella was too young to remember her grandmother, but they struggled with the same set of challenges and faced them in similar ways.

Arbella grew up clever, stubborn and convinced of her own status. Like Margaret, Arbella had claims in Scotland that she never managed to realise. Although she used Margaret's old title, Countess of Lennox, she never secured her father's earldom or his lands. Her financial situation was precarious, especially as Elizabeth had seized the Lennox-Stewarts' English estates, moving Arbella to write that she 'might have recovered a little land, which a most noble great-great-uncle of mine [Henry VIII] gave his niece when he bestowed her of a noble exiled gentleman'.[7] Most dramatically, Arbella married without royal permission. She and her husband, William Seymour, were both imprisoned.

They managed to escape, but whereas Seymour made it out of England and went on to rehabilitation and a long royal career, Arbella was recaptured and died in the Tower.

As for James, he inherited Elizabeth's crown, just as Margaret had hoped. He and every British monarch since have been Margaret's direct descendants. Elizabeth died in 1603, having ruled for forty-five years without naming an heir. There were any number of impediments to James's claim, especially the will of Henry VIII, but after the rule of a child, a Catholic woman and a Virgin Queen, there was only token debate about the right of this adult, married, Protestant Scotsman to claim the English throne.

For England's Catholics, there was hope that this son of the martyred Queen of Scots and grandson of the devout Margaret Douglas would, at the very least, extend them some kind of religious toleration: they were to be disappointed. His heir Charles I did marry a Catholic, however, and his namesake grandson, James II, became the last Catholic ever to sit on England's throne. It is a bitter irony that British Catholics, especially in Ireland and Scotland, would suffer terrible repercussions for their loyalty to the House of Stewart – the very family that Margaret hoped would unite the crowns and restore the British Isles to the Church of Rome.

Although James would never bring Britain back to Rome, he would rule in three kingdoms, and he remembered the grandmother he had never met. He refashioned the Lady Chapel into a proclamation of his Anglo-Scottish heritage and turned Margaret into a kind of dynastic lynchpin. In 1612, James moved his mother's body from Peterborough to Westminster Abbey. He had her reinterred in a new tomb of black and white marble vivified with gold, its long inscriptions telling the story of her life: how she had been Queen of Scotland and of France and heir to the throne of England, but lost her crown and died on a scaffold, only to be vindicated in her son, who was King of Scotland, Ireland and England. She lies between Margaret Beaufort and Margaret Douglas: James declared in gilt and marble that the blood of these three women gave him an indisputable right to the crowns of England and Ireland as well as Scotland.[8]

But Margaret Douglas had always had a talent for adaptation, and as she planned her memorial, she knew that Westminster Abbey was not the place to tell her story. There was no mention of her own claim to the English throne, a claim that had unsettled and even terrified her Tudor cousins and had caused her four long spells of imprisonment. There was no hint at her beliefs, even though she was born in an England of near-universal Catholicism and died sixty-two years later in one that was officially Protestant but riven with religious unrest. There was not a whisper that she and Mary had once been implacable enemies before reconciling, united by their common love for James and by their hope that he would share their Catholic faith rather than the Protestantism that had taken hold of both England and Scotland.

For all the lineage it declares, Margaret's own tomb does not capture the degree to which her blood placed her at the centre of British politics, or the role she played in shaping those politics. Like all the Tudors, she believed profoundly in the importance of family and in the ideal of dynastic monarchy, and that belief, combined with her religion and her unique perspective as a half-Scottish member of the English royal family, led her to devote herself to the pursuit of Catholic British union through dynastic marriage. It is fitting that she dedicated the most enduring expression of her ambitions to her grandson. The Lennox Jewel, crafted to be worn directly over King James VI's heart, sets out Margaret Douglas's British vision in a blaze of sapphire, rubies and gold: *Qvha Hopis Stil Constantly Vith Patience Sal Obteain Victorie In Yair Pretence.*

NOTES

ABBREVIATIONS IN THE NOTES

Add	Additional MSS, British Library, London
CDR Scotland	*Calendar of Documents relating to Scotland*, 2 vols., ed. Markham John Thorpe, London, 1858
Cotton	Cotton MSS, British Library, London
CSP Burghley	*A Collection of State Papers, Relating to Affairs in the Reigns of King Henry VIII, King Edward VI, Queen Mary, and Queen Elizabeth, Transcribed from Original letters and Other Authentick Memorials, left by William Cecill Lord Burghley*, 2 vols., ed. Samuel Haynes, London, 1840
CSP Dom	*Calendar of state papers, domestic series, of the reigns of Edward VI, Mary, Elizabeth 1547–1570*, ed. Robert Lemon, London, 1856
CSP Milan	*Calendar of State Papers and Manuscripts in the Archives and Collections of Milan*, ed. Allen B. Hinds, London, 1912
CSP Rome	*Calendar of State Papers Relating to English Affairs in the Vatican Archives*, 2 vols., ed. J. M. Rigg, London, 1916–26
CSP Scotland	*Calendar of State Papers Relating to Scotland and Mary, Queen of Scots, 1574–1603*, 13 vols., ed. Joseph Bain et al., Edinburgh, 1898–1969
CSP Sim	*Calendar of letters and state papers relating to English affairs, preserved principally in the archives at Simancas*, 4 vols., ed. Martin Hume, London, 1892–4
CSP Spain	*Calendar of State Papers, Spain*, 13 vols., ed. G. A. Bergenroth et al., London, 1862–1954

CSP Venice	*Calendar of State Papers Relating to English Affairs in the Archives of Venice*, 38 vols., ed. Rawdon Brown et al., London, 1864–1947
CSPF	*Calendar of state papers, foreign: Edward VI, Mary, Elizabeth I*, 25 vols., ed. Joseph Stevenson et al., London, William Paterson, 1865–71
E	Records of the Exchequer, National Archives, Kew
GD	Gifts and Deposits, National Archives of Scotland, Edinburgh
Harley	Harley MSS, British Library, London
HM	Historical Manuscripts, Huntington Library and Archives, San Marino
HMC Salisbury	*Calendar of the manuscripts of the Most Honourable the Marquess of Salisbury, preserved at Hatfield House, Hertfordshire*, 24 vols., ed. S. R. Scargill-Bird, London, 1883
Lansdowne	Lansdowne MSS, British Library, London
LP	*Letters and Papers, Foreign and Domestic, of the Reign of Henry VIII*, 21 vols., ed. J. S. Brewer et al., London, 1864–1920
NAS SP	State Papers, National Archives of Scotland, Edinburgh
NLS	National Library of Scotland, Edinburgh
ODNB	*Oxford Dictionary of National Biography*, 60 vols., Oxford, Oxford University Press, 2004
PC	Privy Council Records, National Archives of Scotland, Edinburgh
Prob	Prerogative Court of Canterbury, National Archives, Kew
Sloane	Sloane MSS, British Library, London
SP	State Papers, National Archives, Kew
Talbot	Talbot Manuscripts, Lambeth Palace Library, London

CHAPTER 1: 'O COME YE IN PEACE HERE, OR COME YE IN WAR?'

1 Polydore Vergil, *Anglica Historia*, ed. Dana F. Sutton, Philological Museum, Birmingham, 2010, ch. XXV.

2 Michael K. Jones and Malcolm G. Underwood, *The King's Mother: Lady Margaret Beaufort, Countess of Richmond and Derby*, Cambridge University Press, Cambridge, 1993, pp. 19–25.

3 Alice Hunt, *The Drama of Coronation: Medieval Ceremony in Early Modern England*, Cambridge University Press, Cambridge, 2008, pp. 16–18.

4 Thomas Malory, trans. William Caxton, *Le Morte d'Arthur*, London, 1485, sig. A6r.

5 *CSP Spain*, vol. I, nos. 13–16.

6 *CSP Spain*, vol. I, nos. 34 and 121.

7 John Leland, *De Rebus Britannicis Collectanea*, ed. Thomas Hearne, G. and J. Richardson, London, 1770, vol. IV, p. 254.

8 *CDR Scotland*, vol. IV, no. 1622.

9 *CDR Scotland*, vol. IV, no. 1633.

10 For changing concepts of regency in Scotland, see Amy Blakeway, *Regency in Sixteenth-Century Scotland*, Boydell & Brewer, Woodbridge, 2015.

11 John Guy, 'Tudor Monarchy and Its Critiques', in *The Tudor Monarchy*, Arnold, London, 1997, pp. 78–82.

12 *CSP Spain*, vol. I, no. 210.

13 *CDR Scotland*, vol. IV, nos. 1680–1.

14 Simon Thurley, *The Royal Palaces of Tudor England*, Yale University Press, New Haven, 1993, p. 202.

15 Leland, *Collectanea*, vol. IV, pp. 258–64.

16 Leland, *Collectanea*, vol. V, pp. 373–4. See Job 2:10.

17 *CSP Milan*, vol. I, no. 833.

18 Leland, *Collectanea*, vol. IV, p. 265; J. J. G. Alexander, 'Foreign Illuminators and Illuminated Manuscripts', in *The Cambridge History of the Book in Britain, Volume III: 1400–1557*, ed. Lotte Hellinga and J. B. Trapp, Cambridge University Press, Cambridge, 1999, p. 57; Harley 6986, f. 4r.

19 Leland, *Collectanea*, vol. IV, pp. 289–91. For discussion of Margaret's entry in general and of the apple in particular, see Douglas Gray, 'The Royal Entry in Sixteenth-Century Scotland', *The Rose and the Thistle: Essays on the Culture of Late Medieval and Renaissance Scotland*, Tuckwell Press, East Linton, 1998, pp. 17–22.

20 For Holyrood, see John G. Dunbar, *Scottish Royal Palaces: The Architecture of the Royal Residences during the Late Medieval and Early Renaissance Periods*, Tuckwell Press, East Linton, 1999, pp. 55–70 and Fiona Jamieson, 'The Royal Gardens of the Palace of Holyroodhouse, 1500–1603', *Garden History*, vol. 22, no. 1, Summer 1994, pp. 18–36.

21 Leland, *Collectanea*, vol. IV, pp. 290–6.

22 William Dunbar, 'Welcum of Scotlond to be quene', in *William Dunbar: The Complete Works*, ed. John Conlee, Medieval Institute Publications, Kalamazoo, 2004.
23 Cotton Vespasian FXIII, f. 134r.
24 Cotton Caligula BII, f. 224r.
25 For the pilgrimage, see Jane E. A. Dawson, *Scotland Re-formed, 1488–1587*, Edinburgh University Press, Edinburgh, 2007, p. 66.
26 *LP*, vol. I, nos. 81–2 and 101.
27 *LP*, vol. I, no. 119.
28 *LP*, vol. I, no. 5.
29 *LP*, vol. I, no. 153.
30 *LP*, vol. I, no. 253.
31 See Norman Macdougall, *James IV*, Tuckwell Press, East Linton, 1997, pp. 247–81.
32 Cotton Caligula BIII, f. 30r and *LP*, vol. I, nos. 1504 and 1775.
33 *LP*, vol. I, no. 2246.
34 *LP*, vol. I, no. 2460.
35 Cotton Vespasian FIII, f. 33r.
36 *CSP Spain*, no. II, no. 137.
37 John Skelton, *A ballad of the Scottysshe kynge*, London, 1513.
38 Leland, *Collectanea*, vol. V, p. 361.
39 *CSP Milan*, vol. I, no. 669.
40 *CSP Spain*, vol. II, no. 141; Cotton Caligula BVI, f. 39r; SP 49/1, f. 19r.
41 *LP*, vol. I, no. 2323.
42 *Acts of the Lords of Council in Public Affairs, 1501–1554*, ed. Robert Kerr Hannay, Edinburgh, 1932, nos. 2–4.
43 SP 1/7, f. 35r.
44 David Hume of Godscroft, *The history of the houses of Douglas and Angus*, Edinburgh, 1643, p. 275.
45 Vergil, *Anglica Historia*, ch. XXVII and Raphael Holinshed, *Chronicles of England, Scotland, and Ireland*, London, 1587, vol. VI, p. 838. Hume of Godscroft wrote that the marriage took place with the consent of Henry VIII, who thought that an alliance with the Douglases would be a counterweight to French influence in Scotland, but there is no contemporary evidence of this: see Hume of Godscroft, *The history of the houses of Douglas and Angus*, p. 239.
46 Cotton Caligula BVI, f. 272r.
47 *Acts of the Lords of Council*, no. 22.
48 See, for instance, *LP*, vol. II, nos. 296 and 494.

49 *LP*, vol. II, no. 777.
50 Cotton Caligula BII, f. 224v.
51 Cotton Caligula BII, f. 226r.
52 Cotton Caligula BVI, f. 124r.
53 Cotton Caligula BVI, f. 135r.

CHAPTER 2: CHILDHOOD

1 *LP*, vol. II, no. 1387.
2 *LP*, vol. II, no. 1350.
3 Cotton Caligula BIII, f. 33r-v.
4 Edward Hall, *The vnion of the two noble and illustre famelies of Lancastre & Yorke*, London, 1548, f. 58r-v.
5 *Negociations diplomatiques entre la France et l'Autriche*, 2 vols., ed. Nadré Joseph Ghislain Le Glay, Paris, 1845, vol. I, pp. 107–8.
6 *LP*, vol. II, no. 3136.
7 Cotton Caligula BII, f. 253r.
8 Cotton Caligula BI, f. 247r.
9 Cotton Caligula BI, ff. 261r and 153r.
10 This account is Thomas Bishop's deposition against Margaret in May 1562, SP 12/23, f. 49r. Bishop said that she lived in Scotland 'fouretene yeares', which is the sole mention of where she spent her childhood, though the dates line up only if she lived there until she was nearly fourteen years old, rather than for fourteen years.
11 Cotton Caligula BI, f. 251r.
12 *The register of the Privy Seal of Scotland*, 5 vols., ed. David Hay Fleming et al., Edinburgh, 1908–57, vol. II, 27 March 1529.
13 Cotton Caligula BVII, ff. 447r-v; also transcribed in *The Douglas Book*, 4 vols., ed. William Fraser, Edinburgh, 1885, vol. IV, pp. 172–3.
14 For the education of noblewomen in this period, see Barbara J. Harris, *English Aristocratic Women, 1450–1550: Marriage and Family, Property and Careers*, Oxford University Press, Oxford, 2002, pp. 27–40; see also Linda Pollock, '"Teach her to live under obedience": The Making of Women in the Upper Ranks of Early Modern England', *Continuity and Change*, vol. 4, Special Issue no. 2, August 1989, pp. 231–58.
15 For the link between reading and conversion, see Peter Marshall, 'Evangelical Conversion in the Reign of Henry VIII', in *The Beginnings of English Protestantism*, ed. Peter Marshall and Alec Ryrie, Cambridge University Press, Cambridge, 2002, p. 33.
16 *LP*, vol. III, no. 1274.

17 *LP*, vol. III, no. 1297.
18 *Acts of the Parliament of Scotland*, 12 vols., ed. Thomas Thomson and Cosmo Innes, Edinburgh, 1814–75, vol. II, no. 295.
19 Add MS 24965, f. 273r.
20 Cotton Caligula BVI, f. 424r.
21 Cotton Caligula BII, f. 223r; Cotton Caligula BI, f. 232v.
22 *LP*, vol. IV, no. 1484.
23 Cotton Caligula BII, f. 65r.
24 *LP*, vol. IV, no. 830.
25 *LP*, vol. IV, no. 2487; see also Jamie Cameron, *James V: The Personal Rule 1528–1542*, ed. Norman Macdougall, Tuckwell Press, East Linton, 1998, p. 9.
26 John Duncan to Albany, 29 March 1528, in *Relations Politiques de la France et de l'Espagne avec l'Écosse au XVIe Siècle*, 4 vols., ed. Alexandra Teulet, Paris, 1862, vol. I, p. 67. See also Cameron, *James V*, p. 18.
27 Cotton Caligula BVI, ff. 225v-226r.
28 *LP*, vol. IV, nos. 4457, 4674 and 4701.
29 *CSP Burghley*, vol. I, no. 382.
30 Cotton Caligula BVI, f. 552r.
31 Ibid.
32 Cotton Caligula BVII, ff. 109r-109v. The word in the manuscript is *disherest*.
33 SP 1/55, f. 2r.
34 *LP*, vol. IV, nos. 6220 and 6344.
35 *LP*, vol. IV, no. 6571.
36 *LP*, vol. IV, no. 6586.
37 *LP*, vol. IV, nos. 6738 and 6478.
38 *LP*, vol. V, no. 365.
39 *The Privy Purse Expenses of King Henry the Eighth*, ed. Nicholas Harris Nicolas, William Pickering, London, 1827, p. 98.
40 *LP*, vol. IV, no. 6779.

CHAPTER 3: THE KING'S NIECE

1 Thurley, *Royal Palaces*, p. 48.
2 Hall, *The vnion of the two noble and illustre famelies of Lancastre & Yorke*, ff. 194–5v.
3 Ecclesiastes 10:16.
4 *LP*, vol. V, no. 1254; see also NAS SP 6/44.

5 For details of Mary's household, see Harley 6807, ff. 7r-9v. See *ODNB* for Hussey's career.
6 For an account of Mary's christening and godparents, see Add MS 4712, f. 78r.
7 *LP*, vol. VI, no. 1164.
8 *LP*, vol. VI, no. 1528.
9 *LP*, vol. V, no. 1484. For Chapuys, see *ODNB*.
10 'An Act in restraint of appeals', 24 Hen.VIII, c.12, 1533, *Statutes of the Realm*, 9 vols., ed. John Raithby, London, 1817, vol. III, p. 427.
11 *LP*, vol. VI, no. 524; Anon., *The noble tryumphant coronacyon of quene Anne*, London, 1533.
12 *LP*, vol. VI, no. 1139.
13 *LP*, vol. VI, no. 1296.
14 *LP*, vol. VI, no. 1392.
15 *LP*, vol. VI, nos. 1528 and 1541.
16 *LP*, vol. VII, no. 9.
17 *LP*, vol. VII (Appendix), no. 13.
18 Ibid. For accounts of Alessandro de' Medici, see Nicholas Scott Baker, 'Writing the Wrongs of the Past: Vengeance, Humanism, and the Assassination of Alessandro de' Medici', *The Sixteenth Century Journal*, vol. 38, no. 2, Summer 2007, pp. 307–11, and John M. Najemy, *A History of Florence, 1200–1575*, Blackwell, Oxford, pp. 464–6.
19 Sloane MS 72, f. 213r.
20 Eric Ives, *The Life and Death of Anne Boleyn: 'The Most Happy'*, Blackwell, Oxford, 2004, pp. 231–59; Suzannah Lipscomb, 'The Fall of Anne Boleyn: A Crisis in Gender Relations', in *Henry VIII and the Court: Art, Politics and Performance*, Ashgate Publishing Ltd, Farnham, 2013, pp. 291–9.
21 For discussion of the complexities of authorship in the Devonshire Manuscript, see Chris Stamatakis, *Sir Thomas Wyatt, and the Rhetoric of Rewriting: 'Turning the word'*, Oxford University Press, Oxford, 2012, pp. 151–2.
22 An episode described by Stamatakis, *Sir Thomas Wyatt*, p. 153.
23 Elizabeth Heale, 'Introduction', in *The Devonshire Manuscript: A Women's Book of Courtly Poetry*, ed. Elizabeth Heale, Iter, Toronto, 2012, pp. 3–4. This edition also includes an invaluable transcription of Add MS 17492 in its entirety.
24 Add MS 17492, ff.40r; 81r; 17r; 24v; 72v; 78v; and 80v.

25 Add MS 17492, f. 6v. For discussion of the relationship between these annotations, see Stamatakis, *Sir Thomas Wyatt*, pp. 19–20.
26 *LP*, vol. VI, no. 1111.
27 Irish, 'Gender and Politics in the Henrician Court', *Renaissance Quarterly*, vol. 64, Spring 2011, p. 97.
28 E 36/120, f. 53v.
29 *LP*, vol. X, no. 141.
30 *LP*, vol. X, no. 282.
31 *LP*, vol. X, no. 352.
32 *LP*, vol. X, no. 351.
33 *LP*, vol. X, no. 908.
34 Anne's fall remains a matter of intense debate. See G.W. Bernard, 'The Fall of Anne Boleyn', *The English Historical Review*, vol. 106, no. 420, July 1991, pp. 584–610; E.W. Ives, 'The Fall of Anne Boleyn Reconsidered', *The English Historical Review*, vol. 107, no. 424, July 1992, pp. 651–64; Greg Walker, 'Rethinking the Fall of Anne Boleyn', *The Historical Journal*, vol. 45, no. 1, March 2002, pp. 1–29.
35 *LP*, vol. XII, no. 973; Charles Wriothesley, *A Chronicle of England During the Reigns of the Tudors*, ed. William Douglas Hamilton, Camden Society, London, 1875–7, vol. I, p. 48.
36 Quoted by Susan Brigden, *Thomas Wyatt: The Heart's Forest*, Faber, London, 2012, p. 275.
37 *LP*, vol. X, no. 908.
38 *LP*, vol. VIII, nos. 69–70.
39 See Mortimer Levine, *Tudor Dynastic Problems 1460–1571*, George Allen & Unwin Ltd, London, 1973, pp. 110 and 125.
40 *LP*, vol. VII, no. 337.
41 *LP*, vol. XI, no. 48.

CHAPTER 4: SO HIGH A BLOOD

1 'An act concyning the Attaynder of the Lord Thomas Howard', 28 Henry VIII, c.24, in *Statutes of the Realm*, vol. III, pp. 680–1; *Journal of the House of Lords*, vol. I, 1509–1577, pp. 83–5 and 100–1. See also David M. Head, ' "Beyng Ledde and Seduced by the Devyll": The Attainder of Lord Thomas Howard and the Tudor Law of Treason', *The Sixteenth Century Journal*, vol. 13, no. 4, Winter 1982, pp. 3–16.
2 Quoted in Ives, *The Life and Death of Anne Boleyn*, p. 334.

3 For discussions of the Tower lyrics, see Ruth Ahnert, *The Rise of Prison Literature in the Sixteenth Century*, Cambridge University Press, Cambridge, 2013, pp. 81–90; Heale, 'Introduction', in *The Devonshire Manuscript*, pp. 14–15; Bradley J. Irish, 'Gender and Politics in the Henrician Court', pp. 79–114.
4 Add MS 17492, f. 26r.
5 Add MS 17492, ff. 26r-f.26v and f.29r.
6 *LP*, vol. XIII (ii), no. 1280.
7 Add MS 17492, f. 28v.
8 *LP*, vol. XI, no. 376.
9 *Statutes of the Realm*, vol. III, pp. 680–1; *LP*, vol. X, no. 862.
10 SP 49/4, f. 123r.
11 Add MS 32646, f. 89v.
12 Add MS 17492, f. 93r.
13 SP 1/110, f. 186r.
14 Hall, *The vnion of the two noble and illustre famelies of Lancastre & Yorke*, f. 31r.
15 *LP*, vol. VII, no. 1090.
16 *LP*, vol. VIII, no. 1096.
17 *LP*, vol. VIII, no. 661.
18 *LP*, vol. XI, no. 1396.
19 Cotton Vespasian FXIII, f. 241r; SP 1/113, f. 171r.
20 Cotton Vespasian FXIII, f. 241r.
21 *LP*, vol. XI, no. 147.
22 *LP*, vol. XII (i), no. 532.
23 See William Caxton, *The Golden Legend*, London, 1483, and all subsequent editions except that of 1493.
24 See *Ancient criminal trials in Scotland*, 3 vols., ed. Robert Pitcairn, William Tait, Edinburgh, 1833, vol. I, pp. 187–99.
25 *LP*, vol. XII (ii), nos. 922 and 947.
26 *LP*, vol. XII (ii), nos. 1012 and 1023.
27 Wriothesley, *A Chronicle of England*, vol. I, p. 70.
28 Add MS 17942, f. 88r.

CHAPTER 5: THESE WORLDLY STORMS

1 Cotton Vespasian CXIV (i), f. 104v.
2 Hall, *The vnion of the two noble and illustre famelies of Lancastre & Yorke*, f. 232v.
3 *LP*, vol. XIII (i), no. 995.

4 *LP*, vol. XVI, no. 373 and vol. XII (ii), no. 973.

5 *The Lisle Letters*, 6 vols., ed. Muriel St Clare Byrne, Chicago University Press, Chicago, 1981, vol. V, p. 184; Cotton Vespasian FXIII, f. 241r.

6 Maria Hayward, 'Gift Giving at the Court of Henry VIII: the 1539 New Year's Gift Roll in Context', *The Antiquaries Journal*, vol. 85, no. 1, 2005, pp. 133 and 144.

7 *LP*, vol. XIV (i), no. 625.

8 *LP*, vol. XIII (ii), no. 622 (3).

9 *Privy Purse Expenses of the Princess Mary*, ed. Frederic Madden, London, 1831, p. 86.

10 For the history of Blackheath, see Walter Thornbury and Edward Walford, *Old and New London*, Cassell, Petter & Galpin, London, 1878, vol. VI, pp. 224–36.

11 *LP*, vol. XV, nos. 23 and 179.

12 Hall, *Chronicle*, p. 238. For a detailed discussion of the marriage negotiations and Anne's arrival in England, see Retha M. Warnicke, *The Marrying of Anne of Cleves: Royal Protocol in Early Modern England*, Cambridge University Press, Cambridge, 2000, pp. 1–11 and 127–54.

13 *LP*, vol. XV, nos. 215 and 216.

14 *LP*, vol. XV, nos. 21 and 22; SP 1/157, f. 16v.

15 *Privy Purse Expenses of the Princess Mary*, p. 88.

16 John Drummond, ed. and trans., *Here is a newe boke, called the defence of age*, London, 1540, p. 1; for a series of manuscript extracts, including the dedication, see Sloane MS 72, ff. 213r–216v.

17 Sloane MS 72, f. 214v.

18 For Katherine's life before court, see *LP*, vol. XVI, no. 1320; SP 1/167, ff. 117r-120v; Cotton Otho C.X.41, ff. 250r-252r; *LP*, vol. XVI, no. 1339; SP 1/168, ff. 1r-2r; *LP*, vol. XVI, no. 1398; for Culpepper, see *LP*, vol. XVI, no. 1343 and XVII (appendix), no. 10; for Marillac, see *LP*, vol. XVI, no. 3.

19 *LP*, vol. XVI, no. 1389.

20 *LP*, vol. XVI, no. 1422.

21 *LP*, vol. XVI, no. 1134.

22 For an account of Henry's entry into Lincoln, see Frederic Madden, 'Account of King Henry the Eighth's Entry into Lincoln', *Archaeologia*, vol. 23, January 1831, pp. 334–8, transcribed from Add MS 6113.

23 SP 49/5, f. 57r. For an account of the progress arguing that the invitation came from James, rather than Henry, see R.W. Hoyle and

J. B. Ramsdale, 'The Royal Progress of 1541, the North of England, and Anglo-Scottish Relations, 1534–1542', *Northern History*, vol. 40, no. 2, September 2004, pp. 239–65.

24 *LP*, vol. XVI, no. 1339.

25 SP 49/5, f. 28v.

26 Harley 6986, f. 5r.

27 John Leslie, *The History of Scotland*, Bannatyne Club, Edinburgh, 1830, pp. 157 and 272.

28 See also Julia Fox, *Jane Boleyn: The True Story of the Infamous Lady Rochford*, Ballantine Books, New York, 2009, pp. 257–87; David Starkey, *Six Wives: The Queens of Henry VIII*, Vintage, London, 2004, pp. 644–84.

29 *LP*, vol. XVI, no. 1331.

30 SP 1/167, f. 127v.

31 *LP*, vol. XVI, no. 1426.

32 *CSP Venice*, vol. V, no. 284.

33 SP 1/168, f. 143r.

34 Add MS 32648, f. 21r.

CHAPTER 6: LENNOX

1 The Angus estates had been annexed in the 1540 Parliament; see Cameron, *James V*, pp. 270–1.

2 Add MS 32648, f. 21r.

3 Add MS 32648, f. 21v.

4 *The Hamilton Papers*, 2 vols., ed. Joseph Bain, Edinburgh, 1890–2, vol. I, no. 251.

5 *LP*, vol. XVII, nos. 1230 and 1241; *LP*, vol. XVIII (i), no. 3.

6 *Privy purse expenses of the Princess Mary*, pp. 96 and 100.

7 *Collectanea de Rebus Albanicis*, ed. Iona Club, Edinburgh, 1847, p. 23.

8 *LP*, vol. XVIII (i), no. 12.

9 John Guy, *'My Heart is My Own': The Life of Mary, Queen of Scots*, HarperPerennial, London, 2004, pp. 17–28; Marcus Merriman, *The Rough Wooings: Mary Queen of Scots, 1542–1551*, Tuckwell Press, East Linton, 2000, pp. 111–36.

10 *CSP Venice*, vol. V, no. 194.

11 *Collectanea de Rebus Albanicis*, p. 23; *Hamilton Papers*, vol. II, no. 11.

12 *Hamilton Papers*, vol. I, no. 259; *LP*, vol. XVII, no. 1241 and XVIII (i), no. 44.

13 Alec Ryrie, *The Origins of the Scottish Reformation*, Manchester University Press, Manchester, 2006, pp. 53–64.

14 For a full-length study of Lennox's career, see Sarah Macauley, 'Matthew Stewart, Fourth Earl of Lennox and the Politics of Britain, c.1543–1571', PhD thesis, University of Cambridge, 2006.

15 SP 52/8, f. 45r.

16 Robert Lindsay of Pitscottie, *The History of Scotland*, ed. Robert Freebairn, Edinburgh, 1728, p. 182.

17 *Hamilton Papers*, vol. II, no. 63.

18 *Hamilton Papers*, vol. II, nos. 30 and 26.

19 *Hamilton Papers*, vol. II, nos. 38 and 56.

20 *Hamilton Papers*, vol. II, no. 60.

21 *LP*, vol. XVIII (i), no. 873.

22 See Desiderius Erasmus, *The first tome or volume of the Paraphrase of Erasmus upon the newe testament*, London, 1548, passim.

23 Cited in Katherine Parr, *Complete Works and Correspondence*, ed. Janel Mueller, University of Chicago Press, Chicago, 2011, with annotations described by H. O. Coxe, *Bodleian Library Quarto Catalogues II: Laudian Manuscripts*, ed. R. W. Hunt, Bodleian Library, Oxford, 1973, p. 73. For the probable presentations of *Psalms or Prayers*, see Mueller's introduction to Parr's *Complete Works*, p. 13.

24 For dancing as a pastime, see Sir Thomas Elyot, *The boke named the Gouernour*, London, 1537, p. 88; 'Narrative of the Visit of the Duke de Najera to England, in the year 1543–4; written by his Secretary, Pedro de Gante', ed. Frederic Madden, *Archaeologia*, vol. 23, no. 1, January 1831, pp. 344–5.

25 George Buchanan, *The History of Scotland*, 4 vols., ed. and trans. James Aikman, Blackie, Fullarton & Co., Glasgow, 1827, vol. II, p. 343.

26 'An Acte concerninge thestablishment of the Kinges Maiesties Succession in the Imperiall Crowne of the Realme', 35 Hen.VIII.c.1, in *Statutes of the Realm*, vol. III, pp. 955–8.

27 Maria Hayward, *Dress at the Court of King Henry VIII*, Maney Publishing, Leeds, 2007, pp. 202–3.

28 'Henry VIII to Lord Wharton and Sir Robert Bowes, 26 March 1544', in *The Letters of King Henry VIII: A Selection, with a Few Other Documents*, ed. Muriel St Clare Byrne, Cassell, London, 1968, p. 347.

29 SP 1/10, f. 82v.

30 R. Pollitt, 'An "Old Practizer" at Bay: Thomas Bishop and the Northern Rebellion', *Northern History*, vol. 16, 1980, pp. 60–1.

31 See Talbot MS 3206, f. 89r. Lennox described Bishop as 'long my frende & of long acquentence'.

32 SP 1/87, ff.122r-126v.

33 For a reading suggesting Henry did not want Margaret to accept Lennox's suit, see Macauley, 'Matthew Stewart', p. 80.

34 *CSP Spain*, vol. VII, no. 138; *LP*, vol. XIX (i), no. 799; *Privy Purse Expenses of the Princess Mary*, p. 175. There is a tradition that Henry declared he would be glad to see Margaret's children succeed him if his own line failed, but this seems to be a later invention: the first recorded instance of it is Thomas Fuller, *Church-history of Britain*, John Williams, London, 1655, p. 253.

CHAPTER 7: THE THIRD TIME

1 Cotton Caligula EIV, f. 56v. For early modern Stepney, see *A History of the County of Middlesex*, volume II, ed. T. F. T. Baker, Victoria County History, London, 1998, vol. XI, pp. 1–70.

2 SP 52/20, f. 119r.

3 Add MS 32656, f. 191r. See also Dawson, *Scotland Re-formed*, pp. 163–4.

4 *LP*, vol. XIX (i), no. 779.

5 E/178/2538 no. 4, ff. 1r-3r.

6 'A TempleNewsam Inventory, 1565', ed. and notes by E. W. Crossley, *The Yorkshire Archaeological Journal*, vol. 25, 1920, pp. 92–3.

7 *LP*, vol. XX (ii), no. 824.

8 *LP*, vol. XXII (ii), no. 768.

9 'A TempleNewsam Inventory', pp. 94–100.

10 For this reconstruction of Margaret's movements in 1544–5 and for a full-length study of her second son's life, see Caroline Bingham, *Darnley: A Life of Henry Stuart, Lord Darnley, Consort of Mary Queen of Scots*, Constable, London, 1995, pp. 37–8.

11 John Weever, *Ancient funerall monuments within the vnited monarchie of Great Britaine, Ireland, and the islands adiacent*, London, 1631, p. 539.

12 'A TempleNewsam Inventory', p. 94.

13 This can be surmised from the presence of a poem in Darnley's hand, at Add MS 17492, f. 57r.

14 Sarah Macauley, 'The Lennox Crisis, 1558–1563', *Northern History*, Vol. 41, Sept. 2004, pp. 270–5; SP 50/5, no. 2.

15 See, for instance, Talbot MS 3192, f. 91r.

16 Cotton Caligula EIV, f. 56v.

17 PRO E/23/4, f. 7v.
18 Harley 289, f. 73r.
19 SP 1/225, ff. 76r-79v.
20 Cotton Caligula BVIII, ff. 184–185r.
21 *LP*, vol. XXII (ii), no. 768.
22 Cotton Caligula BVIII, f. 165v.
23 Cotton Caligula BVIII, f. 166r.
24 Add MS 32656, f. 147v.
25 SP 50/5, no. 2; Add MS 35831, f. 66v.
26 'A TempleNewsam Inventory', p. 95; PRO Prob/11/60, f. 93v.

CHAPTER 8: ROUGH WOOING

1 *Ecclesiastical Memorials, relating Chiefly to Religion*, 3 vols., ed. John Strype, Clarendon Press, Oxford, 1822, vol. II, pp. 289–311.
2 Diarmaid MacCulloch, *Tudor Church Militant*, Allen Lane, London, 1999, pp. 20–1; Aysha Pollnitz, *Princely Education in Early Modern Britain*, Cambridge University Press, Cambridge, 2015, pp. 140–98.
3 *CSP Spain*, vol. IX, Van der Delft to the Queen Dowager, 7 March 1547.
4 Add MS 35831, f. 66v.
5 Hume of Godscroft, *The history of the houses of Douglas and Angus*, p. 273.
6 Gervase Phillips, *The Anglo-Scots Wars 1513–1550: A Military History*, Boydell Press, Woodbridge, 1999, p. 201; Sarah Macauley, 'Matthew Stewart', pp. 67–9; *CSP Scotland*, I.63.
7 SP 50/1, f. 124r.
8 Merriman, *The Rough Wooings*, pp. 295–304.
9 Phillips, *The Anglo-Scots Wars*, pp. 215–16; Merriman, *The Rough Wooings*, p. 305.
10 Macauley, 'Matthew Stewart', pp. 71–2.
11 SP 50/4, no. 43 (i).
12 *The Douglas Book*, vol. III, pp. 239–41.
13 SP 50/4, no. 43.
14 Guy, *'My Heart is My Own'*, pp. 40–2.
15 SP 50/5, no. 2.
16 SP 12/83, f. 7r.
17 Cotton Caligula BVIII, f. 184r.
18 Cotton Caligula BVIII, f. 165v.

19 SP 15/2, f. 47v and SP 15/3, f. 8r. See also Macauley, 'The Lennox Crisis', pp. 272–3.

20 John Foxe, *Acts and Monuments*, London, 1563, bk. III, p. 570.

21 See Andrew Pettegree, 'Printing and the Reformation', in *The Beginnings of English Protestantism*, ed. Peter Marshall and Alec Ryrie, Cambridge University Press, Cambridge, 2002, pp. 172–6.

22 MacCulloch, *Tudor Church Militant*, pp. 119–23.

23 It is worth noting that Sir William Sanderson, writing in the mid-seventeenth century, observed that Margaret was 'in King Edward's time in much honour here, but after in adverse fortune'. See *A compleat history of the lives and reigns of Mary, Queen of Scotland and of her son and successor*, London, 1656, p. 87.

CHAPTER 9: IDOLS AND IMAGES

1 John Foxe, *Acts and Monuments*, London, 1570, bk. IX, pp. 1524–5. I am indebted to Dr Tom Freeman for pointing me towards this reference. For discussion of the duty of punishing and correcting heretics, see Alexandra Walsham, *Charitable Hatred: Tolerance and Intolerance in England, 1500–1700*, Manchester University Press, Manchester, 2006.

2 Thomas Cranmer, *A defence of the true and catholike doctrine of the sacrament of the body and bloud of our sauiour Christ*, R. Wolfe, London, 1550, p. 31. See also Diarmaid MacCulloch's discussion in *Thomas Cranmer: A Life*, Yale University Press, New Haven, 1996, pp. 462–9.

3 For Edward's education, see MacCulloch, *Tudor Church Militant*, pp. 25–31 and Aysha Pollnitz, *Princely Education in Early Modern Britain*, pp.140–98. See also John Foxe, *Acts and Monuments*, 1583, bk. IX, p. 1419.

4 2 Kings 22:1 and 23:24. See also Stephen Alford, *Kingship and Politics in the Reign of Edward VI*, Cambridge University Press, Cambridge, 2002, pp. 157–62.

5 *The boke of common praier, and administracion of the sacraments*, London, 1552.

6 SP 50/5, no. 2.

7 See SP 50/5, no. 2 and *CSP Spain*, vol. XI, 28 November 1553.

8 It is worth noting that I differ here from most accounts of Margaret's life, which typically date her identification with Catholicism to the last years of Henry's reign. See *ODNB*; Kimberly Schutte, *A Biography of Margaret Douglas*, Edwin Mellen, New York, 2002, pp. 108–9; Agnes

Strickland, *Lives of the Queens of Scotland*, W. Blackwood and Sons, London, 1854, vol. II, pp. 295–6.

9 For reference, a woman who married before the age of twenty-five was likely to have five children. See Keith Wrightson and David Levine, *Poverty and Piety in an English Village: Terling, 1525–1700*, Clarendon Press, Oxford, 1995, p. 49.

10 The boys were her eldest son, who died young; Henry, lord Darnley and Charles Stewart, who survived to adulthood; and 'A chylde called phillep', born and christened during Mary's reign, per SP 12/22, f. 77r.

11 SP 12/23, f. 48r.

12 SP 68/9, ff. 79r–81v.

13 Add MS 4712, f. 47r.

14 *The Diary of Henry Machyn, Citizen and Merchant-Taylor of London*, ed. J. G. Nichols, J. B. Nichols and Sons, London, 1848, pp. 3–13.

15 *Literary Remains of King Edward the Sixth*, ed. J. G. Nichols, J. B. Nichols and Sons, London, 1857, vol. II, pp. 356–64.

16 Cotton Caligula BVII, f. 447r-v; also transcribed in *The Douglas Book*, vol. IV, pp. 172–3.

17 *Relations Politiques*, vol. I, p. 270.

18 SP 10/14, f. 29r.

19 Alford, *Kingship and Politics in the Reign of Edward VI*, pp. 139–41.

20 SP 10/14, f. 29r.

21 *Acts of the Privy Council of England*, 46 vols., ed. John Roche Dasent et al., London, 1890–1964, vol. III, p. 126.

22 SP 10/15, f. 144r-v.

23 See Eric Ives, *Lady Jane Grey: A Tudor Mystery*, Wiley-Blackwell, Chichester, 2009, pp. 225–38.

CHAPTER 10: BEST SUITED TO SUCCEED

1 *CSP Spain*, vol. XI, 19 October 1553.

2 SP 12/22, f. 77r.

3 *CSP Spain*, vol. XI, 17 November 1553.

4 *CSP Spain*, vol. XI, 28 November 1553.

5 See Elmore Harris Harbison, *Rival Ambassadors at the Court of Queen Mary*, Princeton University Press, Princeton, 1940, pp. 29–32.

6 *Acts of the Privy Council of England*, vol. IV, p. 260 and vol. VI, p. 218; *A History of the County of Middlesex: Volume 3*, ed. Susan Reynolds, Victoria County History, London, 1962, vol. III, pp. 103–11.

7 *Ambassades de Messieurs de Noailles en Angleterre*, 5 vols., ed. René-Aubert Vertot, Paris, 1763 vol. II, pp. 264–6 and 272–4.
8 SP 12/22, ff. 77r-78v.
9 SP 12/23, f. 12v.
10 *Collectanea de Rebus Albanicis*, p. 23.
11 For more on Elder's career, see Alec Ryrie, 'Paths not taken in the British Reformations', *The Historical Journal*, vol. 52, no. 1, March 2009, pp. 4–7.
12 John Elder, *The copie of a letter sent in to Scotlande*, John Wayland, London, 1555, ff. 93v-94r.
13 Cotton Vespasian FIII, f. 37v.
14 SP 12/22, ff. 77r-78v.
15 *CSP Spain*, vol. XII, pp. 204–205.

CHAPTER 11: COUNTESS OF ANGUS

1 Elder, *The copie of a letter*, ff. 4v-7v; *CSP Spain*, vol. XII, 26 July 1554.
2 Elder, *The copie of a letter*, ff. 13r-v and 20r-v.
3 There is no mention of her playing a part in the ceremony, which she almost certainly would have done had she been there, and one of the most detailed accounts of the event was written for Lennox's brother Robert by John Elder, who would have taken particular care to mention the Lennox-Stewarts' role, if any.
4 SP 12/22, f. 77r.
5 SP 12/23, f. 30r.
6 *CSP Sim.*, vol. I, no. 300.
7 *CSP Spain*, vol. XIII, nos. 61 and 92.
8 *CSP Spain*, vol. XIII, nos. 111 and 116.
9 Judith M. Richards, 'Mary Tudor as "Sole Quene"?: Gendering Tudor Monarchy', *The Historical Journal*, vol. 40, Dec. 1997, p. 920.
10 The inscriptions on Margaret's tomb indicate that Charles was her youngest son.
11 See the discussion of Charles's eventual marriage in Chapter 21.
12 See, for instance, Susan Wabuda, 'Equivocation and Recantation during the English Reformation', *Journal of Ecclesiastical History*, vol. 44, no. 2, pp. 237–42; Andrew Pettegree, *Marian Protestantism: Six Studies*, Scolar Press, Aldershot, 1996, pp. 101–3.
13 For a revisionist account of Mary's reign, which stresses the importance of print and reevaluates the burning campaign, see Eamon Duffy, *Fires*

of Faith: Catholic England Under Mary Tudor, Yale University Press, New Haven, 2009.

14 See Walsham, *Charitable Hatred*, pp. 39–43.

15 Harley 289, f. 74r; *CSP Sim.*, vol. I, no. 434.

16 John Jewel to Peter Martyr Vermigli, 7 February 1562, in *The Works of John Jewel, Bishop of Salisbury*, ed. John Ayre, Cambridge University Press, Cambridge, 1801, vol. IV, pp. 1245–6: '[M]ulier supra modum infensa religioni, supra etiam rabiem Marianam'.

17 E 117/14/119, f. 1r.

18 *CSP Burghley*, vol. I, no. 382.

19 The source for this story is Hume of Godscroft's MS *History*, part II.134, quoted by Fraser in *The Douglas Book*, vol. II, p. 285, n. 4, though it does not appear in either the 1643 or 1648 printed versions of his *History of the House of Douglas and Angus*.

20 *CSPF*, Mary, 579.

21 Discussed in Amy Blakeway, 'The attempted divorce of James Hamilton, Earl of Arran, Governor of Scotland', *The Innes Review*, vol. 61, no. 1, Spring 2010, pp. 7–8.

22 For Morton's appearance, career, and character, see *ODNB* and *The Douglas Book*, vol. II, pp. 298–322.

23 SP 51/1, f. 34r.

24 GD 150/328, f. 1v.

25 Guy, *'My Heart is My Own'*, pp. 83–92.

26 Quoted by David Loades, *The Reign of Mary Tudor: Politics, Government and Religion in England, 1553–58*, Longman, Harlow, 1991, p. 336.

27 Psalm 117:23.

28 SP 12/23, f. 12v; 'A TempleNewsam Inventory', p. 95.

29 Carole Levin, 'Parents, Children, and Responses to Death in Dream Structures in Early Modern England', in *Gender and Early Modern Constructions of Childhood*, ed. Naomi J. Miller and Naomi Yavneh, Ashgate, Farnham, 2011, pp. 41–2.

30 Cotton Caligula BVII, ff. 447r-v.

CHAPTER 12: SPOILT CHILDREN OF THE DEVIL

1 Leland, *Collectanea*, vol. V, pp. 307–23.

2 Jane Lawson, ed., *The Elizabethan New Year's Gift Exchanges*, Oxford University Press, Oxford, 2013, pp. 35–6, 45–6 and 20–1.

3 See Judith M. Richards, 'Love and a Female Monarch: The Case of Elizabeth Tudor', *The Journal of British Studies*, vol. 38, April 1999,

p. 148; Kevin Sharpe, 'Representations and Negotiations: Texts, Images, and Authority in Early Modern England', *The Historical Journal*, vol. 42, Sept. 1999, p. 870; Carole Levin, *'The Heart and Stomach of a King': Elizabeth I and the Politics of Sex and Power*, University of Pennsylvania Press, Philadelphia, 1994, pp. 11–16.

4 Quoted in John Guy, *Tudor England*, Oxford University Press, Oxford, 1988, p. 271.

5 John Foxe, *Acts and Monuments*, 1583, bk. X, p. 1442.

6 For a full-length study of Cecil's career, see Stephen Alford, *Burghley: William Cecil at the Court of Elizabeth I*, Yale University Press, New Haven, 2008. For Mildred Cecil, see Pauline Croft, 'Mildred, Lady Burghley: The Matriarch', in *Patronage, Culture, and Power: The Early Cecils 1559–1612*, ed. Pauline Croft, Yale University Press, New Haven, 2002, pp. 283–300.

7 Guy, *'My Heart is My Own'*, pp. 96–8.

8 'Supremacy Act, 1559' and 'The injunctions of 1559', in *Documents Illustrative of English Church History*, ed. Henry Gee and William John Hardy, Macmillan & Co., New York, 1896, pp. 442–8 and 417–42.

9 Margaret Aston, 'Lollardy and Sedition, 1381–1431', *Past and Present*, vol. 17, 1960, pp. 4–5; John Coffey, *Persecution and Toleration in Protestant England, 1558–1689*, Longman, Harlow, 2000, p. 185.

10 Alec Ryrie, 'Reform without Frontiers in the Last Years of Catholic Scotland', *English Historical Review*, vol. 119, no. 480, Feb. 2004, pp. 31–46.

11 Alec Ryrie, 'Congregations, Conventicles and the Nature of Early Scottish Protestantism', *Past & Present*, no. 191, May 2006, pp. 49–53.

12 Raphael Holinshed, *Chronicles of England, Scotland, and Ireland, London*, 1857, vol. V, p. 327; John Knox, *The historie of the reformation of the Church of Scotland*, London, 1644, p. 137. For Knox's appearance, see *ODNB*.

13 Jane E. A. Dawson, *The Politics of Religion in the Age of Mary, Queen of Scots: The Earl of Argyll and the Struggle for Britain and Ireland*, Cambridge University Press, Cambridge, 2002, pp. 87–99; Guy, *'My Heart is My Own'*, pp. 105–6; Roger Mason, *Kingship and the Commonweal: Political Thought in Renaissance and Reformation Scotland*, Tuckwell Press, East Linton, 1998, pp. 159–61.

14 John Knox, *The first blast of the trumpet against the monstrous regiment of women*, Geneva, 1558, p. 33.

15 Dawson, *The Politics of Religion*, p. 99.

16 *Relations Politiques*, vol. I, pp. 376–7 and 400; SP 52/1, f. 309v.

17 Cotton Caligula BIX, f. 86r.
18 *Relations Politiques*, vol. I, p. 376.
19 *CSP Burghley*, vol. I, no. 193.
20 See Macauley, 'Matthew Stewart', pp. 96–8.
21 SP 52/2, f. 316r.
22 SP 52/2, f. 4r.
23 SP 52/2, f. 20r-v.
24 GD1/506/2r.
25 Bond of Manrent by James, duke of Châtelherault and his son, James, earl of Arran, to Archibald, eighth earl of Angus, and James, earl of Morton, 31 May 1560, in *The Douglas Book*, vol. III, pp. 250–1. Discussed in Blakeway, 'The attempted divorce of James Hamilton', p. 19.
26 SP 52/5, f. 65r-v.
27 *CSP Sim.*, vol. I, no. 26.
28 *CSP Sim.*, vol. I, no. 32.
29 SP 52/5, f. 58r.

CHAPTER 13: THE BISHOP AND THE HAWK

1 Giles Godet, *The city of London, as it was before the burning of St Pauls steeple*, London, 1565.
2 James Pilkington, *The true report of the burnyng of the steple and church of Poules in London*, London, 1561.
3 SP 12/23, f. 31r.
4 SP 52/2, f. 53r-v.
5 SP 52/5, f. 55r.
6 SP 52/5, f. 58v.
7 Lennox, writing to Darnley on December 1566, apologised for not using his own hand. See Sloane MS 3199, f. 129r.
8 *CSP Sim.*, vol. I, no. 123. For transcriptions of several of de Quadra's dispatches, see Add MS 26056a.
9 SP 12/23, f. 10v; SP 12/23, f. 30r; Harley 289, f. 75; see Macauley, 'The Lennox Crisis', p. 274, for Elder's work with Darnley in the 1550s.
10 SP 52/6, ff. 68r-69v and 72r-73v; SP 52/6, f. 70r; SP 12/23, f. 30r.
11 SP 52/12, ff. 29r-29v.
12 SP 12/23, ff. 80r-81v.
13 Macauley, 'Matthew Stewart', pp. 101–14.
14 Michael A. Mullett, *Catholics in Britain and Ireland, 1558–1829*, Macmillan, Basingstoke, 1998, pp. 33–54; Keith M. Brown, *Noble*

Society in Scotland: Wealth, Family and Culture, from Reformation to Revolution, Edinburgh University Press, Edinburgh, 2000, pp. 245–7.

15 SP 12/23, ff. 10v.

16 See *ODNB* for details of the religious leanings of Atholl, Sutherland, Cassillis, Bothwell, Sempill and Seton.

17 SP 12/23, f. 30v.

18 SP 12/22, f. 77r.

19 For details of Yaxley's involvement with the Montague affinity, see Michael Questier, *Catholicism and Community in Early Modern England*, Cambridge University Press, Cambridge, 2006, pp. 128–9.

20 *CSP Dom.*, Philip and Mary, vol. X, no. 7; for Yaxley's contacts with Sir Thomas Cornwallis, Mary's controller, Sir John Bourne, one of her secretaries of state, and Sir Thomas Wharton, her Master of Horse, see SP 12/4, f. 166r; SP 12/11, f. 37r; SP 12/16, ff. 33r-37v.

21 SP 12/23, f. 12r; SP 12/14, f. 100r.

22 SP 12/21, f. 81r.

23 Pauline Croft, ' "The State of the World is Marvellously Changed": England, Spain and Europe 1558–1604', in *Tudor England and its Neighbours*, ed. Susan Doran and Glenn Richardson, Palgrave Macmillan, Basingstoke, 2005, pp. 178–9; Guy, *'My Heart is My Own'*, pp.122–3; see also Alford, *The Early Elizabethan Polity: William Cecil and the British Succession Crisis, 1558–1569*, Cambridge University Press, Cambridge, 1998, pp. 78–9.

24 *CSP Sim.*, vol. I, no. 84.

25 *CSP Sim.*, vol. I, nos. 189 and 198.

26 *CSP Sim.*,vol. I, no. 92.

27 *CSP Sim.*,vol. I, nos. 93 and 144.

28 *CSP Sim.*, vol. I, no.218.

29 *CSP Sim.*, vol. I, nos. 84 and 169.

30 *CSP Sim.*, vol. I, no. 173.

31 *CSP Sim.*, vol. I, no. 159.

32 See Jenny Wormald, *Mary Queen of Scots: Politics, Passion and a Kingdom Lost*, Tauris Parke, London, 2001, pp. 103–15; Guy, *'My Heart is My Own'*, pp. 134–57.

33 SP 12/23, f. 47r.

34 SP 12/23, ff. 75r-76v.

35 *CSP Sim.*, vol. I, no. 144.

CHAPTER 14: THE TIME OF OUR TROUBLE

1 Harley 289, ff. 73r-74v; SP 12/22, ff. 77r-78v.
2 SP 12/21, ff. 81r-82v.
3 *CSPF*, vol. IV, nos. 644 and 720.
4 *CSP Sim.*, vol. I, no. 157.
5 John Jewel to Peter Martyr Vermigli, 7 February 1562, in *The Works of John Jewel, Bishop of Salisbury*, vol. IV, pp. 1245–6; SP 52/7, f. 35r.
6 SP 70/36, f. 153v; SP 70/38, f. 18r-18v.
7 SP 70/38, f. 26r; SP 70/38, ff. 8r-13v.
8 *CSP Sim.*, vol. I, no. 169.
9 Add MS 35831, f. 37r.
10 Shakespeare, *Hamlet*, 1.2: 'Tis an unweeded garden that grows to seed/Things rank and gross in nature possess it merely.'
11 SP 12/23, ff. 9r-13v.
12 SP 59/5, f. 155r.
13 SP 12/23, ff. 30r-31v.
14 Luke 9:26. The episode is discussed by Perez Zagorin, *Ways of Lying: Dissimulation, Persecution, and Conformity in Early Modern Europe*, Harvard University Press, Cambridge, 1990, pp. 135–6.
15 See Alexandra Walsham, *Church Papists*, Boydell Press, Woodbridge, 1993, pp. 78–81.
16 Cotton Caligula BVIII, f.165v.
17 SP 12/23, f. 66r.
18 SP 70/38, f. 72r.
19 SP 70/37, f. 67r.
20 SP 70/38, f. 72r.
21 SP 12/23, f. 12r; SP 12/14, f. 100r.
22 SP 59/6, f. 106r.
23 Add MS 35831, ff. 56r-57r.
24 Add MS 35831, ff. 65r-67v.
25 SP 59/6, f. 106r.
26 Cotton Caligula BVIII, f. 299r-299v.
27 SP 12/23, f. 91r.
28 SP 12/23, f. 179r.
29 SP 12/23, f. 117r.
30 SP 12/23, f. 247r.
31 SP 12/24, f. 17r.
32 SP 12/27, f. 12r.
33 SP 12/24, f. 17r.

34 SP 12/23, f. 243r; SP 12/24, f. 73r.
35 SP 12/23, f. 207r.
36 SP 12/23, ff.106r-107v and ff. 111r-112v.
37 SP 12/24, f. 2r.
38 Ibid.
39 SP 12/24, f. 9r.
40 SP 12/25, f. 22r.
41 Ibid.
42 SP 12/25, f. 94r.
43 SP 12/25, f. 123r.

CHAPTER 15: SECRET CHARGE

1 *CSPF*, vol. VI, no. 97.
2 SP 12/27, f. 136v.
3 SP 12/27, f. 200r.
4 SP 12/27, f. 33r.
5 Henry A. Harben, *Historical notes of streets and buildings in the City of London*, H. Jenkins Ltd., London, 1918.
6 SP 12/27, f. 475r.
7 Ibid.
8 *CSP Sim.*, vol. I, no. 198.
9 *CSP Burghley*, vol. I, no. 382.
10 SP 52/8, f. 36r-v; SP 12/28, f. 41r-42v.
11 Lambeth MS 302, f. 312r.
12 John Hales, 'A declaration of the succession of the crown imperial of England', in George Harbin, *The Hereditary Right of the Crown of England Asserted*, Richard Smith, London, 1713, pp. xx–xlii. The bibliography of this tract is discussed in Victoria de la Torre, ' "We Few of an Infinite Multitude": John Hales, Parliament, and the Gendered Politics of the Early Elizabethan Succession', *Albion*, vol. 33, no. 4, Winter 2001, pp. 557–82. Bishop's deposition focuses on the fact that Queen Margaret, rather than Angus, failed to arrive *in animo remanendi*, but the two arguments follow the same structure and use the phrase 'can claim no benefit', see SP 12/23, ff. 9r-13v.
13 *CSP Sim.*, vol. I, nos. 233 and 304.
14 SP 70/63, f. 38r, although there is some debate over Lennox's presence: see Macauley, 'Matthew Stewart', p. 127.
15 *CSP Sim.*, vol. I, nos. 233–4.
16 SP 52/8, f. 13r.

17 SP 70/63, f. 38r.
18 Guy, *'My Heart is My Own'*, pp. 194–5; Macauley, 'Matthew Stewart', p. 133.
19 Cotton Caligula BX, f. 276r.
20 Macauley, 'Matthew Stewart', p. 134.
21 SP 52/9, f. 65r.
22 *CSP Sim.*, vol. I, nos. 233, 234 and 290; Simon Adams, 'The Release of Lord Darnley and the Failure of the Amity', in *Mary Stewart: Queen in Three Kingdoms*, ed. Michael Lynch, Basil Blackwell, Oxford, 1988, pp. 130–1.
23 Add MS 17492, f. 57r.
24 *CSP Sim.*, vol. I, nos. 253 and 251.
25 Macauley, 'Matthew Stewart', p. 142.
26 SP 53/5, f. 157r-v.
27 *CSP Sim.*, vol. I, no. 265.
28 James Melville, *Memoirs of his own life by Sir James Melville of Halhill*, ed. Thomas Thomson, Edinburgh, 1827, pp. 108–30.
29 *CSP Scotland*, vol. IX, no. 51.
30 Guy, *'My Heart is My Own'*, p. 202.
31 *CSP Sim.*, vol. I, no. 273.
32 Cotton Caligula BX, ff. 276v-277r.
33 SP 52/9, ff. 180r-181r.
34 SP 52/9, f. 180r.

CHAPTER 16: RUNNING AT THE RING

1 Lawson, *The Elizabethan New Year's Gift Exchanges*, pp. 110–11.
2 See discussion in Adams, 'The Release of Lord Darnley', pp. 128–33.
3 Melville, *Memoirs*, p. 130.
4 SP 52/10, f. 25r and ff.26r-27v.
5 Melville, *Memoirs*, p. 134.
6 SP 52/10, f. 30r; SP 70/60, f. 100r.
7 SP 52/10, f. 30r.
8 SP 52/10, f. 25r.
9 SP 52/10, f. 41v.
10 *CSP Sim.*, vol. I, no. 286.
11 SP 52/10, f. 27r.
12 *CSP Sim.*, vol. I, no. 292.
13 NLS MS 3657, ff. 18r-20v, and transcribed by Katharine P. Frescoln, 'A Letter from Thomas Randolph to the Earl of Leicester',

Huntington Library Quarterly, vol. 37, Nov. 1973, pp. 83–8. The episode is discussed in detail in Guy, *'My Heart is My Own'*, pp. 193–4. See also R. Coltman Clephan, *The Tournament: Its Periods and Phases*, Methuen & Co., London, 1919, pp. 6–8.

14 Cotton Caligula BX, f. 288r.

15 SP 52/10, f. 49r.

16 SP 52/10, f. 57v.

17 SP 52/10, f. 59r; *CSP Sim.*, vol. I, no. 294.

18 Darnley began showing symptoms of secondary syphilis in early spring. The initial stage can last as long as two months with the secondary stage beginning shortly afterwards, which would be consistent with a date of infection in December 1564 or January 1565.

19 SP 59/9, f. 66r.

20 *CSP Sim.*, vol. I, no. 295.

21 *CSP Sim.*, vol. I, no. 296.

22 Cotton Caligula BX, f. 288v.

23 SP 52/10, f. 79r.

24 GD220/2/1/155, f. 1r-1v. A transcription is available in *The Douglas Book*, vol. III, pp. 255–62.

25 Peter Wentworth, *A pithie exhortation to her Maiestie*, Edinburgh, 1598, p. 15.

26 Cotton Caligula BX, f. 301v.

27 Cotton Caligula BX, ff. 302r-303r.

28 Cotton Caligula BX, f. 307r.

29 *CSP Rome*, vol. I, no. 326; *CSP Sim.*, vol. I, no. 302; *Relations Politiques*, vol. II, pp. 205–7.

30 SP 12/37, f. 78r.

31 *CSP Sim.*, vol. I, no. 304.

32 Ibid.

33 *CSP Sim.*, vol. I, no. 300.

CHAPTER 17: A SON LOST

1 Royal Commission on Historical Monuments of England, *An Inventory of the Historical Monuments in London, Volume 5: East London*, His Majesty's Stationery Office, London, 1930, pp. 69–101; SP 12/37, f. 78r. Both sources agree that she had five attendants, though the former suggests two women and three men, the latter three women and two men.

2 SP 52/10, f. 148r.

3 SP 52/10, f. 159v.

4 *CSP Sim.*, vol. I, no. 307.
5 'A TempleNewsam Inventory', p. 96.
6 E/178/2538 no. 4, f. 1r.
7 *Relations Politiques*, vol. II, p. 241.
8 *CSP Sim.*, vol. I, no. 305; *Relations Politiques*, vol. II, p. 241.
9 SP 52/12, f. 82r; SP 52/13, f. 7r.
10 *CSP Sim.*, vol. I, no. 312.
11 SP 52/11, f. 24v.
12 *CSP Sim.*, vol. I, no. 310.
13 *CSP Sim.*, vol. I, no. 320.
14 See Julian Goodare, 'Queen Mary's Catholic Interlude', in *Mary Stewart: Queen in Three Kingdoms*, ed. Michael Lynch, Basil Blackwell, Oxford, 1988, p. 159.
15 See Robert Keith, *History of the affairs of church and state in Scotland*, 3 vols., ed. John Parker Lawson, Thomas and Walter Ruddimans, Edinburgh, 1844–1850, vol. II, p. 347.
16 Guy, *'My Heart is My Own'*, pp. 228–36; Dawson, *The Politics of Religion*, pp.125–6.
17 Guy, *'My Heart is My Own'*, pp. 235–47.
18 *CSP Sim.*, vol. I, no. 434; Cotton Caligula BIX (i), f. 227v.
19 See Goodare, 'Queen Mary's Catholic Interlude', pp. 159–64.
20 *CSP Burghley*, vol. I, no. 447.
21 *CSP Sim.*, vol. I, no. 337.
22 *Lettres, Instructions, et Mémoires de Marie Stuart, Reine d'Écosse*, 7 vols., London, 1844, vol. I, pp. 311–13.
23 For Darnley and Rizzio, see Guy, *'My Heart is My Own'*, p. 211. For Rizzio, see Keith, *History of the affairs of church and state in Scotland*, vol. II, p. 259, n. 4.
24 Guy, *'My Heart is My Own'*, pp. 244–5.
25 *CSP Sim.*, vol. I, nos. 344 and 349.
26 Guy, *'My Heart is My Own'*, pp. 260–2.
27 *The History of Mary Stewart from the Murder of Riccio until her Flight into England. By Claude Nau her Secretary*, ed. Joseph Stevenson, William Paterson, Edinburgh, 1883, p. 223.
28 *CSP Sim.*, vol. I, no. 357.
29 SP 52/12, ff. 61r and 67v.
30 *Catalogues of the Jewels, Dresses, Furniture, Books, and Paintings of Mary Queen of Scots, 1556–1569*, ed. Joseph Robertson, Bannatyne Club, Edinburgh, 1863, p. 112.

31 See Keith, *History of the Affairs of Church and State in Scotland*, vol. II, pp. 448–9; discussed in more detail by Macauley, 'Matthew Stewart', pp. 176–7.
32 Lawson, *The Elizabethan New Year's Gift Exchanges*, p. 132.
33 See Michael Lynch, 'Queen Mary's Triumph: The Baptismal Celebrations at Stirling in December 1566', *The Scottish Historical Review*, vol. 69, April 1990, pp. 11–13.
34 NLS Adv.Ms.29.3.12, f. 255v.
35 *CSP Sim.*, vol. I, no. 405.
36 UL Oo.VII.47, f. 27v.
37 William Cecil to Sir Henry Norris, 20 February 1567, in *Scrinia Ceciliana*, ed. Francis Bacon, London, 1663, p. 108.
38 *CSP Sim.*, vol. I, no. 408.

CHAPTER 18: MEMORIAL

1 *CSP Sim.*, vol. I, nos. 408–409.
2 *CSP Scotland*, vol. II, no. 477.
3 William Cecil to Sir Henry Norris, 21 March 1567, in *Scrinia Ceciliana*, p. 111.
4 Guy, *'My Heart is My Own'*, p. 309.
5 Cotton Caligula BX, f. 407r.
6 SP 52/12, f. 21r.
7 See 'Heir followis ane Ballat declaring the Nobill and Gude inclination of our King' and 'Heir followis the testament and tragedie of umquhile King Henrie Stewart of gude memorie', in *Satirical Poems of the Time of the Reformation*, ed. James Cranstoun, William Blackwood and Sons, Edinburgh, 1891, vol. I, pp. 31–8 and 39–45.
8 UL Oo.VII.47, ff. 34v and 32v.
9 'Heir followis ane Ballat declaring the Nobill and Gude inclination of our King', in *Satirical Poems of the Time of the Reformation*, vol. I, p. 34.
10 Cotton Caligula DIX, f. 409r.
11 *CSP Sim.*, vol. I, no. 413; SP 12/42, f. 73r.
12 SP 59/13, f. 9r.
13 *CSP Sim.*, vol. I, no. 417.
14 Wormald, *Mary Queen of Scots*, p. 166.
15 Macauley, 'Matthew Stewart', pp. 184–6.
16 Dawson, *The Politics of Religion*, p. 149–50. See also Julian Goodare, 'The Ainslie Bond', in *Kings, Lords and Men in Scotland and Britain, 1300–1625*, ed. Steve Boardman and Julian Goodare, Edinburgh University Press, Edinburgh, 2014, pp. 301–19.

17 *Relations Politiques*, vol. II, p. 299.
18 Dawson, *The Politics of Religion*, pp. 150–1.
19 *CSP Sim.*, vol. I, no. 422.
20 SP 52/13, f. 53r.
21 SP 52/13, f. 36r.
22 *CSP Burghley*, vol. I, no. 447.
23 *CSP Sim.*, vol. I, no. 426.
24 *CSP Sim.*, vol. I, no. 427.
25 Guy, *'My Heart is My Own'*, p. 373; Wormald, *Mary Queen of Scots*, p. 168; Dawson, *The Politics of Religion*, p. 151.
26 *CSP Sim.*, vol. I, no. 429.
27 For the coronation, see Michael Lynch, *Scotland: A New History*, Pimlico, London, 1992, p. 219.
28 *CSP Sim.*, vol. I, no. 434.
29 For discussions of this work, see Margaret Aston, *The King's Bedpost: Reformation and Iconography in a Tudor Group Portrait*, Cambridge University Press, Cambridge, 1993, pp. 23–4; Roland Mushat Frye, *The Renaissance Hamlet*, Princeton University Press, Princeton, 1984, pp. 31–7; Marguerite A. Tassi, *The Scandal of Images*, Susquehanna University Press, Selinsgrove, 2005, pp. 172–3.
30 Transcribed in Tassi, *The Scandal of Images*, p. 173.
31 *CSP Rome*, vol. I, no. 505.
32 SP 12/44, f .83r.
33 SP 12/45, f. 26r.
34 Archibald A. M. Duncan, *Scotland: The Making of the Kingdom*, Mercat Press, Edinburgh, 1992, pp. 161–2.
35 See Dawson, *The Politics of Religion*, p. 155; Guy, *'My Heart is My Own'*, pp. 369–70.
36 *Lettres, Instructions, et Mémoires de Marie Stuart*, vol. II, pp. 102–3.
37 Cotton Caligula BIX (ii), f. 335r.
38 UL Oo.VII.47, f. 27v.
39 SP 53/2, f. 66v. For an in-depth discussion of the Casket Letters, see Guy, *'My Heart is My Own'*, pp. 396–436.

CHAPTER 19: CONSTANT HOPE

1 Elizabeth I, *A Proclamation declarying the vntrueth of certaine malitious reportes deuised and publisshed in the Realme of Scotlande*, London, 1569.
2 Foxe, *Acts and Monuments*, 1570, bk. IX, pp. 1524–5.

3 *CSP Sim.*, vol. II, no. 174.

4 Pollitt, 'An "Old Practizer" at Bay', pp. 69–77; SP 15/17, ff. 104r-105r; *HMC Salisbury*, vol. I, no. 1490; K. J. Kesselring, *The Northern Rebellion of 1569: Faith, Politics, and Protest in Elizabethan England*, Palgrave Macmillan, Basingstoke, 2007, p. 49.

5 Dawson, *The Politics of Religion*, pp. 178–80.

6 Cecil to Sir Henry Norris, 7 February 1570, in *Scrinia Ceciliana*, pp. 179–82. For Moray's death and its aftermath, see Amy Blakeway, 'The Response to the Regent Moray's Assassination', *The Scottish Historical Review*, vol. 99, April 2009, pp. 9–33.

7 *CSP Sim.*, vol. II, no. 177; William Cecil to Sir Henry Norris, 7 February 1568, in *Scrinia Ceciliana*, p. 180.

8 *CSP Sim.*, vol. II, no. 177; Cotton Caligula CI, f. 511r.

9 *CSP Burghley*, vol. I, no. 602.

10 Cotton Caligula CI, f. 511r.

11 'The Regentis Tragedie ending with ane exhortatioun', in Cranstoun, ed., *Satirical Poems of the Time of the Reformation*, pp. 100–7; SP 52/17, f. 51r; discussed in Macauley, 'Matthew Stewart', pp. 210–11.

12 SP 59/16, ff. 182v-183r.

13 Macauley, 'Matthew Stewart', p. 213.

14 Cotton Caligula BIX (ii), f. 451r.

15 *CSP Scotland*, vol. III, no. 135.

16 *CSP Sim.*, vol. II, no. 183.

17 SP 53/5, f. 157r-v.

18 SP 52/17, f. 139r.

19 SP 52/18, f. 30r.

20 Ibid.

21 SP 52/18, f. 41r.

22 Dawson, *Scotland Re-formed*, pp. 272–3.

23 Macauley, 'Matthew Stewart', p. 218.

24 SP 52/18, f. 64r.

25 See Diana Scarisbrick in *Scottish Jewellery: A Victorian Passion*, 5 Continents, Milan, 2009, p. 16; Macauley, 'Matthew Stewart', pp. 139–40; Guy, *'My Heart is My Own'*, p. 99; Strickland, *Lives of the Queens of Scotland*, vol. II, pp. 432–4; Patrick Fraser Tytler, *Historical notes on the Lennox or Darnley Jewel: The Property of the Queen*, Shakespeare Press, London, 1843, pp. 14–16.

26 It is also worth noting that while Margaret was perpetually insolvent, she did receive a gift of £800 from Elizabeth early in 1571, making this

one of the few moments in her life when she could have afforded to commission such a gift. See SP 12/77, f. 80r.

27 For contemporary use of the heart and salamander in the arms of the earldom of Angus, see R. R. Stodart, ed., *Scottish Arms, being A Collection of Armorial Bearings A.D. 1370–1678*, William Paterson, Edinburgh, 1881, p. 97.

28 Tytler, *Historical notes on the Lennox or Darnley Jewel*, p. 46.

29 Diana Scarisbrick, *Jewellery in Britain 1066–1837: A Documentary, Social, Literary and Artistic Survey*, Michael Russell, Wilby, 1994, pp. 94–105 and 134.

CHAPTER 20: THE LADY REGENT

1 SP 53/5, f. 92r.

2 Thornbury and Walford, *Old and New London*, vol. III, pp. 89–95.

3 Macauley, 'Matthew Stewart', p. 225.

4 SP 53/5, ff. 128r-129r.

5 *CSP Scotland*, vol. III, no. 464.

6 NLS Adv.Ms.29.3.12, f. 94r.

7 SP 52/19, f. 98r.

8 SP 53/5, f. 136r.

9 SP 53/5, ff. 157r-v.

10 *CSP Scotland*, vol. III, no. 543.

11 *CSPF*, vol. IX, no. 1238.

12 Lawson, *The Elizabethan New Year's Gift Exchanges*, pp. 151 and 161; SP 12/77, f. 80r.

13 *CSP Scotland*, vol. III, no. 627.

14 Dawson, *Scotland Re-formed*, p. 275.

15 GD 112/39/12/11, f. 1r-v.

16 SP 52/20, f. 170r.

17 NLS Adv.MS.29.3.12, f. 245r-v.

18 NLS Adv.MS.29.3.12, ff. 252v-253r.

19 NLS Adv.MS.29.3.12, f. 253r.

20 NLS Adv.MS.29.3.12, f. 251r.

21 NLS Adv.MS.29.3.12, f. 253r.

22 *CSP Scotland*, vol. III, no. 888.

23 SP 52/21, f. 60r. For Case, see *CDR Scotland*, vol. XX, no. 110 (3).

24 SP 52/21, f. 60r; SP 52/21, f. 48v.

25 NLS Adv.MS.29.3.12, f. 255v.

26 John Spottiswood, *The history of the Church of Scotland*, London, 1655, pp. 256–7; SP 52/21, f. 106r.
27 Spottiswood, *The history of the Church of Scotland*, p. 257. Spottiswood's is the most detailed account of Lennox's death, though it is worth bearing in mind that his family had ties to the Lennox's and that he accords the earl a notably good death; nonetheless, it is similar to the account given by Drury to Cecil on 10 September at SP 52/21, ff. 90r-91v.
28 *CSP Scotland*, vol. IV(Appendix), no. 2.
29 SP 52/21, f. 151r.
30 *The progresses and public processions of Queen Elizabeth*, ed. John Nichols, London, 1788, vol. I, p. 99, nn. 3 and 282.
31 Cotton Caligula CIII, f. 240r.
32 SP 52/21, f. 75r.
33 SP 59/19, f. 22r.
34 *CSP Sim.*, vol. II, no. 198.
35 *CSP Sim.*, vol. II, no. 279.
36 Cotton Caligula CI, f. 511.
37 GD 124/15/6, f. 1r.
38 Holinshed, *Chronicles*, vol. V, p. 412.

CHAPTER 21: A LONE WOMAN

1 SP 12/83, f. 7r.
2 GD 124/15/6, f. 1r; for the falcons, see GD 124/15/7, f. 1r.
3 SP 12/83, f. 7r.
4 Alford, *Burghley*, p. 146.
5 Alford, *Burghley*, pp. 139–47.
6 *The register of admissions to Gray's Inn, 1521–1889*, ed. Joseph Foster, Hansard, London, 1889, p. 43.
7 Peter Malliet to Henry Bullinger the Younger, 26 May 1572, in *The Zurich letters, second series, comprising the correspondence of several English bishops and others with some of the Helvetian reformers, during the reign of Queen Elizabeth*, ed. Hastings Robinson, Cambridge University Press, Cambridge, 1845, p. 121.
8 *CSP Scotland*, vol. IV, no. 122; SP 52/22, f. 83r.
9 Add MS 33531, f. 109r.
10 *CSPF*, vol. X, no. 763.
11 *CSPF*, vol. X, no. 824; SP 52/23/1, f. 6v.

12 *CSP Scotland*, vol. IV, no. 474.
13 *CSPF*, vol. X, no. 823.
14 Add MS 33531, ff.113r-114v; cf. *CSP Scotland*, vol. IV, no. 703.
15 SP 52/25, f. 192r.
16 *Correspondance Diplomatique*, vol. VI, no. 249.
17 *CSP Sim.*, vol. II, no. 403.
18 SP 12/99, f. 25r.
19 PC 2/10, f. 269v.
20 SP 12/99, f. 25r.
21 SP 12/99, f. 25r.
22 For the life of Bess of Hardwick, see David N. Durant, *Bess of Hardwick: Portrait of an Elizabethan Dynast*, Cromwell, Newark, 1988; Guy, *'My Heart is My Own'*, p. 435.
23 SP 12/99, f. 26r.
24 Cotton Caligula CIV, f. 303r.
25 SP 12/199, f. 25r.
26 Ibid.
27 Shrewsbury to Burghley, 27 December 1574, in *Illustrations of British History*, ed. Edmund Lodge, John Chidley, London, 1838, vol. I, pp. 47–9.
28 SP 12/99, f. 23r.
29 SP 12/99, f. 26r.
30 See Susan Doran, *Monarchy and Matrimony: The Courtships of Elizabeth I*, Routledge, London, 1996, pp. 142–3; Natalie Mears, *Queenship and Political Discourse in the Elizabethan Realms*, Cambridge University Press, Cambridge, p. 53.
31 See Michael Questier, 'Practical Antipapistry during the Reign of Elizabeth I', *The Journal of British Studies*, vol. 36, Oct. 1997, p. 373.
32 Cotton Caligula CIV, ff. 306r-307v.
33 *Lettres, instructions et mémoires de Marie Stuart*, vol. IV, p. 258; for Mary's irritation with Bess of Hardwick following the marriage, see Guy, *'My Heart is My Own'*, p. 449.
34 *Correspondance Diplomatique*, vol. VI, p. 299.
35 *Correspondance Diplomatique*, vol. VI, p. 293.
36 *HMC Salisbury*, vol. XIII, no. 447.
37 *Lettres, instructions et mémoires de Marie Stuart*, vol. VII, p. 240; see Emily Jackson, *A History of Hand-Made Lace*, L. Upcott Gill, London, 1900, p. 190.

CHAPTER 22: WATCHES AND DIALS

1 See W. A. Eden et al., *Survey of London: Volume 28, Brooke House, Hackney*, London County Council, London, 1960, pp. 19–22 and 52–75.

2 Transcribed by Agnes Strickland, *Letters of Mary, Queen of Scots*, H. Coburn, London, 1843, vol. III, pp. 123–4.

3 *Lettres, instructions et mémoires de Marie Stuart*, vol. VII, p. 240.

4 SP 53/10, f. 71r-v.

5 *Lettres, Instructions, et Mémoires de Marie Stuart*, vol. IV, p. 355.

6 SP 52/27, f. 5r.

7 Harley 289, f. 196r.

8 SP 46/30, f. 333r.

9 Richard Robinson, *A record of auncient histories*, London, 1595, ff. 1r-3v. Though it seems to have been first printed in 1595, a later edition dates the writing to 1577 (see 1602, f. 3r).

10 Lancelot-Voisin, sieur de la Popelinière, *The historie of France the foure first bookes*, London, 1595, f. 4r.

11 William Camden, *The historie of the life and death of Mary Stuart Queene of Scotland*, London, 1624, pp. 123–4.

12 *Lettres, Instructions, et Memoires de Marie Stuart*, vol. IV, pp. 397–9.

13 Holinshed, *Chronicles*, vol. V, p. 415.

14 GD 124/15/6, f. 1r.

15 For child burials, see Patricia Phillippy, 'A Comfortable Farewell: Child-loss and Funeral Monuments in Early Modern England', in *Gender and Early Modern Constructions of Childhood*, ed. Naomi J. Miller and Naomi Yavneh, Ashgate, Farnham, 2011, p. 21.

16 See Melville, *Memoirs*, p. 127 and Marjorie Swann, *Curiosities and Texts: The Culture of Collecting in Early Modern England*, University of Pennsylvania Press, Philadelphia, 2001, pp. 16–22.

17 SP 52/2, f. 6r.

18 For Margaret's will, see PRO Prob/11/60, f. 93r-v.

19 HM 90, f. 15r.

20 *Lettres, instructions et mémoires de Marie Stuart*, vol. V, pp. 31–2.

21 SP 52/27, f. 52v.

22 For the coffin, see Jodocus Crull, *The Antiquities of St Peter's, Or, the Abbey-Church of Westminster*, E. Bell et al., London, 1722, p. 135.

23 For details of Margaret's funeral, see SP 52/27, f. 30r and College of Arms, London, Dethick's Funerals, vol. 1 (I), f.155r-v.

24 John Phillips, *An epitaphe on the death of the right noble and most vertuous lady Margarit Duglasis good grace*, London, 1578. See also John Phillips, *A commemoration of the right noble and vertuous ladye, Margrit Duglasis good grace*, London, 1578.

EPILOGUE: KING HENRY'S CHAPEL

1 Niccolò Machiavelli, *The Prince*, trans. Peter Bondanella, Oxford University Press, Oxford, 2005, p. 84.
2 *CSP Scotland*, vol. V, no. 374.
3 *CSP Scotland*, vol. V, no. 370.
4 SP 12/152, f. 30r; SP 12/153, f. 84r.
5 SP 12/152, f. 30r; Lansdowne 34, f. 4r.
6 SP 53/12, f. 83r.
7 Arbella Stewart to Sir Henry Brounker, in *The Letters of Lady Arbella Stuart*, ed. Sara Jayne Steen, Oxford University Press, Oxford, 1994, p. 151.
8 For an account of James's redesign of the Lady Chapel, see Peter Sherlock, 'The Monuments of Elizabeth Tudor and Mary Stuart: King James and the Manipulation of Memory', *Journal of British Studies*, vol. 46, April 2007, pp. 263–89.

BIBLIOGRAPHY

Manuscript Sources

British Library, London
Additional, Cotton, Harley, Lansdowne Sloane

Cambridge University Library, Cambridge
Oo.VII.47

College of Arms, London
Dethick's Funerals, vol. 1 (I)

Huntington Library and Archives, San Marino
Historical Manuscripts

Lambeth Palace Library, London
Lambeth MS 302, Talbot Manuscripts

National Archives, Kew
E 36/120, E/178/2538, E/23/4, Prob/11/60, SP 1, 10, 12, 15, 49–53, 59, 68, 70

National Archives of Scotland, Edinburgh
GD 1/506/21, GD 124/15/6, GD 150/328, GD 220/2/1, PC 2/10, SP 6/44

National Library of Scotland, Edinburgh
NLS Adv.MS.29.3.12, NLS MS 3657

Primary Sources

'Account of King Henry the Eighth's Entry into Lincoln', ed. and trans. Frederic Madden, *Archaeologia*, vol. 23 (January 1831), pp. 334–8.

Acts of the Lords of Council in Public Affairs, 1501–1554, ed. Robert Kerr Hannay, Edinburgh: 1932.

Acts of the Parliament of Scotland, 12 vols., ed. Thomas Thomson and Cosmo Innes, Edinburgh: 1814–75.

Acts of the Privy Council of England, 46 vols., ed. John Roche Dasent et al., London: 1890–1964.

Ambassades de Messieurs de Noailles en Anglettere, 5 vols., ed. René-Aubert Vertot, Paris: 1763.

Ancient criminal trials in Scotland, 3 vols., ed. Robert Pitcairn, Edinburgh: 1833.

Anonymous, *The noble tryumphant coronacyon of quene Anne wyfe vnto the moost noble kynge Henry the viij*, London: 1533.

The boke of common praier, and administracion of the sacraments, London: 1552.

Buchanan, George, *The History of Scotland*, 4 vols., ed. and trans. James Aikman, Glasgow: Blackie, Fullarton & Co., 1827.

Calderwood, David, *The History of the Kirk of Scotland: Volume I*, ed. Thomas Thomson, Edinburgh: 1842.

Calendar of Documents relating to Scotland, 2 vols., ed. Markham John Thorpe, London: 1858.

Calendar of letters and state papers relating to English affairs, preserved principally in the archives at Simancas, 4 vols., ed. Martin Hume, London: 1892–4.

Calendar of the manuscripts of the Most Honourable the Marquess of Salisbury, preserved at Hatfield House, Hertfordshire, 24 vols., ed. S. R. Scargill-Bird, London: 1883.

Calendar of State Papers and Manuscripts in the Archives and Collections of Milan, ed. Allen B. Hinds, London: 1912.

Calendar of state papers, domestic series, of the reigns of Edward VI, Mary, Elizabeth 1547–1570, ed. Robert Lemon, London: 1856.

Calendar of state papers, foreign: Edward VI, Mary, Elizabeth I, 25 vols., ed. Joseph Stevenson et al., London: William Paterson, 1865–71.

Calendar of State Papers Relating to English Affairs in the Archives of Venice, 38 vols., ed. Rawdon Brown et al., London: 1864–1947.

Calendar of State Papers Relating to English Affairs in the Vatican Archives, 2 vols., ed. J. M. Rigg, London: 1916–26.

Calendar of State Papers Relating to Scotland and Mary, Queen of Scots, 1574–1603, 13 vols., ed. Joseph Bain et al., Edinburgh: 1898–1969.

Calendar of State Papers, Spain, 13 vols., ed. G. A. Bergenroth et al., London: 1862–1954.

Camden, William, *The historie of the life and death of Mary Stuart Queene of Scotland*, London: 1624.

Catalogues of the Jewels, Dresses, Furniture, Books, and Paintings of Mary Queen of Scots, 1556–1569, ed. Joseph Robertson, Edinburgh: Bannatyne Club, 1863.

Caxton, William, *Legenda aurea*, London: 1483.

Collectanea de Rebus Albanicis, consisting of Original Papers and Documents relating to the history of the Highlands and Islands of Scotland, ed. the Iona Club, Edinburgh: 1847.

A Collection of State Papers, Relating to Affairs in the Reigns of King Henry VIII, King Edward VI, Queen Mary, and Queen Elizabeth, Transcribed from Original letters and Other Authentick Memorials, left by William Cecill Lord Burghley, 2 vols., ed. Samuel Haynes, London: 1840.

Correspondence diplomatique de Bertrand de Salignac de la Mothe Fénélon, 6 vols., ed. Charles Purton Cooper, Pans: Panckoucke, 1838.

Coxe, H. O., *Bodleian Library Quarto Catalogues II: Laudian Manuscripts*, ed. R. W. Hunt, Oxford: Bodleian Library, 1973.

Cranmer, Thomas, *A defence of the true and catholike doctrine of the sacrament of the body and bloud of our sauiour Christ*, London: R. Wolfe, 1550.

Cranstoun, James, ed., *Satirical Poems of the Time of the Reformation*, 2 vols., Edinburgh: William Blackwood and Sons, 1891–3.

Crull, Jodocus, *The Antiquities of St Peter's, Or, the Abbey-Church of Westminster*, London: 1722.

The Devonshire Manuscript: A Woman's Book of Courtly Poetry, ed. and introduced by Elizabeth Heale, Toronto: Iter, 2012.

The Diary of Henry Machyn, Citizen and Merchant-Taylor of London, 1550–1563, ed. J. G. Nichols, London: J. B. Nichols and Sons, 1848.

Documents Illustrative of English Church History, ed. Henry Gee and William John Hardy, New York: Macmillan & Co., 1896.

The Douglas Book, 4 vols., ed. William Fraser, Edinburgh: 1885.

Drummond, John, ed. and trans., *Here is a new boke, called the defence of age*, London: 1540.

Dunbar, William, 'Welcum of Scotlond to be Quene', in *William Dunbar: The Complete Works*, ed. John Conlee, Kalamazoo: Medieval Institute Publications, 2004.

Ecclesiastical memorials, relating chiefly to religion, and the reformation of it, and the emergencies of the Church of England, under King Henry VIII, King Edward VI and Queen Mary I, 3 vols., ed. John Strype, Oxford: Clarendon Press, 1822.

The Egerton Papers, ed. J. Payne Collier, London: 1841.

Elder, John, *The copie of a letter sent in to Scotlande*, London: John Wayland, 1555.

Elizabeth I, *A Proclamation declarying the vntrueth of certaine malitious reportes deuised and publisshed in the Realme of Scotlande*, London: 1569.

Elyot, Thomas, *The boke named the Gouernour*, London: 1537.
Erasmus, Desiderius, *The first tome or volume of the Paraphrase of Erasmus upon the newe testament*, London: 1548.
Foxe, John, *Acts and Monuments of the Church*, London: 1563, 1570 and 1583.
Frescoln, Katharine P., 'A Letter from Thomas Randolph to the Earl of Leicester', *Huntington Library Quarterly*, vol. 37 (November 1973), pp. 83–8.
Fuller, Thomas, *Church-history of Britain from the birth of Jesus Christ until the year M.D.C.XLVIII endeavoured by Thomas Fuller*, London: John Williams, 1655.
Godet, Giles, *The city of London, as it was before the burning of St. Pauls steeple*, London: 1565.
Hales, John, 'A declaration of the succession of the crown imperial of England', in George Harbin, *The Hereditary Right of the Crown of England Asserted*, London: H. Jenkins Ltd., 1713, pp. xx–xlii.
Hall, Edward, *The vnion of the two noble and illustre famelies of Lancastre & Yorke*, London: 1548.
The Hamilton Papers, 2 vols., ed. Joseph Bain, Edinburgh: 1890–2.
Hayward, Maria, 'Gift Giving at the Court of Henry VIII: The 1539 New Year's Gift Roll in Context', *The Antiquaries Journal*, vol. 85 (2005), pp. 126–75.
Holinshed, Raphael, *Chronicles of England, Scotland, and Ireland*, London: 1587.
Hume of Godscroft, David, *The history of the houses of Douglas and Angus*, Edinburgh: 1643.
Illustrations of British History, Biography, and Manners, in the Reigns of Henry VIII, Edward VI, Mary, Elizabeth, & James I, in Three Volumes, Second Edition, ed. Edmund Lodge, London: John Chidley, 1838.
Jewel, John, *The Works of John Jewel, Bishop of Salisbury*, 8 vols., ed. John Ayre, Cambridge: Cambridge University Press, 1801.
Journal of the House of Lords: Volume I, 1509–1577, London: 1767.
Keith, Robert, *History of the affairs of church and state in Scotland*, 3 vols., ed. John Parker Lawson, Edinburgh: 1844–50.
Knox, John, *The first blast of the trumpet against the monstrous regiment of women*, Geneva: 1558.
— *The historie of the Reformation of the Church of Scotland, London: 1644.*
la Popelinière, Lancelot-Voisin de, *The historie of France the foure first bookes*, London: 1595.

Lawson, Jane A., ed., *The Elizabethan New Year's Gift Exchanges, 1559–1603*, Oxford: Oxford University Press, 2013.

Leland, John, *De Rebus Britannicis Collectanea*, 6 vols., ed. Thomas Hearne, London: G. and J. Richardson, 1770.

Leslie, John, *The history of Scotland, from the death of King James I. in the year M.CCCC.XXXVI, to the year M.D.LXI*, Edinburgh: Bannatyne Club, 1830.

Letters and Papers, Foreign and Domestic, of the Reign of Henry VIII, 21 vols., ed. J. S. Brewer et al., London: 1864–1920.

The Letters of King Henry VIII: A Selection, with a Few Other Documents, ed. Muriel St Clare Byrne, London: Cassell, 1968.

Letters of Mary, Queen of Scots and Documents connected with her Personal History, ed. Agnes Strickland, 3 vols., London: H. Coburn, 1843.

Lettres, Instructions, et Mémoires de Marie Stuart, Reine d'Écosse; Publiés sur les Originaux et les Manuscrits du State Paper Office de Londres et des Principales Archives et Bibliothèques de l'Europe, et accompagnés d'un Résumé Chronologique par le Prince Alexandre Labanoff, 7 vols., London: 1844.

Lindsay of Pitscottie, Robert, *The history of Scotland: from 21 February, 1436 to March, 1565*, ed. Robert Freebairn, Edinburgh: 1728.

The Lisle Letters, 6 vols., ed. Muriel St Clare Byrne, Chicago: Chicago University Press, 1981.

Literary Remains of King Edward the Sixth, 2 vols., ed. J. G. Nichols, London: J. B. Nichols and Sons, 1857.

Machiavelli, Niccolò, *The Prince*, trans. Peter Bondanella, Oxford: Oxford University Press, 2005.

Malory, Thomas, trans. William Caxton, *Le Morte d'Arthur*, London: 1485.

Melville, James, *Memoirs of his own Life by Sir James Melville of Halhill*, ed. Thomas Thomson, Edinburgh: 1827.

'Narrative of the Visit of the Duke de Najera to England, in the year 1543–4; written by his Secretary, Pedro de Gante', ed. Frederic Madden, *Archaeologia*, vol. 23 (January 1831), pp. 344–57.

Nau, Claude, *The History of Mary Stewart from the Murder of Riccio until her Flight into England. By Claude Nau her Secretary*, ed. Joseph Stevenson, Edinburgh: 1883.

Negociations diplomatiques entre la France et l'Autriche durant les trentes premières années du XVIe siècle, 2 vols., ed. André Joseph Ghislain Le Glay, Paris: 1845.

Parr, Katherine, *Complete Works and Correspondence*, ed. Janel Mueller, Chicago: University of Chicago Press, 2011.

Phillips, John, *A commemoration of the right noble and vertuous Ladye, Margrit Duglasis good grace*, London: 1578.

— *An epitaphe on the death of the right noble and most vertuous lady Margarit Duglasis good grace*, London: 1578.

Pilkington, James, *The true report of the burnyng of the steple and church of Poules in London*, London: 1561.

The Privy Purse Expenses of King Henry the Eighth, from November MDXXIX, to December MDXXXII, ed. Nicholas Harris Nicolas, London: William Pickering, 1827.

Privy purse expenses of the Princess Mary, daughter of King Henry the Eighth, afterwards Queen Mary, with a memoir of the princess, and notes, ed. Frederic Madden, London: 1831.

The progresses and public processions of Queen Elizabeth, vol. I., ed. John Nichols, London: 1788.

The register of admissions to Gray's Inn, 1521–1889, ed. Joseph Foster, London: Hansard, 1889.

The register of the Privy Seal of Scotland, 5 vols., ed. David Hay Fleming et al., Edinburgh: 1908–57.

Relations Politiques de la France et de l'Espagne avec l'Écosse au XVIe Siècle, 4 vols., ed. Alexandra Teulet, Paris: 1862.

Robinson, Richard, *A record of auncient histories*, London: 1595 and 1602.

Royal Commission on Historical Monuments of England, *An Inventory of the Historical Monuments in London, Volume 5, East London*, London: 1930.

Sanderson, William, *A compleat history of the lives and reigns of Mary, Queen of Scotland, and of her son and successor, James the Sixth*, London: 1656.

Scrinia Ceciliana, mysteries of state & government of the late famous Lord Burghley, and other grand ministers of state, in the reigns of Queen Elizabeth, and King James, being a further additional supplement of the Cabala, ed. Francis Bacon, London: 1663.

Skelton, John, *A ballad of the Scottysshe kynge*, London: 1513.

Spottiswood, John, *The history of the Church of Scotland*, London: 1655.

Statutes of the realm, 9 vols., ed. John Raithby, London: 1817.

Stewart, Arbella, *The Letters of Lady Arbella Stuart*, ed. Sara Jayne Steen, Oxford: Oxford University Press, 1994.

Stodart, R. R., ed., *Scottish Arms, being a Collection of Armorial Bearings A.D. 1370–1678*, Edinburgh: 1881.

'A Temple Newsam Inventory, 1565', ed. E. W. Crossley, in *The Yorkshire Archaeological Journal*, vol. 25 (1920), pp. 91–100.

Vergil, Polydore, *Anglica Historica*, ed. Dana F. Sutton, Birmingham: Philological Museum, 2010.

Weever, John, *Ancient funerall monuments within the vnited monarchie of Great Britaine, Ireland, and the islands adiacent*, London: 1631.

Wentworth, Peter, *A pithie exhortation to her Maiestie*, Edinburgh: 1598.

Wriothesley, Charles, *A Chronicle of England During the Reigns of the Tudors*, 2 vols., ed. William Douglas Hamilton, London: Camden Society, 1875–7.

The Zurich Letters, second series, comprising the correspondence of several English bishops and others with some of the Helvetian reformers, during the reign of Queen Elizabeth, ed. Hastings Robinson, Cambridge: Cambridge University Press, 1845.

Secondary Sources

Adams, Simon, 'The Release of Lord Darnley and the Failure of the Amity', in *Mary Stewart: Queen in Three Kingdoms*, ed. Michael Lynch, Oxford: Basil Blackwell, 1988, pp. 123–53.

Ahnert, Ruth, *The Rise of Prison Literature in the Sixteenth Century*, Cambridge: Cambridge University Press, 2013.

Alexander, J. J. G., 'Foreign Illuminators and Illuminated Manuscripts', in *The Cambridge History of the Book in Britain, Volume III: 1400–1557*, ed. Lotte Hellinga and J. B. Trapp, Cambridge: Cambridge University Press, 1999, pp. 47–64.

Alford, Stephen, *Burghley: William Cecil at the Court of Elizabeth I*, New Haven: Yale University Press, 2008.

— *Kingship and Politics in the Reign of Edward VI*, Cambridge: Cambridge University Press, 2002.

— *The Early Elizabethan Polity: William Cecil and the British Succession Crisis, 1558–1569*, Cambridge: Cambridge University Press, 1998.

Aston, Margaret, *The King's Bedpost: Reformation and Iconography in a Tudor Group Portrait*, Cambridge: Cambridge University Press, 1993.

— 'Lollardy and Sedition, 1381–1431', *Past and Present*, vol. 17 (April 1960), pp. 1–44.

Baker, Nicholas Scott, 'Writing the Wrongs of the Past: Vengeance, Humanism, and the Assassination of Alessandro de' Medici', *The Sixteenth Century Journal*, vol. 38 (Summer 2007), pp. 307–27.

Baker, T. F. T., ed., *A History of the County of Middlesex: Volume 11, Stepney, Bethnal Green*, London: Victoria County History, 1998.

Bernard, G. W., 'The Fall of Anne Boleyn', *The English Historical Review*, vol. 106, no. 420 (July 1991), pp. 584–610.

Bingham, Caroline, *Darnley: A Life of Henry Stuart, Lord Darnley, Consort of Mary Queen of Scots*, London: Constable, 1995.

Blakeway, Amy, *Regency in Sixteenth-Century Scotland*, Woodbridge: Boydell & Brewer, 2015.

— 'The Attempted Divorce of James Hamilton, Earl of Arran, Governor of Scotland', *The Innes Review*, vol. 61, no. 1 (Spring 2010), pp. 1–23.

— 'The Response to the Regent Moray's Assassination', *The Scottish Historical Review*, vol. 99 (April 2009), pp. 9–33.

Brigden, Susan, *Thomas Wyatt: The Heart's Forest*, London: Faber, 2012.

Brown, Keith M., *Noble Society in Scotland: Wealth, Family and Culture, from Reformation to Revolution*, Edinburgh: Edinburgh University Press, 2000.

Cameron, Jamie, *James V: The Personal Rule, 1528–1542*, East Linton: Tuckwell Press, 1998.

Clephan, R. Coltman, *The Tournament: Its Periods and Phases*, London: Methuen & Co., 1919.

Coffey, John, *Persecution and Toleration in Protestant England, 1558–1689*, Harlow: Longman, 2000.

Croft, Pauline, ' "The State of the World is Marvellously Changed": England, Spain and Europe 1558–1604', *Tudor England and its Neighbours*, ed. Susan Doran and Glenn Richardson, Basingstoke: Palgrave Macmillan, 2005, pp. 178–202.

— 'Mildred, Lady Burghley: The Matriarch', *Patronage, Culture, and Power: The Early Cecils 1559–1612*, ed. Pauline Croft, New Haven: Yale University Press, 2002, pp. 283–300.

Dawson, Jane E. A., *Scotland Re-formed, 1488–1587*, Edinburgh: Edinburgh University Press, 2007.

— *The Politics of Religion in the Age of Mary, Queen of Scots: The Earl of Argyll and the Struggle for Britain and Ireland*, Cambridge: Cambridge University Press, 2002.

Doran, Susan, *Monarchy and Matrimony: The Courtships of Elizabeth I*, London: Routledge, 1996.

Duffy, Eamon, *Fires of Faith: Catholic England under Mary Tudor*, New Haven: Yale University Press, 2010.

Dunbar, John G., *Scottish Royal Palaces: The Architecture of the Royal Residences during the Late Medieval and Early Renaissance Periods*, East Linton: Tuckwell Press, 1999.

Duncan, Archibald A. M., *Scotland: The Making of the Kingdom*, Edinburgh: Mercat Press, 1992.

Durant, David N., *Bess of Hardwick: Portrait of an Elizabethan Dynast*, Newark: Cromwell, 1988.

Eden, W. A. et al., *Survey of London: Volume 28, Brooke House, Hackney*, London: London County Council, 1960.

Fox, Julia, *Jane Boleyn: The True Story of the Infamous Lady Rochford*, New York: Ballantine Books, 2009.

Frye, Roland Mushat, *The Renaissance Hamlet*, Princeton: Princeton University Press, 1984.

Goodare, Julian, 'The Ainslie Bond', *Kings, Lords and Men in Scotland and Britain, 1300–1625*, ed. Steve Boardman and Julian Goodare, Edinburgh: Edinburgh University Press, 2014, pp. 301–19.

— 'Queen Mary's Catholic Interlude', *Mary Stewart: Queen in Three Kingdoms*, ed. Michael Lynch, Oxford: Basil Blackwell, 1988, pp. 154–70.

Gray, Douglas, 'The Royal Entry in Sixteenth-Century Scotland', *The Rose and the Thistle: Essays on the Culture of Late Medieval and Renaissance Scotland*, ed. Sally Mapstone and Juliette Wood, East Linton: Tuckwell Press, 1998, pp. 10–37.

Guy, John, *'My Heart is My Own': The Life of Mary, Queen of Scots*, London: HarperPerennial, 2004.

— 'Tudor Monarchy and its Critiques', *The Tudor Monarchy*, ed. John Guy, London: Arnold, 1997, pp. 78–109.

— *Tudor England*, Oxford: Oxford University Press, 1988.

Harben, Henry A., *Historical Notes of Streets and Buildings in the City of London*, London: H. Jenkins Ltd., 1918.

Harbison, Elmore Harris, *Rival Ambassadors at the Court of Queen Mary*, Princeton: Princeton University Press, 1940.

Harris, Barbara J., *English Aristocratic Women, 1450–1550: Marriage and Family, Property and Careers*, Oxford: Oxford University Press, 2002.

Hayward, Maria, *Dress at the Court of King Henry VIII*, Leeds: Maney Publishing, 2007.

— 'Gift Giving at the Court of Henry VIII: The 1539 New Year's Gift Roll in Context', *The Antiquaries Journal*, vol. 85 (September 2005), pp. 126–75.

Head, David M., ' "Beyng Ledde and Seduced by the Devyll": The Attainder of Lord Thomas Howard and the Tudor Law of Treason', *The Sixteenth Century Journal*, vol. 13 (Winter 1982), pp. 3–16.

Hoyle, R. W. and J. B. Ramsdale, 'The Royal Progress of 1541, the North of England, and Anglo-Scottish Relations, 1534–1542', *Northern History*, vol. 40, no. 2(September 2004), pp. 239–65.

Hunt, Alice, *The Drama of Coronation: Medieval Ceremony in Early Modern England*, Cambridge, Cambridge University Press: 2008.

Irish, Bradley J., 'Gender and Politics in the Henrician Court: The Douglas-Howard Lyrics in the Devonshire Manuscript (BL Add 17492)', *Renaissance Quarterly*, vol. 64 (Spring 2011), pp. 79–114.

Ives, Eric, *Lady Jane Grey: A Tudor Mystery*, Chichester: Wiley-Blackwell, 2009.

— *The Life and Death of Anne Boleyn: 'The Most Happy'*, Oxford: Blackwell, 2004.

— 'The Fall of Anne Boleyn Reconsidered', *The English Historical Review*, vol. 107, no. 424 (July 1992), pp. 651–64.

Jackson, Emily, *A History of Hand-Made Lace*, London: L. Upcott Gill, 1900.

Jamieson, Fiona, 'The Royal Gardens of the Palace of Holyroodhouse, 1500–1603', *Garden History*, vol. 22, no. 1 (Summer 1994), pp. 18–36.

Jones, Michael K. and Malcolm G. Underwood, *The King's Mother: Lady Margaret Beaufort, Countess of Richmond and Derby*, Cambridge: Cambridge University Press, 1993.

Kesselring, K. J., *The Northern Rebellion of 1569: Faith, Politics, and Protest in Elizabethan England*, Basingstoke: Palgrave Macmillan, 2007.

la Torre, Victoria de, ' "We Few of an Infinite Multitude": John Hales, Parliament, and the Gendered Politics of the Early Elizabethan Succession', *Albion*, vol. 33 (Winter 2001), pp. 557–72.

Levin, Carole, 'Parents, Children, and Responses to Death in Dream Structures in Early Modern England', *Gender and Early Modern Constructions of Childhood*, ed. Naomi J. Miller and Naomi Yavneh, Farnham: Ashgate, 2011, pp. 38–49.

— *'The Heart and Stomach of a King': Elizabeth I and the Politics of Sex and Power*, Philadelphia: University of Pennsylvania Press, 1994.

Levine, Mortimer, *Tudor Dynastic Problems 1460–1571*, London: George Allen & Unwin Ltd, 1973.

Lipscomb, Suzannah, 'The Fall of Anne Boleyn: A Crisis in Gender Relations', *Henry VIII and the Court: Art, Politics and Performance*, ed. Thomas Betteridge and Suzannah Lipscomb, Farnham: Ashgate Publishing, 2013, pp. 287–305.

Loades, David, *The Reign of Mary Tudor: Politics, Government and Religion in England, 1553–58*, Harlow: Longman, 1991.

Lynch, Michael, *Scotland: A New History*, London: Pimlico, 1992.

— 'Queen Mary's Triumph: The Baptismal Celebrations at Stirling in December 1566', *The Scottish Historical Review*, vol. 69 (April 1990), pp. 1–21.

Macauley, Sarah, 'Matthew Stewart, Fourth Earl of Lennox and the Politics of Britain, c.1543–1571', PhD thesis, University of Cambridge: 2006.

— 'The Lennox Crisis, 1558–1563', *Northern History*, vol. 41 (September 2004), pp. 267–87.

MacCulloch, Diarmaid, *Tudor Church Militant*, London: Allen Lane, 1999.

— *Thomas Cranmer: A Life*, New Haven: Yale University Press, 1996.

Macdougall, Norman, *James IV*, East Linton: Tuckwell Press, 1997.

Marshall, Peter, 'Evangelical Conversion in the Reign of Henry VIII', *The Beginnings of English Protestantism*, ed. Peter Marshall and Alec Ryrie, Cambridge: Cambridge University Press, 2002, pp. 14–37.

Mason, Roger, *Kingship and the Commonweal: Political Thought in Renaissance and Reformation Scotland*, East Linton: Tuckwell Press, 1998.

Mears, Natalie, *Queenship and Political Discourse in the Elizabethan Realms*, Cambridge: Cambridge University Press, 2005.

Merriman, Marcus, *The Rough Wooings: Mary Queen of Scots, 1542–1551*, East Linton: Tuckwell Press, 2000.

Mullett, Michael A., *Catholics in Britain and Ireland, 1558–1829*, Basingstoke: Macmillan, 1998.

Najemy, John M., *A History of Florence, 1200–1575*, Oxford: Blackwell, 2006.

Oxford Dictionary of National Biography, 60 vols., Oxford: Oxford University Press, 2004.

Pettegree, Andrew, 'Printing and the Reformation', *The Beginnings of English Protestantism*, ed. Peter Marshall and Alec Ryrie, Cambridge: Cambridge University Press, 2002, pp. 157–79.

— *Marian Protestantism: Six Studies*, Aldershot: Scolar Press, 1996.

Phillippy, Patricia, 'A Comfortable Farewell: Child-loss and Funeral Monuments in Early Modern England', *Gender and Early Modern Constructions of Childhood*, ed. Naomi J. Miller and Naomi Yavneh, Farnham: Ashgate, 2011, pp. 17–37.

Phillips, Gervase, *The Anglo-Scots Wars 1513–1550: A Military History*, Woodbridge: Boydell Press, 1999.

Piacenti, Kirsten Aschengreen and John Boardman, *Ancient and Modern Gems and Jewels in the Collection of Her Majesty the Queen*, London: Royal Collection Enterprises Ltd, 2008.

Pollitt, Ronald, 'An "Old Practizer" at Bay: Thomas Bishop and the Northern Rebellion', *Northern History*, vol. 16 (1980), pp. 59–84.

Pollnitz, Aysha, *Princely Education in Early Modern Britain*, Cambridge: Cambridge University Press, 2015.

Pollock, Linda, ' "Teach her to live under obedience": The Making of Women in the Upper Ranks of Early Modern England', *Continuity and Change*, vol. 4, Special Issue no. 2 (August 1989), pp. 231–58.

Questier, Michael, *Catholicism and Community in Early Modern England*, Cambridge: Cambridge University Press, 2006.

— 'Practical Antipapistry during the Reign of Elizabeth I', *Journal of British Studies*, vol. 36, no. 4 (October 1997), pp. 371–96.

Reynolds, Susan, ed., *A History of the County of Middlesex: Volume 3*, London: Victoria County History, 1962.

Richards, Judith M., 'Love and a Female Monarch: The Case of Elizabeth Tudor', *The Journal of British Studies*, vol. 38 (April 1999), pp. 133–60.

— 'Mary Tudor as "Sole Quene"? Gendering Tudor Monarchy', *The Historical Journal*, vol. 40 (December 1997), pp. 895–924.

Ryrie, Alec, *The Origins of the Scottish Reformation*, Manchester: Manchester University Press, 2010.

— 'Congregations, Conventicles, and the Nature of Early Scottish Protestantism', *Past & Present*, vol. 191 (May 2006), pp. 45–76.

— 'Reform without Frontiers in the Last Years of Catholic Scotland', *The English Historical Review*, vol. 119 (February 2004), pp. 27–56.

— 'Paths not Taken in the British Reformations', *The Historical Journal*, vol. 52 (March 2009), pp. 1–22.

Scarisbrick, Diana, *Scottish Jewellery: A Victorian Passion*, Milan: 5 Continents Editions, 2009.

— *Jewellery in Britain 1066–1837: A Documentary, Social, Literary and Artistic Survey*, Wilby: Michael Russell Publishing Ltd, 1994.

Schutte, Kimberly, *A Biography of Margaret Douglas, Countess of Lennox (1515–1578): Niece of Henry VIII and Mother-in-Law of Mary, Queen of Scots*, New York: Edwin Mellen, 2002.

Sharpe, Kevin, 'Representations and Negotiations: Texts, Images, and Authority in Early Modern England', *The Historical Journal*, vol. 42 (September 1999), pp. 853–81.

Sherlock, Peter, 'The Monuments of Elizabeth Tudor and Mary Stuart: King James and the Manipulation of Memory', *Journal of British Studies*, vol. 46 (April 2007), pp. 263–89.

Stamatakis, Chris, *Sir Thomas Wyatt and the Rhetoric of Rewriting: 'Turning the word'*, Oxford: Oxford University Press, 2012.

Starkey, David, *Six Wives: The Queens of Henry VIII*, London: Vintage, 2004.

Strickland, Agnes, *Lives of the Queens of Scotland and English Princesses Connected with the Regal Succession of Great Britain, Volume II*, London: W. Blackwood and Sons, 1854.

Swann, Marjorie, *Curiosities and Texts: The Culture of Collecting in Early Modern England*, Philadelphia: University of Pennsylvania Press, 2001.

Tassi, Marguerite, *The Scandal of Images: Iconoclasm, Eroticism, and Painting in Early Modern English Drama*, Selinsgrove: Susquehanna University Press, 2005.

Thornbury, Walter and Edward Walford, *Old and New London: A Narrative of its History, its People, and its Place*, 6 vols., London: Cassell, Petter & Galpin, 1878.

Thurley, Simon, *The Royal Palaces of Tudor England: Architecture and Court Life 1460–1547*, New Haven: Yale University Press, 1993.

Tytler, Patrick Fraser, *Historical Notes on the Lennox or Darnley Jewel: The Property of the Queen*, London: Shakespeare Press, 1843.

Wabuda, Susan, 'Equivocation and Recantation during the English Reformation: The "Subtle Shadows" of Dr Edward Crome', *Journal of Ecclesiastical History*, vol. 44 (April 1993), pp. 224–42.

Walker, Greg, 'Rethinking the Fall of Anne Boleyn', *The Historical Journal*, vol. 45, no. 1 (March 2002), pp. 1–29.

Walsham, Alexandra, *Charitable Hatred: Tolerance and Intolerance in England, 1500–1700*, Manchester: Manchester University Press, 2006.

Church Papists, Woodbridge: Boydell Press, 1993.

Warnicke, Retha M., *The Marrying of Anne of Cleves: Royal Protocol in Early Modern England*, Cambridge: Cambridge University Press, 2000.

Wormald, Jenny, *Mary Queen of Scots: Politics, Passion and a Kingdom Lost*, London: Tauris Parke, 2001.

Wrightson, Keith and David Levine, *Poverty and Piety in an English Village: Terling, 1525–1700*, Oxford: Clarendon Press, 1995.

Zagorin, Perez, *Ways of Lying: Dissimulation, Persecution, and Conformity in Early Modern Europe*, Cambridge, MA: Harvard University Press, 1990.

ACKNOWLEDGEMENTS

I am very grateful to the archivists and librarians of the British Library, the Cambridge University Library, the College of Arms, the Huntington Library and Archives, Lambeth Palace Library, the National Archives at Kew, the National Archives of Scotland, the National Library of Scotland and the University of York. My thanks as well to the kind and welcoming staff at Tantallon and Temple Newsam, and especially to Ian Franklin and Daniel Jackson at Hampton Court.

During my PhD I had the support of the Archbishop Cranmer Trust at the Cambridge Faculty of History and the Gonville Research Fund at Gonville and Caius College. The latter made it possible for me to undertake both my MPhil and my PhD, and my thanks go to the Graduate Tutors, especially David Holburn and Ruth Scurr. The Huntington offered me a marvellous, productive month as a visiting fellow and I am forever indebted to Juan Gomez, Steve Hindle and Carolyn Powell.

John Guy set me on the trail of the Countess of Lennox when I was a second-year undergraduate and has been the best of supporters and mentors ever since. I could not ask for a more inspiring PhD supervisor than Alexandra Walsham.

Many historians have taken the time to discuss aspects of this project with me and to lend their insight and expertise. My particular thanks to Stephen Alford, for acting as my supervisor during Michaelmas 2011; Alan Bryson, for sharing his transcriptions of the Talbot–Cavendish correspondence; Tom Freeman, for pointing me towards the references to Margaret and Lennox in *Acts and Monuments*, and for ceaseless encouragement with this and other projects; Julian Goodare, for making me think harder about Lennox's medical history; Leanda de Lisle, for championing this book; Simon Macdonald, for a conversation about lockets; Catherine Medici-Thiemann, for a discussion of *Leicester's Commonwealth*; and François Rigolot, for taking the time to share his work on the poetry of Mary, Queen of Scots. Members of the Dorothy Dunnett Society, the Sixteenth Century Society and the Cambridge Graduate Research Day all graciously listened to papers on aspects of the project and offered helpful questions. Many thanks as well to the Forum at the Stratford Shakespeare Festival.

Still others have been kind enough to read drafts of the manuscript and give me feedback. My MPhil examiners gave me wise and constructive suggestions. Kate Davison, Sean Heath, Michael O'Sullivan and Joan Redmond read the whole thesis and improved it enormously. Peter Wills has been reading my writing for more than a decade and has never once failed to make it better. To Amy Blakeway – who not only introduced me to the Edinburgh archives, utterly revised my view of the second Earl of Arran, and was endlessly willing to talk Scottish history over every meal of the day in every café from Cambridge to New Orleans, but also read the entire manuscript – my very deepest gratitude.

Cambridge has been my academic home for seven years and thanks are inadequate for the Fellows of Caius, especially David Abulafia, Andrew Bell, Melissa Calaresu, Cally Hammond, Emma Hunter, Huw Jones, Peter Mandler and Sujit Sivasundaram, and of Selwyn, particularly John Morrill and David Smith. The 2008–11 Caius historians, 2011–12 Early Modern MPhils and my fellow PhD candidates challenged my every idea about history and let me shoehorn the Countess of

Lennox into each class and seminar we shared. My own students have been a constant source of new insights. Finally, the Early Modern British and Irish Seminar never fails to make my Wednesday.

Much of the research for my PhD and for this book took me to London, where I have had the enormous good fortune to belong to Goodenough College. I will be forever grateful to Alan, Caroline, Mandy, the Book Club, the Drama Society, the Dean's Seminar and the wonderful Goodenough community.

The marvellous Anna Power suggested this book and I am wholeheartedly grateful for that and for everything else. It has been a joy working with the team at Bloomsbury, and my thanks go to everybody: my wonderful editors Bill Swainson and Michael Fishwick, for ideas and encouragement that did so much to shape the book; Richard Mason, for his brilliant copy-editing; Anna Simpson, for managing the entire process; Marigold Atkey and Imogen Denny, for keeping me organised; George Gibson and Callie Garnett, for their countless wise suggestions and their kind welcome to New York.

Eternally patient friends on both sides of the Atlantic have helped more than they know. In particular, my thanks to Adam and Rivka, in the hope that someday I will be able to repay all their kindness; Aislinn, Harriet, James, Katie, Liesbeth and Simone, for many an early modern discussion; Allegra, Andrew, Ariel, Charlie, Elle, Flossie, James, Kat, Liz, Rodger and Vincent, who have never stopped asking after Margaret and have been tireless cheerleaders; Jong, for answering all manner of odd medical questions; Max and Sam, who let me turn the living room into an office; and Simon, for being endlessly willing to hear this story.

Above all, my thanks go to my family: my grandparents, unstinting with their love and support; my sisters Rachel, who makes sure there is always Gaelic music when I come home, and Bronwyn, intrepid explorer, writer and all-round inspiration; my aunts and uncles, who have never stopped encouraging me; Hamish and Alfred, faithful reading, writing and running companions. To Aunt Frances: I think you would have liked this one. To my mother, who is the first and best of Margarets, and my father, who read every word of every draft and without whom I would not be a writer: this book is for you.

INDEX

INDEX

A NOTE ON THE AUTHOR

MORGAN RING was born and raised in Toronto. She read History at Cambridge, where she is now completing her PhD. She held the Francis J. Weber Fellowship at the Huntington Library and holds the Gonville Studentship at Gonville and Caius College. *So High a Blood* is her first book.

A NOTE ON THE TYPE

The text of this book is set in Fournier. Fournier is derived from the *romain du roi*, which was created towards the end of the seventeenth century from designs made by a committee of the Académie of Sciences for the exclusive use of the Imprimerie Royale. The original Fournier types were cut by the famous Paris founder Pierre Simon Fournier in about 1742. These types were some of the most influential designs of the eight and are counted among the earliest examples of the 'transitional' style of typeface. This Monotype version dates from 1924. Fournier is a light, clear face whose distinctive features are capital letters that are quite tall and bold in relation to the lower-case letters, and *decorative italics, which show the influence of the calligraphy of Fournier's time.*